"This is a wonderful, inspiring book. Give it to your friends. It truly helps us understand that you can have it all, just not all at the same time. Some of the best moments for women may come later in life and *What's Next?* can help you realize your dreams."

—NANCY BRINKER, founder of the Susan G. Komen Foundation for breast cancer research and Komen Race for the Cure

What's Next?

Women Redefining Their Dreams in the Prime of Life

RENA PEDERSON

with Dr. Lee Smith

A Perigee Book

Perigee Books
Published by The Berkley Publishing Group
A division of Penguin Putnam Inc.
375 Hudson Street
New York, New York 10014

First edition: April 2001

Published simultaneously in Canada.

The Penguin Putnam Inc. World Wide Web site address is
http://www.penguinputnam.com

Library of Congress Cataloging-in-Publication Data

Pederson, Rena.
    What's next? : women redefining their dreams in the prime of life / by
Rena Pederson with R. Lee Smith.
        p.   cm.
Includes bibliographical references.
ISBN 0-399-52678-1
    1. Middle aged women—Psychology. 2. Middle aged women—Attitudes.
3. Middle aged women—Conduct of life. I. Smith, R. Lee. II. Title.

HQ1059.4 .P43 2001
305.244—dc21
                                                                    00-068474

Printed in the United States of America

10   9   8   7   6   5   4   3   2

Contents

Acknowledgments

This book would not have been possible without the encouragement of Bob Buford who gave me the inspiration for this book, and the assistance of Dr. Lee Smith, a psychologist and highly regarded executive coach. Lee has conducted many seminars for women and business leaders around the country. She developed most of the self-help questions for the chapters in this book and provided thoughtful counsel along the way.

Bob and his wife Linda provided steady support and advice as well as dozens of leads to interviews. Their colleagues at the Buford Foundation, B. J. Engle and Gayle Carpenter added their able assistance.

I also would like to thank:

- My sons, Gregory Gish and Grant Gish, for their patience, constant support, and computer assistance.

- All the women who so graciously gave of their time for interviews.

- Those who devoted time to reviewing early drafts and made countless helpful suggestions: Ellen Kampinsky, Libby Norwood, Debra Decker, Paula Peters, Bill Cornwell, Karen Newsom, Ann Carruth, Diana Holbert, Wissie Thomson.

- Bill Blackburn for legal assistance and steady encouragement.

- Carol Stabler, who made house calls to rescue computer files.

- Rita Cox, Dick Collins, and Cappy McCarr for helping make connections.

- Those who shared financial expertise: Buddy Ozanne, Pamela Yip, Marion Asnes.

- Jo Giese for providing many suggestions for interviews and lessons learned from her book, *A Woman's Path*.

- Susan Sanders for help drafting the original proposals.

- My minister, the Rev. Mark Craig, for his inspiration.

- All the members of my Bible study, for their prayers.

- My dear and faithful secretary, Carol Portele, the only saint you'll find in a newsroom.

- My patient editor, Jennifer Repo, who has a sharp eye and sharp pen, but a thoughtful way.

Introduction

"I want to be all that I am capable of becoming."
—KATHERINE MANSFIELD, WRITER

When I first became an editor, a friend sent me a coffee mug that read, "The Career Woman's Checklist for Success: Dress like a lady. Act like a man. Work like a dog." I laughed and drank lots of coffee out of that mug. But after more than ten years of watching the sun go down from my desk, it dawned on me that it *was* a dog's life. Like Lily Tomlin says, the trouble with the rat race is that even if you win, you're still a rat.

Don't get me wrong. The newspaper business has been very good to me. In many ways, I have been blessed. I have had lunch in the White House and have flown on Air Force One. I've floated down the Amazon at sunset and have seen the Kremlin in the moonlight. I've interviewed welfare mothers in housing projects, murderers on death row, and Nobel Prize winners. I have seen some of the most fascinating figures of our time up close—from physicist Stephen Hawking, in his talking wheelchair, to the "Iron Lady," Margaret Thatcher.

But my business can be soul-draining. When I worked for United Press International, the labor guild members protested the callous work practices with buttons that said, "Use 'em up.

Burn 'em out. Throw 'em away." That's a good summation of the relentless pressure in the news business overall. Although there was a better climate where I had been working than at most newspapers, the inherent demands of daily deadlines and dealing continuously with controversy can take its toll, like working in an emergency room.

As I neared fifty, I found myself burned out by the pace and the pressure of trying to "succeed" as a single working mom. Like many women of the "baby boomer" generation, I bought into the proposition that you could have it all—"bring home the bacon and fry it in the pan." That is, if you could cook in your sleep. After years of trying to run the corporate marathon in high heels, I found myself too pooped to enjoy what little time off I had. Could I keep up the pace until retirement? Did I really want to? What would I be missing in life if I hung on to the status quo? My sons were graduating from school soon. Couldn't that be a graduation for me, too? But to what? Renewing yourself at middle age is not easy. As F. Scott Fitzgerald famously said, "There are no second acts in America." It's difficult to rewrite yourself.

Then I happened to read a lovely little book called *Halftime,* written by a businessman named Bob Buford. Bob, the owner of a cable television company in East Texas, went through the heartache of losing his only son in a tragic drowning accident. He came to the realization that devoting most of his energy to making money was a hollow pursuit. He decided to devote the rest of his life to church and charity projects. And he wrote an inspiring book about how to make a new beginning at midlife.

One day over lunch I told him that it was a terrific book, but I found it difficult to identify with the transformation process because all the examples were rich guys. Most women aren't millionaires or CEOs, I told him. The formula for change did not apply as neatly to them. Women have less financial freedom. They often feel bound to take care of their families before themselves. So I suggested he write a sequel showing women how to reinvent their lives.

"Why don't *you* write it?" he said gently.

To my surprise, I heard myself saying, "All right. I will."

And a journey of discovery began.

I had always wanted to write a book and this seemed like a tailor-made topic. I began a personal odyssey, a quest to find a more fulfilling "second half" for myself and, at the same time, find lessons to share with other women.

For the next few years, I interviewed dozens of women around the country who had transformed their lives in midstream. I learned something from each one of them. I gained new insights about this card game called Life. Several things became quickly apparent:

Middle age is not what it used to be. Back in 1808, Napoleon wrote to Josephine, "I have been to a ball in Weimar. The Emperor Alexander dances, but I don't. Forty is forty." But today you can dance on for several more decades, thanks to Advil and an extended life expectancy. You can ride a pink Harley-Davidson on your sixtieth birthday, as Texas Governor Ann Richards did, or become a flight attendant at seventy, as Evelyn Gregory of North Carolina did. Now that many legal barriers have been removed and cultural stereotypes discarded, middle age can be the most liberating time of all for women, a time when they can finally do what they really want.

A remarkable number of social trends are converging. This is contributing to the tendency for those in the age range of forty to sixty to have a "midlife crisis."

- *Time stress:* Growing numbers of workers who feel tethered to their desks want relief from the relentless time pressure of a 24/7 world. They are yearning for a more "balanced" life.

- *Material overload:* Thanks to a sustained economic boom for the last eight years, many people have grown tired of the age of acquisition and are seeking a simpler life that is not money driven.

- *Corporate chill:* The competitive pressure that has produced more mega-mergers and acquisitions has also made corporations even more impersonal, decreasing employee loyalty and increasing the longing for connectedness to other human beings.

- *Back to nature:* Those who have toiled most of their life in urban office buildings without green space or in a cookie-cutter suburban scene are feeling a hunger to savor the outdoors, enjoy nature, soak up beauty.

- *Self-realization:* Women who devoted themselves to their family for many years or who dedicated themselves to blazing a path in business are now seeking ways to express their neglected talents by taking up arts like painting, photography, or singing.

- *The legacy thing:* Baby boomers who began adulthood in the feel-good, do-good ethos of the 1960s are now feeling the urge to do something meaningful while they still can. Like the ghost of Hamlet's father crying "Remember me, remember me," they are looking for a way to make their life count, to leave a legacy.

- *Spiritual chic:* The more candid expression of spiritual beliefs by political leaders is coinciding with the move to use faith-based groups to address social problems— providing unprecedented opportunities for middle-aged women who are yearning for a way to apply their spiritual beliefs.

When you combine all these trends, you get a unique climate for change. Not all the women I interviewed credited their faith with giving them courage to try a new direction, but as it turned out, the majority did and the others clearly had a strong moral compass to guide them. It reminded me that for many years I had been so busy I had neglected my own beliefs. I had been going through the motions. As I worked on this book, I started taking time to think more about faith, to pray about problems, to get back in touch with God. It was like coming home to a warm bath after a long, dusty trip.

I suspect that there are many more women who want to revitalize their lives and are looking for a road map, just as I was. You can read this book simply as a collection of profiles about contemporary women, or you can use the profiles as case studies and guide yourself with the questions in each chapter. I hope *What's Next?* will be a companion on your journey of discovery. Asking the right questions is how you begin to find answers.

- How do you learn to listen to that little voice inside of you?

- How do you filter out the voices of well-meaning people who say "don't"?

- How can you get away from the busy-ness and much-ness of life to find peace of mind?

"It seems to me we can never give up longing and wishing while we are thoroughly alive. There are certain things we feel to be beautiful and good, and we *must* hunger after *them*."
—GEORGE ELIOT (MARY ANN EVANS), NOVELIST

- If you could add one accomplishment to your life, what would it be?

- How would you like to be remembered?

- How can you be sure of what you need to do?

To be perfectly honest, I didn't know what I wanted to do when I started out, other than to write a book that would be helpful for others. Should I stay where I was until my two sons got out of college? Should I try writing a novel? Or that children's book I'd been thinking about? I was paralyzed by indecision. But like the pilgrim on a journey, I learned from the wise women I met on the road. I hope you do, too.

Chapter One

There Is Still Time

"Is that all there is?"

—PEGGY LEE, SINGER-SONGWRITER

If you're past forty, you're in good company. Some 38 million women are in the age bracket of forty to sixty-five. Hillary Clinton and Farrah Fawcett are in their fifties. Meryl Streep and Lindsay Wagner, the "Bionic Woman," have turned fifty. Tipper Gore is a grandmother. Gloria Steinem is in her sixties and recently married for the first time.

One out of three Americans is now approaching that midlife zone. And according to the *Wall Street Journal*, every eight seconds, someone in the United States will be turning fifty as the baby boom hits middle age. Back in the 1800s, Fyodor Dostoyevsky thought forty was an "extremely old age," and grumbled, "To live longer than forty years is bad manners; it is vulgar, immoral." But these days, there are millions in that predicament. It is a time of reckoning. Gravity has begun to have its way with you. A flat stomach is probably a distant memory. You may have to borrow someone's reading glasses to read the menu. You find yourself thinking that Alan Greenspan would be interesting to know. The only noisy joint you know is your knee. You eat bran. You actually watch the

Weather Channel. And read the obituaries in the paper, calcu-
lating who was older than you.

It begins to dawn on you that the first half of your life went by
as fast as a teenager in a new car. Welcome to halftime in the game
of life. By now, you've had your share of hard knocks and disappointments. You may have discovered that the corporate treadmill
wears you down. You may have deferred your dreams while you
served your husband and children. You may be sighing, as Bette
Davis did in the movie *Old Acquaintance,* "It's late, and I'm
very tired of youth and love and self-sacrifice." So what's next?

There is lots of advice in the glossy magazines about how to
survive menopause, how to nip this and how to tuck that. But
there's not much of a practical template on how to reinvent
yourself, how to reinvigorate your life, or how to accomplish
something that is meaningful to you and the world. However,
there's time for a second chance. It's not too late to begin a second career, or start a parallel career, or remain in the same
career, but in a way that feels better.

As you reach the middle part of your life, you may hear the
clock ticking louder and start worrying that you won't find
whatever it is that gives you a sense of fulfillment in the days
allotted to you. A poignant example comes to mind. Once I was
lucky enough to interview Princess Grace and Prince Rainier of
Monaco. She was in her late forties by then, a little heavier than
in her starlet years, but still stunningly beautiful, with regal
poise. He was graying at the temples, a little paunchy, and
looked bored. I knew she had been interviewed hundreds if not
thousands of times, as a movie star and as a royal celebrity.
Hoping to find a question she had never been asked, I suggested
that she had everything that other people wished for—beauty,
fame, fortune, a picture-perfect family. So what did she wish for
when she made a wish, while blowing out a candle or tossing a

coin in a fountain? She paused and thought for what seemed like a very long time. Just as I was mentally kicking myself for having asked a dumb question, she said softly, "Health for my children." How wise, I thought, and how like a mother.

Then, to my surprise, she turned to her husband, Prince Rainier, who was sitting next to her. She said to him with an arched eyebrow, "Well?" He took the challenge and thought for a moment about what he would wish for. It was going to be hard to top her thoughtful gesture. Then he said, as softly as she had, one word, "Time." She nodded her head in agreement as if to say, "Yes, that's it." And of course, it is. You can have all the beauty and money in the world, but time is still your enemy. As it turned out, she died not long after, in a car crash while she was riding with her daughter Stephanie. She was fifty-two.

Sadly, she didn't get the time to compose another chapter in her remarkable career. Other celebrities have provided good examples of new directions that can be taken at midstream: at midlife, Audrey Hepburn was an advocate for starving children around the world. Shirley Temple Black became a capable ambassador. Poet Maya Angelou, now in her seventies, teaches at Oxford and sponsors community projects to help the poor in the South.

Those who do get the time to try something different, especially something that uses neglected gifts or something more altruistic, should not hesitate to do so. Life is not over until it's over. You must find a way to use your autumn days well. But where and how to begin?

You may begin by answering these questions:

1. What do you want to do?

2. How do you want to be remembered?

3. What are you waiting for?

People often think of their twenties as a starting time, but there's no reason why you can't start something new several decades later. Make time your friend. There is still plenty of time to try something else rather than chug along the same track with little enthusiasm. Midlife is an invitation to conscious living.

Let's look at the experience of Anna Quindlen. At the beginning of the 1990s, she was at the top. Star columnist at the *New York Times*. Pulitzer Prize winner. It was rumored she was on the fast track to become one of the chief editors at the most prestigious newspaper in the country. However, she walked away from it all in 1994. Her goal was to become a novelist. But judging from the reaction, you would have thought she had announced she was running off to join the circus in Argentina. Some friends wanted to know, "What's the *real* story? Did she have a tiff with the higher-ups?" One ultraconservative commentator wrote that it showed women had no business in the workplace to begin with. Other critics suggested she was setting a bad example for young women, who might give up their own careers to embrace home life. A subway conductor asked her, "How's retirement?" He assumed that writing novels was not really working. A feminist activist wrote a letter to the editor that began, "How can you do this to us?" And a corporate mogul told a friend of hers that her decision proved that "women are afraid of success."

The *Times* news story was headlined "Quindlen Leaving *Times* to Be a Full-time Novelist," but most of the other news stories played up the domestic angle that she wanted to spend time with her family. In truth, she had already been working at home for five years as a columnist, but most reporters played up the home-and-kids theme instead of the novelist angle.

She later told a graduating class at Mount Holyoke that

when she quit, "the cries of the world of 'theys' said I was nuts. But I'm not nuts. I'm happy." Thank goodness she listened to her heart. And not to the colleagues who wanted her to reach for the next rung at the *Times*. Not to those who wanted her to stay the intellectual poster girl for "Working Women with Families."

Four years later, Anna Quindlen could be found happily promoting her third novel, *Black and Blue*. It climbed onto the best-seller lists faster than you could say, "I told you so." A movie version of her first novel, *One True Thing*, was made into a movie starring Meryl Streep and William Hurt, and would later be nominated for a handful of Academy Awards.

When we talked, she said she wants to keep writing novels and get better at it. Does she miss reporting? Yes, she admitted. "It's how I got to learn life. I got to watch a heart transplant. Saw what goes on at night in a police precinct. I had access to a world you never see in the ordinary course of things. Reporting is the best job in the world. But if you don't really need to do it, you shouldn't."

In a way, her journalistic training helped her make the decision to leave the *New York Times*. As she put it, "The great advantage of being a columnist is that you have this ability to argue with yourself. The left brain fights it out with the right brain. I had a number of pitched discussions in my head before I left the *Times*—'Do I want to do this?'

"The truth was I had never stayed in high-profile jobs very long. The time to leave was while you're still hot. It's never the same for you or the readers if you don't. I thought five years was enough. Particularly when you are involved in incendiary topics and a woman. I had finished *One True Thing*. I was growing and developing as a novelist in ways I wanted to work on. Some people said, 'Why not do both?' I had spent four years writing the first novel and doing two columns a week. Now I wonder, how did I do that? Where did I fit the writing in?

"Success isn't success unless it is on your terms," she continued. "Too many women live with someone else's idea of success. Trying to be the perfect wife, the perfect mother, the perfect career woman. They are all hollow in their own way."

Another thing that helped her make her departure decision, she said, was the growing awareness that time is not totally unlimited. And she's right. Many people procrastinate, thinking, "Oh, I'll do this tomorrow," but sometimes tomorrow never comes. Anna's mother had died of ovarian cancer just after turning forty. She took time off from Barnard to help nurse her mother through her last difficult months, an experience that provided some of the wisdom in *One True Thing*. Then her father-in-law died at the age of fifty-two. And her husband's brother's wife died at forty. "I'm more keenly aware that the phrase 'all the time in the world' is not the same as I thought when I was fifteen," she says. "Ask yourself: If the doctor said you had eighteen months to live, would you live in a materially different way? If so, doesn't that tell you something? If I had eighteen months, I'd like my life exactly as it is now."

Typically her day starts early with a brisk walk for a couple of miles. (To prevent osteoporosis and for solitude, she says.) While her husband, attorney Gerald Krovatin, heads to the office, she takes their three children to school. When she gets back, she spends about an hour tending to home business or professional calls. Then she hits the computer and works on her novels from 9:30 A.M. to 2:30 P.M. "You can't make stuff up after three," she says. "You can write, but you can't dream the same way. So then I work on speeches or mail." Then it's more carpool. Meatballs and tomato sauce for dinner. Homework and dishes. The whole glorious, noisy business of life.

That rumbustious home life in Hoboken is very much a part of her writing process, she says, because it means she continues growing as a woman and as a novelist. "You bring all the people you are to the table when you write," she says. "One of the people I am most convincingly is a mother." That's why she empathized with the line in *Black and Blue* that "our kids give us courage." She explained, "Our kids prepare us—at three A.M., someone comes busting in the door and demands that you be fully alive for them. Being responsible for other human beings does give you courage. It is a transforming experience."

When she talked about making soup and planning sleepover parties for her daughter, she sounded like one of your best friends from high school or college. I immediately felt as if I had known her for a long time. I was stranded with the flu in New York, so I had to conduct the interview by phone instead of visiting her home in Hoboken as planned. She was empathetic. She and her daughter had been down with the flu just a few weeks before. "We spent most of the week on the sofa together watching bad TV," she said.

She credits her faith with providing a center to her life, "a level of confidence and clarity." She explained, "I've learned don't sweat the small stuff, and it *is* all small stuff. Faith gives you that. It helps you deal with life and death and goodness and empathy and bad reviews." Attending Mass every Sunday, she says, "gets me up for the week." Did it play a role in her career change? She answered, "It's hard to separate my faith from anything in my life. It's like my liver or my kidneys. It is very much a part of me and how I see the world."

Indeed, in her last column for the *Times*, she paid tribute to all the people who volunteered in homeless shelters, who ministered to prostitutes, who taught in inner city schools. She said the "everyday angels" in today's world were rape counselors, the good cops, the nuns, the librarians. After twenty years as a reporter, she marveled, she had not become more cynical, but more idealistic because of what she saw. "Life will be hard, politics will be mean, money will be scarce, bluster will be plentiful. Yet somehow, good will be done," she wrote. She thanked those who had set an example by standing "in opposition to the spiritual isolationism that makes icicles of our insides and a hard little lump of coal of our hearts." She warned, "If we do not reach out, it is we who will be alone." Then she ended the column with a Christmas wish: "Those who shun the prevailing winds of cynicism and anomie can truly fly."

And she flew away.

Her advice today for others wondering when and how to shift gears is, "You need to follow your heart. At a certain point, you have to screen out everybody's voices. Like people saying you can't let them down. Like people saying your children will be gone in a few years, don't give up your rung on the ladder. Listen to your own voice. The great thing about being alive now is we really can have serial lives. You can be a reporter . . . then a landscape architect . . . a novelist," she said. "Ten years from now I will give all the speeches and sit on boards."

Sure enough, more than a year later, she added another new variation. She joined *Newsweek* as a columnist, filling the back-of-the-book slot previously held by the esteemed Meg Greenberg of the *Washington Post*. Since the column would run only every other week, Ms. Quindlen would still have time for her novels and kiddoes. No wonder she told a graduating class at Villanova that year to "get a life. A real life, not a manic pursuit of the next promotion, the bigger paycheck, the larger house.

"Do you think you'd care so very much about those things if you blew an aneurysm one afternoon, or found a lump in your breast?" she asked them. "Get a life in which you notice the smell of salt water pushing itself on a breeze over Seaside Heights, a life in which you stop and watch how a red-tailed hawk circles over the water gap or the way a baby scowls with concentration when she tries to pick up a Cheerio with her thumb and first finger."

She likes to tell college women to put aside the messages our culture sends through its advertising, its entertainment, its disdain and its approval of how to behave. "Say no to the Greek chorus that thinks it knows the parameters of a happy life, when all it knows is the homogenization of human experience. Listen to the voice inside you that tells you to go another way."

Anna Quindlen's insistence on finding her own way is a reminder to follow your own instincts and remember that you can do whatever you set your heart upon. I've always been inspired by journalist Hazel Brannon Smith, the feisty editor of the Lexington, Mississippi, *Advertiser*. She was not content to settle for life as a secretary. "I don't plan to take dictation, I plan to give it," she insisted. For seventeen years she wrote about the racist policies in her little Southern town despite a hate-filled boycott and, as a result, won a Pulitzer Prize.

Not everyone can win a Pulitzer, of course. Or write a movie that Meryl Streep will star in. But you can follow your

> "One is not born a woman, one becomes one."
> —SIMONE DE BEAUVOIR, WRITER

best instincts and believe that life isn't over when you reach forty. Surely we can become more gutsy as we get older. Surely we can become less concerned with what "they" think. In truth, being self-conscious about doing something is really being they-conscious, concerned about what they would think. And that's like letting someone else drive your car for you, all your life, determining which road you will take and where you will go.

The first step in deciding "what's next?" is to find the time to stop and think, "Who am I now?" Perhaps you need to look in the mirror and get to know yourself again. You must ask yourself what kind of person you want to become. That often means you must remember the person you meant to be before life and necessity stepped in. You must find the time to dream again. What is it you really want to do with the time you have left? Take a time-out to reflect on your life's timeline. Review all the ups and downs. Enumerate the highlights, your accomplishments. Never forget how far you have come. Acknowledge the strengths on which you can build the second half. Leverage what you have learned when deciding what you will do next. You may find it helpful to get a long piece of butcher paper, stick it to a wall, and lay out your timeline. Use colored markers to highlight different significant events. When it is done, step back and view your life.

1. What were the highlights?

- Elementary School
- Middle School
- High School

- College
- Marriage and Children
- Early Career
- Recent Career

2. Like Anna Quindlen's loss of her mother, what were the heartbreaks from which there was the greatest learning? Determine what your greatest strengths are from all that has happened. Write this in a journal. What do you wish you had done that you can do now?

3. For what are you most grateful? List all the things that come to mind.

4. What is that still small voice in you telling you to do? Could it be God with a purpose in mind?

5. What really attracts and interests you? What activities get you excited when you think about them? Is it time for you to use long-neglected gifts? Or perhaps you feel a call to do something that helps others?

6. Develop an exit plan if you want to try something new. Imagine how long you should stay in your current situation and plan how you could leave on your terms. Sometimes women leave their jobs emotionally before they leave physically. What you should plan in advance is an amicable divorce. Keep in mind the kind of moxie it took for Anna Quindlen to walk away from the pinnacle of power. Imagine how you could make your move. Compose a life.

The crux of the matter is to find the kind of work that you want to do in the second half of your life and that the world needs to have done. Other women in this book decided that

"Life is a process of becoming, a combination of states we have to go
through. Where people fail is that they
wish to elect a state and remain in it.
This is a kind of death."
—ANAÏS NIN, WRITER

their calling was to start a
restaurant, to help the homeless, to make quality television
programs, to run for public
office, to leave public office, to
sing part-time, to teach cooking, to help villagers in South
America, to join the family
business and spend more time at home. There's no one model.
You have to decide what fits you at this stage of life, what feels
more fulfilling than what you did before. You have to decide
who you mean to be.

Now, as they say, in a Dickens novel, read on, dear friend.
And you will learn, as I did, how other women learned to
choose what's next for themselves.

Chapter Two

Follow Your Passion

"To love what you do and feel that it matters—how could anything be more fun?"

—KATHARINE GRAHAM, PUBLISHER

Following your great passion in life need not involve great risk. Yes, you may need the courage to change some aspects of your life. You may need the gumption to stick with it. But primarily you will just need to follow your best instincts. Is there something that makes you smile with satisfaction? Or something that gives your life a sense of purpose? Shouldn't it be a big part of your life?

One of the great joys of life is losing track of time because you are so caught up in what you are doing that you are not aware of the time passing by ("Wow—is it three o'clock already?"). You might find yourself humming as you go along. That's because you are doing what you were wired to do. Perhaps your passion involves an artistic gift—painting, playing music, flower arranging, ceramics—or having a knack for something like interior design, strategic planning, teaching others. What makes most people feel good at the end of the day is finding what the Buddhists call "right livelihood"—the idea that what you do for a living should be a natural extension of your personality.

Julia McWilliams Child discovered her first great passion in her early thirties: husband Paul Child, an urbane coworker at the Office of Strategic Services, predecessor of the CIA. He was several inches shorter and ten years older than she was. They met in Ceylon, now known as Sri Lanka, and discovered a mutual fondness for Chinese food and eventually each other.

Julia Child didn't discover her second great passion—cooking—until her late thirties. She didn't write her famous cookbook, *Mastering the Art of French Cooking,* until she was forty-nine. And she was fifty-one when she became a household word as the delightfully irreverent host of *The French Chef* on public television.

As the year 2000 was ushered in, she was eighty-seven, still cooking on PBS, and enjoying every moment of her food fame. She is often credited with demystifying French cooking for Americans and in the process sparking the gourmet food movement. She provided Americans with an alternative to casseroles made with canned Campbell's soup. She guided them to fresh ingredients and exotic tastes like truffles and fennel.

There was little in her well-to-do background to presage her transformation to Super Chef, other than the fact that she grew up hungry because she grew up tall (six feet two inches). At Smith College, Julia McWilliams was best known for her zest for living, which included driving her friends around in her black Ford convertible. When World War II broke out, she gamely volunteered for the OSS. She was working as an office manager in Asia when she met and married Paul. Then when he was transferred to Paris, Julia fell in love again. Her first meal fresh off the boat was oysters, sole meuniere, and Chablis. The experience opened up a new world to her.

"I was just inspired by the food," she told me. She said she had been looking for a career for a long time. But when she went to college in the 1930s, women weren't supposed to do very much with their educations. Only 5 percent of the female population went to college at the time and it was a rarity for women to earn a degree. "You could be a teacher or a secretary," she said. "You were supposed to get married and do laundry. I started cooking after I was married because I learned I *loved* it. I had no training. There was no cooking training in the U.S., really. Then when I got to Paris—one taste of that food and I was *hooked*."

At first she was considered a bit odd in her Parisian circle for doing her own cooking and shopping. Even more out of the ordinary, she decided in 1949, at the age of thirty-seven, to enroll in the world-famous Cordon Bleu cooking school. She was the only woman in the class. After six months, she left the class, but kept studying privately with the instructor and started practicing her skills at dinner parties for friends. Soon she was introduced to Simone "Simca" Beck, a Frenchwoman who shared her passion for cooking and was to become her recipe coauthor. They set to work translating the best of French cooking into understandable recipes.

The rest is culinary history. She became the first female member of the American Chef's Society. She went on to star in eight television series and to publish eleven books. She founded the American Institute of Wine and Food. In our conversation, Ms. Child rattled off her chronology with self-effacing brevity: "I was lucky to have something I was passionately interested in. I was lucky nobody was doing much with French cooking then. Then the Kennedys came into the White House and French cooking was the cat's whiskers! Then public television came along and they needed some excitement and there I was. I was just lucky that the time was right. And I *loved* every minute of it!"

What she leaves out are the long hours of work, testing and retesting recipes until they were foolproof. There were occasional creative differences with Simca. The cookbook was not an overnight success. The first publisher backed out. It took ten long years to get *Mastering the Art of French Cooking* published. But the response in 1961 was dramatically positive. Within three months, the recipe collection had sold twenty thousand copies. By 1970, it had sold more than a million copies.

The Childs were living in Cambridge, Massachusetts, when Julia was invited to participate in a book interview program on Boston's public television station. Sensing the difficulty of "telling" a recipe, she brought along her own hot plate, apron, copper bowl, whip, and a dozen eggs to demonstrate. Letters and calls poured in from viewers who wanted to learn more. So WGBH-TV launched Julia in the first televised cooking show, *The French Chef,* in 1963.

Television was still a young medium and Julia Child was like nothing else seen on TV before. In her first show, she peered into a cooking pot and said, "What do we have here? The big, bad artichoke. Some people are afraid of the big, bad artichoke!" Then she patted a row of naked chickens on the tail and introduced them as "Miss Broiler, Miss Fryer, Miss Roaster. . . ." Some critics mocked her, but viewers loved her loopy humor and frank explanations. She livened up things with zesty imagery ("The dough should feel like a baby's bottom"). And she got right to the point ("Use the electric mixer and go whole hog"). She was known for her funny mistakes on the program. When the top of the blender flew off while she was grinding olives, she deadpanned, "Oh, well, who needs the mechanical age anyway."

Her soufflés sometimes fell, just like other things in life. And, as we should do sometimes, she laughed. Once when loud noises from the studio interrupted, she improvised and said it was probably the plumber. She would even advise, "If you're alone in the kitchen and you drop the lamb, you can always just pick it up. Who's going to know?"

From most accounts, she is not a religious person in a traditional sense, but prefers proving her values in relationships with a "love thy neighbor" approach to others. She cared devotedly for Paul when he slipped into Alzheimer's disease and lost all memory of her. After he died in 1994, she poured more of her energies into her family and enormous circle of friends around the world. You might sum up her boundless drive as *bouter en avant*—to barrel on through life. When a friend said she had always wanted to ride in one of the electric carts at the airport, Julia exclaimed she always wanted to drive one. At eighty, she was still lugging her own bags across crowded airports and quipping, "I wonder what old people do."

At eighty-five, she completed a new PBS series with chef Jacques Pepin, called *Jacques and Julia Cooking at Home*. The twenty-two–part series was filmed in her kitchen in Cambridge. She also is now on the Internet with "Gourmet Guide" and is a plucky Web surfer. She finds the Internet useful to locate books, such as cookbooks from London, or to order products, like French cheese directly from France.

When we talked, she had just spent a month in Italy and jetted to a food and wine gala in Disneyland. "The mail is *awful*," she said. "I can't see my desk for the mail. It's dreadful!" But as for giving any thought to slowing down, she said with some surprise, "Why should I?" When her nieces and good friends told her she shouldn't drive her car anymore, she said it was hell because she couldn't rush down to the store and buy parsley on a whim. She said she would just get used to asking others for transportation and would learn to ride the bus.

Likewise, she didn't find it all that remarkable that she began her TV career at the age of fifty. Perhaps that's because she's never been afraid to be different. She approached life as something to be savored, not deferred. Or as she once said, "Life itself is the proper binge."

She told *Esquire* with typical modesty in 2000, "The measure of achievement is not winning awards. It's doing something that you appreciate, something you believe is worthwhile. I think of my strawberry soufflé. I did that at least twenty-eight times before I finally conquered it."

She said she hoped other women would be emboldened by her example to turn their avocations into a vocation. "Go ahead and *do* it. If you find what you love doing, just get some more training, if necessary, and have at it! Start right in," she advised. "And I hope you will be as lucky as I was. Find something you really *love* doing. Be *passionate*."

Like many women, Julia Child parlayed what had been considered a domestic skill into a career. Many women who are talented cooks open restaurants, bakeries, or catering services. Women who are skilled seamstresses often set up shop so they can make alterations for those who are less skilled. Women who took music lessons as children often become teachers themselves, but even at midlife they can still find ways to perform even if it's as a volunteer to bring joy to nursing homes. Women who dreamed as young girls of becoming a photographer, like the daring Margaret Bourke-White of *Life* magazine, but tended to families instead may later find the time to take photo courses at a community college and start a portrait business.

> "Listen to the passion of your soul, set the wings of your spirit free; and let not a single song go unsung."
> —SYLVANA ROSSETTI, WRITER

What activity makes you feel "in sync?" You must keep seeking what fits you best, what you were designed for. There is a difference between doing things out of economic necessity and doing things because you're wild about doing them. Some women have gotten very good at what they do out of duty, but dread going to work in the morning because they don't enjoy it. You owe it to yourself to keep looking for something that you have a "bent" for and then find a way to get more of it into your everyday schedule.

At midlife, you may hunger for the breathing space to reexamine what you're doing with your life. Try journaling your responses to these questions:

1. What gets you excited and happy about life?

2. What do you notice that you are attracted to do?

3. What would you be doing if you could truly do what *you* want to do? Put another way, what would you do for free?

4. What did you really enjoy doing as a little girl?

5. Are you more interested in people? Or task?

6. Do you like things indoors, or outdoors?

> "Success can come in many areas, such as motherhood, business, or volunteering. It can be finding something that leads you to say, 'Nothing I ever did made me feel this important.'"
> —ELIZABETH DOLE

7. How will you direct your passion once you identify it?

8. Who would be a good mentor for that passion?

After you've written your thoughts out, it might be easier to talk this over with a good friend, coach, or mentor.

E ven if you think you don't have any significant talent, you can still find a purpose in life that gives you a sense of forward direction. Having a personal mission to pursue can be just as energizing as a creative urge. When you feel an intense drive to do something, most likely you are being directed to live the life you were meant to live. Having a mission orients, roots, and balances a person. It can give you a reason to get up in the morning and keep you going strong.

Elizabeth Dole is one of those women who has never doubted her main mission—public service. She just keeps looking for new ways to serve. Whenever polls are taken of potential women presidents or vice presidents, Elizabeth Hanford Dole always leads the list. Her resume is unparalleled: two-time cabinet official, service in five administrations, head of the Red Cross, GOP presidential candidate in 1999. Because she has conducted all those missions with integrity, she has remained one of the most admired women in the country for more than three decades.

We first talked in 1998 when she was leading the Red Cross and trying to decide whether to make a run for the presidency. She began by apologizing that she couldn't shake hands—she had fallen and broken her arm while rushing to do errands when she had some free time. She presses herself through demanding schedules because she fervently believes in what she is doing.

Typically, in one month that year she spoke in five cities, hosted a three-day fiftieth anniversary convention for the Red Cross, and delivered five commencement speeches. She couldn't keep up that pace if she didn't believe it was for a good cause.

She took a gamble when she segued from politics to heading the Red Cross, which provides half the nation's blood supply. She was in her midfifties. She could have parlayed her political capital into a high-powered lobbying job, the plush door of choice among the Beltway crowd. She could have rotated onto lucrative corporate boards. But Elizabeth Dole chose the Red Cross. It fit better with her great passion to serve.

When she became president of the organization in 1991, blood banking was shaken by scares about safety. With the spread of HIV and hepatitis B and C, taking a job in blood banking was asking for trouble. Congress was investigating. So was *60 Minutes*. Most former politicians would have run the other way. Elizabeth Dole saw it as a mission. And rolled up her tailored sleeves. Many in the Red Cross operation advised her to get out of blood services to avoid controversy and liability. "People were frightened," she recalls. "But when you think that giving blood is the gift of life, when you think that every two seconds someone in this country needs blood, we really had no choice. . . . Something had to be done. We had to look outside the boxes. We couldn't let America down." So she launched a gutsy campaign to modernize the Red Cross. Seven years later, virtually every aspect of the blood-collecting operation had been overhauled. Even Democrats on Capitol Hill started singing the praises of Republican Elizabeth Dole's improvements at the Red Cross.

No doubt about it, she has achieved a superstar status in public life. She has been on magazine covers and the late-night shows. She wowed the national TV audience at the 1996 GOP convention by having a talk show–style chat with the audience. The idea was to show support for her husband Bob, who was the presidential nominee. But many commentators came away admiring *her*. NBC's Tom Brokaw predicted that folks in living rooms across the country would be turning to each other and asking, "Wow, why isn't she on the ticket?"

What they didn't know was she had plenty of practice with the talk-show technique at Red Cross appearances across the country. In Salt Lake City, she walked into the audience with a microphone to interview volunteers. She shared tears with a survivor of a tornado. She congratulated a hundred-year-old volunteer, who gushed, "I *love* this lady!" Whereupon the embarrassed Mrs. Dole corrected softly, "No, it's the Red Cross you love."

It was perhaps inevitable that the widespread admiration for her work at the Red Cross would tempt her to segue back into politics. A *USA Today*–CNN Gallup poll in June 1998 showed she could edge out Al Gore to win the presidency. Indeed, polls showed she would even trounce Hillary Clinton in a hypothetical contest.

But she did not make the decision to run without considerable soul-searching about what it would demand of her personally, what it would do to her marriage, what example it would set for other women. To follow her true heart, she would have to leave her job at the Red Cross, because she could not conduct partisan activity as the head of a nonprofit agency. She would be on the road campaigning at least a year. She would have to raise money for herself, rather than for others. Her personal life would be open to inspection and distortion like never before.

Yet she believed that the time was long overdue for a

woman president. A woman had not been on a major party ticket since 1984, when Representative Geraldine Ferraro ran for vice president on the Democratic ticket with Walter Mondale. There were very few women in the country in as good a position as Elizabeth Dole to run in the 2000 race.

> "Women share with men the need for personal success, even the taste for power, and no longer are we willing to satisfy those needs through the achievements of surrogates, whether husbands, children, or merely role models."
> —ELIZABETH DOLE

So she decided to go for it at the age of sixty-three.

Close friends say Elizabeth Dole's husband was among those urging her to run. He joked that she was his last chance to get in the White House. Jay Leno greeted her candidacy on *The Tonight Show* by cracking, "According to *Newsweek* magazine, Elizabeth Dole is planning to resign as head of the American Red Cross, which means one of two things. She's either going to run for president, or, now that her husband, Bob, is on Viagra, she no longer has time to work."

Having her husband become the national spokesperson for erectile dysfunction could have been embarrassing, but Mrs. Dole handled the first questions with admirable good humor, saying teasingly that her only comment was, "It is a good drug." Still, he put her campaign at a disadvantage when he told an interviewer he also might contribute to her rival, Sen. John McCain. She diplomatically responded, "I told him I loved him. I told him he was in the woodshed."

Out on the campaign trail, she drew large crowds of college students and put her talk-show skills to good use, working crowds with aplomb. She took tough stands that her male competitors ducked. Supporting gun reforms, she came up with the memorable line, "You don't need an assault weapon to protect your family."

She ran a more than respectable campaign and drew larger numbers of young people to her appearances than most of the other candidates. She was second in the polls when she quit because of the difficulty of raising enough money to keep up with George W. Bush. She had raised $5 million with 108 fundraisers, no small task. But Governor Bush, the front-runner, already had raised $57 million, an insurmountable advantage. As she said when gracefully bowing out, "It's money, money, money."

Still, despite the fact she has lived so much of her life in the public, everyday people may not know much about what makes Elizabeth Dole tick. To find out, you have to get past her political persona to the other facets of her life. Once the topic was shifted away from politics in our first talk, Mrs. Dole seemed to open up more. She talked long past the expected time for the interview once she ventured into her early career, her marriage, and roles for women.

I asked her about her decisions to put her own career on hold twice to boost her husband's political career. How did she feel about taking a leave of absence from the Cabinet in 1976, when her husband ran as vice president with Gerald Ford, and from the Red Cross in 1996, when he ran for president? She said she took time to be with the campaigns because she felt strongly she should do anything she could to help him. "I can't imagine it any other way. I am blessed with a beautiful marriage. I can't imagine just saying, 'Good-bye, Bob, good luck, and I'll see you when it's over.' I very much wanted to be a part of it," she explained. Remembering the challenges of the '96 campaign, when she was often called to substitute for him at campaign events with little notice, she said she would prod herself on by saying to herself, "Elizabeth, you've got to do this. Bob's got to be on the other side of the country and you need to do this."

She tries to emphasize to women's groups the importance of being flexible about roles they assume at different seasons of their lives. "What we fought for is the right to decide what's best for us, for our families. There doesn't have to be *one* way. In my own professional experience, I had a lot of wonderful challenges. But it doesn't have to be a paid position to be meaningful. I think each woman should be free to try to define success."

She admits she grew up in an era when girls were required to take home economics and boys took shop. In fact, her mother wanted her to major in home economics. But homemaking was not her passion, politics was. She started early as president of a bird club in third grade. She ran for freshman president in high school and lost. Undaunted by the loss, she kept on seeking leadership positions, winning more often than losing. And she thwarted her mother's ambitions for her by majoring in political science at Duke University.

Though homemaking wasn't her future, she always takes pains to show respect for the demands of home and family. Here's what she said in the dual autobiography she wrote with her husband, *The Doles—Unlimited Partners:*

Today, many of the bosses are women and some of the typists are men. Diversity is the hallmark of the modern American woman. We wear the robes of a judge, the face mask of a surgeon, the pinstripes of a banker. We teach on campuses, peer through lab microscopes, design buildings and run businesses. Some of us write the laws that other women enforce. Some build rockets for others to ride into space. The most energetic of all run a home and raise a family. No role is superior to another.

At home, she says, she does the grocery shopping, he walks the dog. Both joke about their "power couple" relationship. Once she quipped to Bob Strauss at the VIP Gridiron Dinner that a reporter had asked her husband whether being married to a powerful woman made him feel emasculated. She said she interrupted, "Hold it, cupcake, I'll take that one." And her husband laughed harder at the joke than anyone.

In person, Mrs. Dole looks coolly composed and treadmill trim. The day of our first interview, she had on a pale peach silk suit and pearls, which perfectly complemented her barely perceptible freckles and creamy complexion. She looked much younger than her years. She studiously manages to be feminine and authoritative at the same time, listening carefully and responding, "Right, right," while thinking through her answers. She is cautious, a habit acquired no doubt after three decades in the Washington shark tank. But she was easy to be with, exuding a kind of wary grace.

Her journey has been guided to a great extent by her faith. She was most comfortable when talking about how important her faith has been in her life. She said her spiritual devotion was inculcated in her at an early age in her hometown of Salisbury, North Carolina, by her maternal grandmother, "Mom" Cathey. Although not particularly well-off, her grandmother's faith was such that when one of her sons was killed by a drunk driver, she donated the life insurance payment to build a hospital wing in his memory in a far-off church mission in Pakistan.

That so impressed young Elizabeth that she still mentions it in conversation and speeches. And over the years, Mrs. Dole has been known to quietly perform similar acts of charity or compassion, helping pay for chemotherapy for a classmate, dropping everything to be at the side of a friend in need. One coworker in the Reagan administration was amazed to find a candy striper uniform on the back of Mrs. Dole's office door one day. Somehow she was making time to volunteer each week to help the sick and the elderly.

She often cites Mom Cathey as her role model and praises her for practicing what she preached. When it became necessary for her grandmother to go into a nursing home in her nineties, she told her granddaughter, "Elizabeth, there might be some people there who don't know the Lord and I can read the Bible to them."

Yet Mrs. Dole candidly admits that when she became a workaholic Washington power broker, she lost touch with her faith for a time. As she sometimes says in her speeches, God was stuck somewhere in her Rolodex between "Gardening" and "Government" until she was in her forties. She decided then that her career had become too all-consuming. She realized she needed to refocus on faith. She admits, "I needed to submit my resignation as master of my own universe."

She found a pastor who helped her see "what joy there can be when God is the center of life, and all else flows from that center." She joined a spiritual growth group that meets each Monday night. And she began Bible study with other Senate wives. Since then, she has participated in a series of Bible study and prayer groups. For most of her Red Cross tenure she had a weekly Bible study group that met in her office. She told me she also tries to find thirty minutes every day for prayer, Bible study, and solitude. "You have a source of strength that is beyond your own," she said.

She revealed with a girlish laugh that when a friend needs a special prayer, she calls her mother (who was ninety-nine in the year 2000) and says, "Mother, turn on your network!" And with quiet feeling, she says of her grandmother's faith, "As I look back, I cannot remember an unkind word ever escaping her lips or ungracious deed marring her path." The impression is left that she would love for others to be able to say that about her someday.

As you might expect, she does have critics. There are tales that she wears out staff because of her perfectionism. There are those who snicker about the sincerity of her faith. But, by and large, the only real knock you hear about Elizabeth Dole is that she is a stickler for detail who insists on being overprepared and in control. So what? That's small chum in the Washington fishbowl, where character assassination is a blood sport.

Mrs. Dole has long been what some call a "stealth feminist," promoting advancement for women in government and instituting innovations like day care for the children of transportation workers. When she speaks to young women, she urges them to find something that they feel passionately about. She tells them that a sense of mission is essential for her and for them: "If you are going to put so much energy into something, you must care about it. A job is right for me, but you have to find what is *right* for you, what gives *you* a sense of mission."

Likewise her advice for women wondering what to do at midlife: "Having a passion for what you are doing is *very* important." Then she tells about seeing some employees waiting at the door of an office building at 3:30 P.M. for the end of the day to come. "And I was nearly knocked down at the door by them," she marveled. "I thought, 'How sad that it doesn't have any more meaning for them!' I just stood there for a few minutes, thinking about it. If you can find something you care about, that's the important thing."

It was clear that working with the Red Cross was not just an interregnum between political appointments, it was an assignment that fit with her sense of mission/passion. She personally consoled the families of victims after the Oklahoma bombing incident. She traveled to Zaire to survey refugees from the Rwanda massacres. Tears filled her eyes as she recalled seeing people who were dying of cholera or dysentery, where she had to step over dead bodies. "The memory will haunt me the rest of my life," she says. "If you can make some difference to people who have such dire needs, it's very rewarding work."

It's clear Elizabeth Dole's mission is to serve, not to be served. Her advice to "follow your passion" may seem obvious sense, but the truth is many women do what's dutiful or doable instead. They often don't give themselves permission to turn their daydreams into reality. But finding your "bliss" is doable, too. It's the option you should try *first,* not last. The alternative is becoming one of those people waiting at 3:30 P.M. for the end of the workday to come.

But *how* to determine what your passion, your calling, your underused gift may be? One device that is sometimes recommended is to imagine you had only a year to live. What would you be doing if you were not doing what you're doing now? Or, put another way, if you could write your own obituary now, what would you want it to say?

Yet another test is to ask yourself how you would like your children to see you. Are you plodding along stolidly, going through the motions, marking time? Or are you showing them how to take risks to have a more authentic life?

Who was it you wanted to be before life pushed and pulled

you in different directions? Is there a daring young girl in you who had to settle for being a compliant woman?

Could you start taking classes in a subject that has always interested you?

Do you have a strength—like a facility with computers, making crafts, a sense of style—that could be turned into a full-time pursuit?

If you're good at organizing your book club or leading your alumnae group, would you like to try public service at some level?

Rethink your thoughts. Stretch. Both Elizabeth Dole and Julia Child have stretched conventional notions of women's work to pursue their passion. To find your passion, you must recognize who you are. Remember who you wanted to be. Decide who you still could be.

I like the way Carolyn G. Heilbrun, a scholar and a mystery writer, described a fictional detective in one of her books:

> But most important, she has become braver as she has aged, less interested in the opinions of those she does not cherish, and has come to realize that she has little to lose, little any longer to risk, that age above all, both for those with children and those without them, is the time when there is very little "they" can do for you, very little reason to fear, or hide, or not attempt brave and important things.

Chapter Three

Give Yourself Permission

"Think wrongly, if you please, but in all cases think for yourself."
—DORIS LESSING, AUTHOR

Women have always worked. They have worked with children on their backs in the fields, doing miserable stoop labor. They have worked with children at their side in dank factories. And they have worked in the home, up at dawn to begin cooking, sewing, canning, cleaning. That long first era of working women, however, was largely on male terms. This new era is more on female terms. Women fought hard in the twentieth century for the right to work in all aspects of business. And women steamed ahead. In 1970, some four out of ten women worked. Today six out of ten are in the workforce. What's needed now is for women to know when it's okay to stop. You should be able to give yourself permission to stop or switch careers without stigma. We each have to ask ourselves, at different stages of our lives, what time it is. Time to stay, or time to move on.

Susan Molinari chose to work in the political arena for her first career. If you saw Congresswoman Molinari deliver the keynote address at the 1996 GOP convention, you might have assumed she had everything going her way. She was the highest-ranking woman in the House of Representatives. Her husband,

Rep. Bill Paxton, was being touted as a potential Speaker of the House. And they had a photogenic new baby, Susan Ruby.

But what the audience didn't know was that her biggest moment in the sun was also her swan song. She had played center-stage politics, but her heart was no longer in it. Although she handily won reelection that fall to her Staten Island district, Susan Molinari resigned the next summer. At forty, Susan Molinari had decided she wanted to spend more time with her young family. So she took a job as host of a new CBS program on Saturday mornings.

The transition wasn't easy. And if you are considering a change, you should be prepared to stretch yourself, which isn't any easier in life than it is in an exercise class. "There is so much to learn," Susan admitted in an interview at the Hyatt Regency in Dallas later that year. "The TV people all make it look easy, but there's so much work and preparation. It's a lot harder to ask the questions and bring everything together on time than it is to be on the other side of the table."

While she said she didn't miss the long days and nights of money-raising and vote-getting, she said she did miss the comfort of a job she knew how to do well. As she put it, "Now when I work, we sit down afterward and talk about what I did *wrong*. It's a healthy exercise since 90 percent can be corrected . . . but it is an adjustment when you're forty."

It was also difficult dealing with criticism that she had "betrayed" women's rights and her constituents by dropping out. Some feminist critics complained that she was quitting so her husband, Rep. Bill Paxton, also a member of Congress from New York, could have the spotlight and move up the leadership ladder. Political detractors said she should have decided what to do about her family before seeking reelection.

"I can answer for myself," she said. "I woke up one day with a different set of priorities. I was first elected to office at twenty-six. I was the youngest member of Congress. But when I had my daughter at thirty-nine, I said, 'This is where my priorities should be.'" She had been in Congress for seven years and on the city council for four years. CBS offered her a more flexible schedule. Now she gets to see Susan Ruby at breakfast and dinner. So there were benefits worth the effort to change.

Indeed, she dedicated her recent book, *Representative Mom,* to Susan Ruby, saying the baby girl had changed her world. She said she now thinks about her child twenty-four hours a day and feels guilty and lonesome when she is away. "I think of you when you are asleep upstairs and wonder if I'm doing it right. I think of you learning and growing, and I feel proud that you are my daughter. I think of you and wonder what you think of me. I think of you, and I thank God (and my own mother). I think of you and decide to put down my pen and go inside to play with you instead."

Her departure from Congress was considered a loss for centrist Republicans who wanted to move the party more to the middle. As a party leader, she could have helped recruit more women and moderates. Likewise, women's advocates regretted that her departure meant giving up seniority, which is essential to winning prize committee chairs. When she left, no women chaired committees in the House.

But her example made a point worth making as the 1990s drew to a close: that women should be able to get on and off the career ladder just like men who leave a corporation to start a business of their own or to sail around the world. "Women need to relax and give themselves a break! Too many have fought for rights that they won't give themselves permission to enjoy. This is a lecture to myself," Susan said and laughed at herself. She added, "I'm not done." She had been in a political career for fifteen years, she explained. "I always had to see the next step—Senate, governor? I thought someday I would try my hand at the Senate. But I no longer had the fire in the belly. I had not thought about quitting. I had been working twenty-four hours a day, seven days a week when I had a child. And around that time CBS started calling about a job, offering me less hours than in Congress. It seemed like the perfect answer to me."

She paced around the room as she talked, a compact bundle of energy. "Being at the top is not necessarily success," she said as she moved a vase of flowers away that she seemed allergic to. "I have a friend who was finance director for George Bush at the age of twenty-two. She was afraid to go on vacation."

When the CBS offer came up, she said she discussed it a lot with her husband, who helped her sort out the issues. That's an important consideration for married women. You should bring your spouse into your planning from the beginning, not at the end. Things will go better if he feels included, not excluded. Susan confirmed, "He was supportive. During the two weeks when I was making the transition to CBS, he even got Susan Ruby sleeping through the night and drinking from a sippy cup."

Does she have regrets? "No. I loved being a member of Congress. But it is a constant challenge at CBS. It is an opportunity to create. A title you can keep. I never felt particularly comfortable with titles in the first place."

When she started her political career, she was the first woman and the first Republican on the New York City Council. She recalled that one of the men on the council said he doubted if she could find the "little girl's room." "He might think it today, but he wouldn't say it," she said with a raised eyebrow and a laugh. Being a woman now has become an asset, she said, as the political parties see the value of the female voting block. She is proud that she got a bill passed to give the proceeds from special postage stamps to breast cancer research. She was outspoken on tough issues from abortion to Bosnia. She took Susan Ruby with her in her stroller to the hearing where she pressed generals for answers about allegations of sexual harassment at the Aberdeen Proving Ground.

Yet despite her steady track record of success, it was always a struggle to get people to take her seriously because of her diminutive size. She was a short blond who looked like everyone's granddaughter. As she explained in her book, petite women get pigeonholed unfairly as lightweights or pawns of powerful men. "That didn't change much even once I had a real record to stand on. There I'd be, in a war zone in Bosnia, and some reporter, usually female, would comment on how I was dressed, then turn to my male colleague for answers to questions of substance," she said.

To this day, she hates being described as "perky" and says, "What was I supposed to do, eat myself into a stupor so I would seem more weighty? Dye my hair salt and pepper? Wear platform shoes? Imagine the controversy that would have created! And when did perky get a bad name? How did being lively and optimistic become a liability? Is dressing in black and weighing yourself down with public angst really morally superior? Why is it chic to smoke cigars and tacky to chew gum? Or okay to play golf, but not lead cheers?" She remembers her irritation when other representatives called her "Susie" on the floor of the House as a way of belittling her position on the issues. It only made her work harder.

Having a sense of humor has helped her keep things in perspective, she said. That and a strong sense of faith. As she put it, "I looked up at forty and discovered I didn't have all the answers. But I did have faith to come back to." She had attended an all-girls Catholic school through high school, but had been moving too fast to think about spiritual matters. Now, she says, prayer and discussion are a larger part of her life. She tries once a day to pause for a quiet moment, even if it has to be on a plane or before the TV show. "I feel that prayerful sense most when I hold my baby. That's as much God as anyone will ever feel."

When she was a child, her mother, Marguerite, struggled with health problems, so her grandmother helped raise her. "Mama Sue," her namesake, became her best friend. Susan described her as a sort of Auntie Mame figure with platinum hair and off-the-shoulder blouses, who let her drive early and teased her to gain weight. She remembers her grandmother would say funny things like, "Put some meat on yer bones because men like something to grab." Susan said she never left her grandmother's side when she was dying. "I knew she was tired, but she was hanging on while I was there. So I told her I knew she was tired and wanted her to go to sleep and see her friends. I told her, 'You can go now. I'm going to have a girl and she's going to know all about you.'"

She got tears in her eyes as she spoke about her grandmother and had to get up and get a Kleenex. For a moment, the bravado, the cheeky confidence she showed the TV and Capitol Hill audiences was gone. But just as quickly, she came back to the subject and charged on.

She thinks that other women should "just do it. Women often think things will come to an end if we fail. We hesitate to begin a new career at forty or fifty. It *is* easier when you are twenty-six or twenty-seven to try something new. But you have to learn to block the noise out." She believes we are entering a defining time for women in America. She explains, "There are incredible changes in all our lives. Sometimes we need to stop and ask, 'Do we really know where we're going?' We need to take time to celebrate. And give ourselves a break. Now that we have clout, it won't mean a thing if we don't have a sense of self-respect. People said to me, 'How could she do this to us?' They said, 'You set us back!' We've got to stop eating our own. We need to get self-respect and respect the choices of others. Career women should be able to climb higher—or stop climbing—without ostracism. At the same time, single mothers need understanding. Welfare mothers need resources. Not constant criticism."

She carried that theme into her speech to a luncheon of businesswomen. She told them that all the progress women have made in general won't mean anything if each one does not use it to enhance her personal growth. Likewise, she told them all the new medical research, which now includes women in case studies, won't help if women are reluctant to see their doctor and they put their own health last. And she told them, "All the antiviolence legislation won't help if you don't have enough self-worth to leave an abusive relationship." She encouraged each woman in the room to stretch, take risks, and not be afraid of failure. "If we all do something for ourselves, our daughters will have it better."

She said her father, longtime Staten Island politician Guy Molinari, encouraged her to seek public office, saying, "Step right up there and try. It's okay if you don't make it, but you will have tried." Still, she acknowledged, if there had been a son before her, she probably would not have been encouraged to try politics. "We still tend to give different messages to our daughters than to our sons," she said.

What message would she like to leave to her daughter? "Not to wait until she's thirty-nine to realize who she is," she said without hesitation.

Postscript: A few months later, Susan Molinari's husband, Bill Paxton, resigned from his leadership position in the House of Representatives and announced he would not seek another term, saying he wanted to spend more time with his family. And CBS announced that she was leaving her job after nine months "by mutual agreement."

When we talked again, she was happily teaching a course on politics at the Kennedy School of Government at Harvard University. "I was raised to say you don't have regrets in life. There are enough things that can go wrong, that make a bad career choice seem minor. But I can't say it was a bad choice, because CBS did compensate me very well for our parting. So I can't tell you that I am sorry I did that. The truth is I learned things I *didn't* want to do. That's an important lesson. It was a year when I had to stay free of politics. Which bothered me a lot. I realized I had lost an important part of my life, my ability to comment and participate in politics. I had always thought politics was something I could just walk away from. But when (as a journalist) you can't even write a check to support a candidate or be seen talking to one candidate longer than another, you feel that loss."

Does that mean she would consider running for office again? "Personally, no," she said, but she would be glad to help others. She said one thing she learned from her chapters in politics and television was that "stretching yourself and failing is not necessarily the *worst* thing that can happen in life. It gives you a chance to grow. It gives you a chance to test what you're good at. It gives you a broader experience in life. It's all part of the journey. Every step makes you a little stronger."

She said she realizes now that her CBS chapter was a "nice rerouting." She soon was to give birth to another baby girl, Katherine Mary ("Katie"). She opened her own consulting firm in Washington, D.C., and was writing a column called "Capitol NOW" for an Internet site. Her husband has become known as one of the most powerful lobbyists in the capital, a "go-to" man that big interests go to when they want things done.

I remained impressed with her struggle to do things her way, not as the heir to her father's congressional seat, not as a quiescent political wife, but as a fully engaged woman with dreams of her own. As she admitted, the chipper lady that TV viewers saw at first was somewhat a façade. Like many American women, she still struggles with the nagging "need to be nice" and self-doubt. But she found the gumption to change direction. And came out of the experience with a clearer definition of who she was.

Like Susan Molinari, your first attempt at a new direction may not be successful. Remember the wisdom of the monk who was asked by a visitor what they did in the monastery all day. The monk replied, "Well, we fall and we get up and we fall and we get up and we fall and we get up." Falling down is no dishonor, but staying down might be. Pick up your sticks and try again. Can you become anything you want? Maybe not. But you can become something you like better.

Sometimes liking something better starts with doing something "significant" with your life. As you get older, you realize it's time to do something serious. But it's not always easy to make a difference. You have to give yourself permission to reach out of your everyday existence. Amira Matsuda had been content to be a dutiful mother and wife. Born and raised in Iraq, a devout Muslim, she saw her role first and foremost as tending to her family. But increasingly, her conscience called on her to do something about the children who were starving in Iraq.

Her own four children in North Dallas lived in comfort thanks to the success of her husband, a Japanese businessman with an international company. Living in a predominately Judeo-Christian culture, where the Muslim faith is often little understood, she had found herself drawn to explain that culture to others. She had started volunteering for the Arabic Heritage Society and she took another step by organizing joint programs with other faith groups. She returned to Iraq to visit her ailing mother and she saw the sanctions imposed after the Desert Storm showdown in 1990 were taking more of a toll on everyday people than on dictator Saddam Hussein. Children were especially vulnerable, without adequate materials for school, without medicines or vaccines.

She knew it was a diplomatic tightrope to walk, trying to explain to Americans that the sanctions were harming children, the sick, and the elderly instead of weakening Saddam Hussein. But she knew that little of the real suffering was making its way into the mainstream media, so she felt she had to find some way to share what she saw on her trips home. In 1999 she took a video camera with her on one of her visits home to Iraq. She recorded the crowded conditions in the schools and the shockingly ill-equipped hospitals, where children languished without basic medical supplies. It was difficult dealing with government officials to get permission to film. She had to be careful not to say or do anything that brought harm to her family. But she pressed on. At forty-two, Amira has the determination of a woman who has had to deal with three cultures, having learned to operate in her husband's Asian surroundings as well as suburban America and emerging Iraq. She listens intently, her dark eyes flickering behind metal frame glasses, then she moves right ahead.

Her amateur video footage was edited down to fifteen minutes on her return and given more polish with a narrative by a local Arab historian. The scenes show how the infrastructure has deteriorated under the embargo after the Desert Storm conflict. The hospitals have beds without sheets and are infiltrated by insects. They reek of refuse. Syringes are often used a half dozen times. Diseases like cholera and dysentery are prevalent. The World Health Organization estimates that the deaths of six to seven thousand children a month can be attributed to the United Nations sanctions and children can be seen sitting two and three at a desk in bare-walled schools and scavenging in trash heaps.

It's a primitive, brief, but well-meaning piece of propaganda. It was shown in 1999 and 2000 to local church groups and at the Dallas Peace Center. Global leaders didn't take note, but Amira did feel that she had helped some Americans look at the situation differently. Choosing her words very carefully, she made it clear she was not trying to create sympathy for the Iraqi leader, but to create more understanding about the prolonged damage the sanctions were doing to everyday people who are trapped under the dictatorship.

Her observations largely corroborate those of United Nations reports. And increasingly the argument is being made by humanitarian groups that other means need to be sought to pressure Saddam Hussein, because he has been siphoning away oil revenues for his military uses rather than allowing the distribution of food and medicine.

"The purpose of life, after all, is to live it, to taste experience to the utmost, to reach out eagerly and without fear for newer and richer experience."
—ELEANOR ROOSEVELT

It's a nightmarish situation with no easy answers, but to Amira's credit, she has tried to speak up for the sick and the elderly who do not deserve the punishment of the world. After she produced her modest video, she took another step to help by organizing a dinner to raise money for medicine, which she personally took to Iraq to make sure the children received it.

Amira Matsuda had no grand illusions that her simple mission would change policy, but she wanted to help as many children as she could. She sees that as being in keeping with her faith, which requires charity as the third pillar of Islam. Those who are comfortable are supposed to share with the unfortunate. The Koran counsels that people should "walk the straight path." For Amira that means doing what she can in her own way. In the process, she has provided a model for her children.

Life is about reinterpreting and revising. You have to decide how to spend your days, because in the end that is how you will have spent your life. Sometimes that means putting on the brakes instead of bearing down on the accelerator. That's what Brenda Barnes, the forty-three-year-old chief executive officer of Pepsi Cola, did in 1997. The business world was taken by surprise when she announced she was leaving to concentrate on raising her three children. Yet it was understandable why the Pepsi exec was burned out. Her schedule reportedly began at 3:30 A.M. and required two or three nights a week away from home. Ms. Barnes explained when she resigned that she was tired of watching videotapes of her children's school plays and missing birthdays. She wanted to be able to spend more time with her three children. Yet her resignation launched big headlines in the *New York Times* and the *Wall Street Journal*. Feminists branded her a Benedict Arnold; traditionalists said it showed working moms were returning to family values. And yet by blazing her own path, Brenda Barnes proved the wisdom of following your heart. The epilogue to her story is that a host of blue-chip companies (Sears, LucasArts, Avon, *New York Times,* Starwood Hotels and Resorts) sought her for board positions because they wanted someone who could think for herself. A year after resigning, she was on five corporate boards and two national nonprofit boards. She was still in the business world, but on her terms.

When I tracked her down, she had moved from New York back to her home area of Chicago, where she had a family network. She said she now has time to go on vacation and teach her daughter's religion class. "For the first time, I have time to spend with family and friends and siblings," she told me. "I have not looked back once. There is so much in the world to explore that you don't realize when you are consumed by something else."

Did she feel she had hurt the chances for other women on the corporate track? She said she did not think so, but admitted she had worried about it. "Even if I didn't outwardly say it, I put that guilt trip on myself, too. You know, 'I can't let womanhood down.' You get told a hundred times you're a role model, you're a role model. You carry the weight of that. I thought the longest time before I made my decision about what it would say, less to the women, but to the corporations who employed women. Finally I came to the conclusion, I can't worry about that. Who, male or female, has given twenty-two years to the same company? I did. I can't discount that." She felt she had earned the right to leave. She gave herself permission to walk away.

"What's happened is people didn't have a choice in the past. Women now have more choices. I've told women forever, be yourself. Don't try to be someone you're not. It won't work. Figure out what's important and make your choices. Realize what tradeoffs you're making and get comfortable with it. You can't do everything. Only you can decide what is right for you. But consciously do it and be happy with it, because you're choosing your life."

Perhaps you need to get away from the noise of the "caring" crowd and begin to think about your life's journey. Have you wandered along and just let things evolve, made wrong turns and wound up somewhere you didn't want to be?

Or have you intentionally designed your life's path?

To begin to get a clear view, ask yourself: Are you driving your life or is someone else? What is the caring crowd saying you "should" do?

1. Make a list of what your parents or significant others wanted you to be when you grew up. What were the subtle, yet strong messages? When you chose a major in college, was it one of your own choice, or someone else's? How have you tried to be a "good girl" and satisfy your family obligations/expectations?

2. Try to imagine what your life will be like in five or ten years if you continue on the path you are on. Where does

all you are currently doing lead? Are you sure you want to go? If you originally chose your career, do you still feel attracted by it?

3. If not, what wheels have you set in motion to transform your life—such as education or saving money for a business venture? What would success "on my terms" mean for you?

4. Can you think of some tools to deal with criticism? Get a support group and use them.

5. Is there a fear of failure if you strike out on your own life's path? How willing are you to try something that may not work?

Remember what Anne Sullivan, Helen Keller's devoted teacher, advised: "No matter what happens, keep on beginning and failing. Each time you fail, start all over again, and you will grow stronger until you find out you have accomplished a purpose—not the one you began with perhaps, but one you will be glad to remember."

Chapter Four

Take Care of Yourself

"If you think you can, you can. And if you think you can't, you're right."

—MARY KAY ASH, FOUNDER OF MARY KAY COSMETICS

Once while attending a conference in Washington, D.C., I was struck by an anecdote that Lesley Stahl of CBS News told. She shared the difficulty of trying to keep up with a high-pressure career, a husband, and children. She said she found it amusing when magazines painted her as the image of the successful career woman. She reached down behind the podium and pulled up a tattered shopping bag from a department store. "This is how organized I am," she admitted with a laugh. "I rushed out today and had to throw everything in a shopping bag because I couldn't get it in my purse."

She had struggled with "doing it all," she said, until a male colleague advised her to visualize her life as juggling a series of balls. "One ball is your job, one ball is your family, one ball is your spouse, one ball is your own health. You can't keep them all in the air at the same time. You have to choose which ones are the glass balls that you don't dare drop and which ones are the rubber balls that you can let bounce and try again." For her, the glass balls were her children. The rubber balls were her job, which would somehow function without her; her husband, who could be persuaded to understand; and her own needs, which usually came last.

That accounting probably is fairly typical for women. They usually put their own emotional and physical needs last while they dutifully serve others. Today's woman walks a tightwire, balancing in her arms the groceries, the cell phone, the cleaning she picked up for her mate, the dog that needs to go to the vet, the canned goods for the church holiday drive, the homework that someone forgot, the airline tickets for the vacation that needs to be rescheduled, the magazine that tells her how to be sexy, the best-seller she doesn't have time to read. It's a staggering load. A decade or two can go by before you have time to sit down and look around.

There is no nobler cause than spending yourself to help others, but at some point, many women realize they have spent most of their lives being dutiful or trying to do what was expected of them by others. They yearn for other ways to express themselves, ways that give them a sense of accomplishment and a sense that their life has counted for something. Often they want the gratification of earning money on their own or just feeling fulfilled. At midlife they want a shot at a richer life.

In many ways, we are all in sales. We have to convince our spouses or children to pitch in and help. We have to convince our bosses we are doing a good job. We cajole our friends into donating or volunteering for

> "I read a definition of women's needs. To the age of fourteen, a woman needs good health and good parents. From fourteen to forty she needs good looks. From forty to sixty she needs personality. From sixty on, I'm here to tell you that what she needs is cash."
> —MARY KAY ASH,
> QUOTING SOPHIE TUCKER

our causes. We are a nation of salespeople. Selling products, projects, ideas, ourselves. But to be a good salesperson, you have to first believe in yourself. You have to take care of yourself and have confidence in yourself. And set goals that you can stretch to reach.

Shirley Nelson Hutton, a legendary sales director with Mary Kay Cosmetics, is a beautiful example of how to transform your life by learning how to project yourself positively. She was the first sales director at Mary Kay to break the $1 million mark and earned a record $7 million in commissions during her career. Looking back, she says the secret of her success was not just being able to set goals for herself, but being able to help her sales members feel good about themselves. Most women, she learned, "are so busy taking care of their husbands and children, they don't take care of themselves." "You have to be emotionally and physically healthy, or you have nothing to give to others," she explained. "It's so true. Who's your best friend? I am."

Shirley learned to fend for herself at an early age. She grew up in an apartment over a movie theater in Willmar, Minnesota. Her father worked for the railroad and her mom managed a dress shop. She started work at the age of eleven to help make ends meet, first as a baby-sitter making ten cents an hour, then as a maid for her mother's boss making fifty cents an hour. She worked her way through college by teaching Red Cross swimming lessons and helping at the college library.

Then along came Joe. She married Joe Hutton when she was twenty and still in college. He was an All-American basketball player who went on to play for the Minnesota Lakers. He opted to coach rather than continue a pro career. They ultimately had four children, two boys and two girls.

When she was pregnant with her third child, she was approached by a modeling agency. She found that laughable, considering her condition. But living on a teacher's salary wasn't easy, so she gave it a try. With her striking blond good looks, she was a natural for a modeling career, which led to commercials on television. The CBS affiliate in Minneapolis recognized her talent and hired her to interview guests on a noon news show. It was good exposure, but it only paid $11,000 a year. So she took buses to work. In order to buy a secondhand car, she saved money by doing her own hair and makeup. The break of her lifetime came when a Mary Kay sales rep offered her a complimentary facial. She was impressed with the results and invited five people on her TV show to talk about Mary Kay. So many people signed up as customers and consultants as a result of the broadcasts that Mary Kay Ash, the founder of the company, came to Minnesota herself to see what was happening. She quickly saw it made sense to recruit Shirley as a sales associate since she was already getting terrific results for the company.

Direct sales wasn't a career Shirley had considered at midlife—she was forty-three by then. But she was attracted by the flexible hours, the tax benefits of running a business from home, and the genuine concern for women in the organization. She saw that Mrs. Ash understood that women needed recognition and just payment for the work they did well.

Even though she started at the very bottom, in her first year she earned $1,000 a month—plus two fur coats. By her third year, she was making $60,000 a year. Each year she aimed to hit a higher plateau, and she did: $100,000 then $250,000 then $400,000. In her final year before retiring, she earned close to a million dollars. It was a meteoric, record-setting career:

- She won eight mink coats, ten pink Cadillacs, several diamond bumblebee pins (the symbol of the company), and shopping sprees at Neiman Marcus.

- In her very best month, she received the highest commission check the company ever paid anyone—$83,000.

- She recruited some fifty thousand women, enough to populate a good-sized city. Some twenty thousand of those were still on the job when she retired.

- She was the No. 1 national sales director for many years and ultimately was named the executive national sales director emeritus.

- One of her daughters became a national sales director as well and they made company history in 1994 as the first mother-daughter NSD team.

With her chic style, Shirley Hutton became a striking role model. Saleswomen who wanted to succeed copied her hairstyles, her meticulous grammar, and her poised delivery. When her hair was long, people told her she looked like Dina Merrill. When it was shorter, they said she looked like Angie Dickinson.

Today, well into her sixties, she still looks like a movie star and talks with the candor of someone who has known success and disappointment: Her marriage ended in divorce after thirty years. It was eighteen more years before she would remarry. Both of her sons wrestled with drinking problems and she struggled to help them, learning in the process about the deep human need for self-esteem and how to communicate at a heartfelt level. Both of her daughters had difficulties having children, one losing twins while five months pregnant. She made it through those wrenching years with a bedrock faith. Today, she says her children "are all well and wonderful with families of their own, but it was a struggle getting through all that."

In her book, *Pay Yourself What You're Worth,* which she wrote in 1988, she shares some of the lessons she learned about setting goals to take you forward to a better life. Those pointers include:

1. Be realistic, so the goal is reachable.

2. Be specific.

3. Be flexible because the goals may change as you grow.

4. Set reasonable time limits.

5. Be able to describe your goal to someone trustworthy.

Often she was that "someone trustworthy" for other women and she would invariably reassure them, "I know you have it in you. Just think the best of yourself and for yourself."

Her daughter recalled at her retirement roast that many evenings her mother would get calls during dinner from women needing a pep talk. She joked that her mom would always say, "I was just thinking about you, Midge." Shirley chuckles that it was partly the truth. "I was always thinking about somebody, 'You can do it. I know you can.'" Recipients of the Shirley Hutton pep talks would say that she helped them believe in themselves when nobody else did.

She says she learned about the importance of building self-confidence when going through counseling with her sons. "I was able immediately to relate it to my work because I saw the same problems every day. When some women just couldn't get out and face the rejection of sales pitches, we started to teach self-esteem classes on how important it was to feel good about yourself. So many women have been put down in their lives and subjected in a lot of ways. I would try to take them back to wherever it was they felt rejection or felt they had failed. Usually they would realize that something happened to them when they were children. Maybe it was verbal abuse. They were told they would never amount to anything. Or physical abuse. Or sexual abuse. Emotional abuse. All kinds of dysfunction. So I would start a session by talking about self-esteem. I couldn't teach them to sell if they couldn't get out of the house. If the problems were serious enough, I would urge them to go to community centers, where counseling would not cost a lot of money, or find other professional help."

She believes that most often the low self-worth was the result of negative messages the women had gotten growing up: "You're no good." "You spilled your milk." "You dummy." "No one in our family ever did that." "What makes you think you can go off and do that?" "Your sister could probably do that well, but not you." "You can't do that without my permission."

Her observations echo the landmark research by Harvard psychologist Carol Gilligan in 1982, which showed that after age eleven, girls start "unlearning" some of their youthful spirit of independence and adventure because of negative societal messages. From puberty on, in advertising and on television as well as in movies, the message most often given to girls is that their basic worth relates to the ability to attract and keep the attention of men. They do not get as many messages that their happiness may depend on making something interesting of their own lives.

A Girls Inc. survey in 2000 showed that young women still need encouragement to be independent: more than 50 percent said "girls are expected to speak softly and not cause trouble,"

63 percent said "girls are under a lot of pressure to please everyone," and 65 percent said "girls are expected to spend a lot of time on housework and taking care of younger brothers and sisters."

Over the years Shirley Hutton listened to thousands of stories of women who had not received any encouragement to pursue their dreams. They had never been told they had potential, so they doubted they would succeed, even though they had joined the sales business out of a need to succeed at something. Among other things, she would encourage them to pattern their consciousness with positive messages, like "I can do this . . . I am worthy of a better life . . . I am a caring person . . . I am a capable person . . . I can do well." She told them to expect highs and lows and learn from both. She advised them to treat themselves as their own best friend. For example, she would encourage them to buy cut flowers and put them on the desk to remind them they deserve beauty.

"All sales is psychology," she confided. "You can learn the technique, how to close the sale, ask the order. They can learn that, but they won't have the courage to go out and speak to people unless they feel good about themselves." No wonder the inscription on the wall of the sumptuous Mary Kay headquarters in Dallas is: "Dedicated to the thousands of women who dared to step out of their 'comfort zones' and use their God-given talents and abilities, realizing that God did not have time to make a nobody—just a somebody." Mrs. Ash modestly has said that she considers all the women to be her daughters and that all she did was what a mother would do when she says, "Come on, honey, come on, you can do it; you can do it!"

But Mary Kay has certainly done well by her sales daughters. At one point, her company had more female employees earning more than $50,000 per year than any other in the country. She has handed out more than $92 million worth of pink Cadillacs. Today the bonuses have been updated to suit the times. There are no more "politically incorrect" fur coats. Top sellers can earn fax machines and workout equipment, or a sport utility vehicle. Her system of personal growth has brought new resources to women in thirty-three countries, from Guatemala to Russia.

Indeed, as I researched Shirley Hutton's career at Mary Kay Cosmetics, a testament to the power of positive thinking and exuding a positive self-image, I discovered that the story of Mary Kay Ash herself is a case study in self-improvement. When she was growing up in Houston, Mary Kay had the responsibility of caring for her brothers and sisters after school because her mother worked fourteen-hour days as a restaurant manager. Her father had tuberculosis and was an invalid most of his life, so her mother got up at five A.M. to support the family. In the afternoons, she would call seven-year-old Mary Kay at home with directions on how to prepare dinner ("First you go get two potatoes . . .").

Mary Kay married at seventeen and moved to Dallas with her new husband. When he went off to serve in World War II, she had to go to work to support their three children. She didn't want to leave them at home, knowing firsthand how lonely that could be, so she took a job in direct sales, first with children's books, then with cookware. To her surprise, when her husband came home from the war, he announced that he no longer wanted to be married. "It was the lowest point in my life," she revealed in her autobiography, *Mary Kay*. Though she had developed a sense of worth for her abilities as a wife and mother, on that day she felt "like a complete and total failure." She later admitted, "Nothing had ever struck me so hard."

She worked for the next twenty-five years as a saleswoman for Stanley Home Products. But she grew increasingly disappointed at the lack of opportunities in sales management for women. There were many times when she was asked to take a male salesman out on the road to train him, and after six months of training, he would be brought back to Dallas, made her superior, and given twice her salary. She chafed when told that the men had families to support, because she did, too. Even more insulting, she felt, was the way women's ideas were rarely respected. As she recalled later, she was silently outraged when she presented a marketing plan only to have it dismissed with, "You're thinking just like a woman!" She vowed to herself that someday thinking like a woman would be considered an asset.

She "retired" in frustration in 1963 when yet another man she had trained was promoted above her. The retirement only lasted a month. During that time, she sat down at her kitchen table to write a book to help women survive in the male-dominated business world. She made two lists: one contained the good things she had seen in companies for which she had worked. The other featured the things she thought could be improved. When she looked at the lists, she realized she had created a great marketing plan for a company. And she decided to start that company, selling beauty products instead of home products.

Mary Kay Inc. was launched in 1963 with five thousand dollars she scraped together. She got some used office equipment and hired her twenty-year-old son Richard Rogers to help her, at half his previous salary. Several bumpy years later, she married businessman Mel Ash, and he encouraged her to hang in there and keep growing the company. She later confessed she did not have any financial goals when she started. Her main goal, she said over and over in her speeches and writing, was to help women. "I wanted to provide opportunities for them to create better lives. . . . My objective was to give women the opportunity to do anything they were smart enough to do." The company now has 500,000 sales consultants and retails $2 billion a year.

Mary Kay saw her role as motivating others to improve their lives and typically would greet employes in the hall with "How are you?" When they would reply, "Oh, I'm good," she would correct with a smile, "No, you're great." The next time she saw them, they would respond, "I'm great!" In her own way, she was a proponent of positive patterning, long before Maxwell Maltz made "Psychocybernetics" popular. She used to say that whenever she met someone she would try to imagine him or her wearing an invisible sign saying, "Make me feel important!" She would respond to the sign immediately by building the other person up rather than herself; then they would both come away feeling better.

She was fond of pointing out that the word *enthusiasm* comes from a Greek word meaning "God within" and she was straightforward about encouraging her employees not to neglect their spiritual life. She was not embarrassed to say her business plan was "God first, family second, and business third." As she explained in her business advice book, *You Can Have It All,* "Making God and family top priorities does not demean the role that work plays in our lives. After all, where do we spend more of our waking hours than at work? Career may rank only third, but it is well ahead of a long list of other activities." She also advised that women could imbue their workdays with their spiritual values. "Our belief in God should never be checked at the door when we punch a time clock. Faith is a twenty-four-hour-a-day commitment. Many women have made the mistake of changing their beliefs to accommodate their work; it must be the other way around. No circumstance is so unusual that it demands a double standard or separates us from our faith."

She knew from her own experience how difficult it can be to balance work and home life. She showed keen insights into the difficulties facing contemporary women who were trying to be "superwomen." She worried that the phrase "having it all" had promised freedom to women in recent years, but at the same time had added responsibilities that shot stress levels off the charts. There weren't enough hours in the day for women to operate at peak performance in full-time jobs and still tend to the needs of home, husband, and children. "This relentless pace means something has to give," she advised. "Priorities have to be established."

Setting priorities for herself meant that she would get up at five A.M. to do paperwork, so she would be free for her husband, Mel, in the evenings. For other women it may mean limiting travel while children are school-aged. For others, it may be keeping yourself healthy, by giving yourself permission for tennis matches with friends or perhaps a therapeutic massage. Just as Lesley Stahl had to evaluate which balls she could drop, you should consciously decide how to rotate your responsibilities. But the key is to try not to neglect yourself in the process.

As Mary Kay cautions, it is important that gains made in the workplace not be negated by deep personal losses. It is important that we keep sight of what really matters in life. As she put it, "If we lose our families and our faith in the process of developing our careers, then we have failed."

That said, Mary Kay has understood that many women work out of necessity, not choice. Many women have difficult home lives to deal with. Her foundation has consistently been a leader in providing assistance to women in need, most recently providing strong support for battered women's shelters and opposing domestic violence.

She often would counsel women to plan their lives with the same care and detail that they would plan a vacation. She shrewdly observed that people often will spend weeks dreaming and planning a trip, making hotel reservations, renting a car, studying sites, then return home and go back to an unsatisfying routine as if on automatic pilot. Why not put that same effort and enthusiasm into planning a better life?

When women asked for her autograph, she would sign next to it "Matthew 25:14–30"—the parable of the talents. She believed that people were meant to use their gifts and increase what God has given them; when they do, they will be given more. That's certainly proven true for the thousands of women she has mentored.

Mary Kay was wise from the outset that beauty comes from inner happiness and equilibrium as much as any miracle cream. In truth, she wasn't selling rouge and powder, she was selling hope, self-worth, and faith. She coached sales directors like Shirley Hutton to "praise their trainees to success."

"When a woman with a negative self-image comes to feel good about herself, she changes into a different person," she said. "Some women think it's acceptable to sacrifice their own growth for their family's sake. What they don't realize is that their growth excites the whole family and gives its members permission to grow, too. Never turn down an opportunity to grow."

Her psychology is right on target. Taking care of yourself and believing in yourself is a major part of improving your life. This is not the same as narcissism or vanity. It's a matter of maintaining a healthy outlook. Your health and well-being may be at stake if you are neglecting yourself. You also aren't helping your family by becoming a drudge.

Just like the parents who are told on an airplane to fit the mask to their own faces first before affixing one on their child, we must love and care for ourselves before we can love and take care of others. Start saying "no" to things that aren't absolutely essential and don't bring you joy. Start saying "yes" to things that give you forward momentum. Give yourself permission to compose a different life. As Mary Kay observed, "Most people live and die with their music still unplayed. They never dare try." Play your music.

To get started, you will need to acknowledge certain things about you.

1. How well do you really know yourself? Get a piece of paper and identify the following about yourself:

   - Strengths
   - Talents
   - Values
   - Needs
   - Styles of communication
   - Decision-making leadership

2. Then name several ways you appreciate yourself in these areas every day. (If you are not currently appreciating yourself, determine how you will begin.)

3. Ask yourself, how does your presence in a business or personal relationship exhibit your self-esteem and self-caring? What are you willing to do to make that even better than it is now?

4. How do you care for yourself physically? Do you have a constructive health regimen?

5. Do you need to change your "look" to reflect the new you that you want to present to the world? What impression do you want to communicate?

6. How do you care for yourself spiritually? Remember the advice: "Love your neighbor as yourself." Often we just hear the first part of that verse, but the other important part is to love yourself.

7. If there have been times when you meditated or journaled, how was that helpful to you? How will you do that on a regular basis?

Do you have balance in your life? Don't feel guilty if you don't. It's an ideal that is difficult for everyone. But keep trying to set priorities. It is a never-ending process. You may be able to have it "all," but not at once. Some things you will need to do full-time, some half, then perhaps back to three-quarters. You may not be able to balance your schedule perfectly, but you can find balance within yourself. Be here. Live in the present moment by making conscious decisions about what you want to be doing now.

The goal should be to present a face to the world that is confident and caring. You not only can start today, you can start right now.

> "Character contributes to beauty. It fortifies a woman as her youth fades. A mode of conduct, a standard of courage, discipline, fortitude and integrity can do a great deal to make a woman beautiful."
> —JACQUELINE BISSET, ACTRESS

❦

Chapter Five

Find Time for Solitude

"What is your purpose, what is your calling? What I know for sure is if you ask the question the answer will come. What I know for sure is, you have to be willing to listen for the answer. You have to get still enough to learn it and hear it and pay attention, to be fully conscious enough to see not just with your eyes but through them to the truth of who you are and what you can be."

—OPRAH WINFREY

Spend some time with a woman who has navigated a midlife crossing and she will tell you that seeking time alone to sort out things was a key factor. Not time to worry, but to meditate. Not just for introspection, but for inspiration. Having some peace and quiet helps you to open up and discover ideas and goals that you may not be aware of. But you can't take stock when your nerves are jangled and you're on the run. It's important to set aside solitude time. It's important to get off the fast track, off the treadmill, away from the car phone, away from the to-do list, long enough to fill your well again. It can be as simple as A-B-C.

A—find time to be Alone, as a first priority for yourself, not the last. No matter what their faith, transitional women said seeking solitude helped them develop a new spiritual foundation that gave them the strength to do what they needed to do. Think of it as resting in God, sitting still in the comforting presence of a friend.

B—add Beauty to that time. Remember, this is not solitary punishment. It is the essence of life, examining who you are and what you are doing, not merely rushing from problem to problem. Retreat to lovely surroundings—the woods or your garden. Or fill your spirit with music. Life *is* beautiful if you take time to think of it that way.

C—make this time Constructive, not just a quieter opportunity for hand-wringing. Make it a goal to separate what's important in your life from what's merely urgent. Try to leave each session with a positive thought, either about someone or something constructive you can do for yourself or others.

There are many different ways to make good use of time alone. Homemaker Susan Baker found she sometimes had to shut the door to the noise of everyday life to keep herself centered as she dealt with new phases at midlife. She went from single mom to matriarch of a combined family of eight when she married James A. Baker III. Then she went from coordinating carpools to coordinating cocktail receptions when he became Secretary of State. And she emerged in her fifties as a nationally recognized leader in helping the homeless. To navigate those transitions, she sought solitude and spiritual guidance.

Today she recalls in speeches that twenty-five years ago, her life was in pieces. She was divorced from a husband who had been an alcoholic. At one point, she was so angry about the divorce and frustrated with the demands of raising her three young children by herself that she remembers going in the bedroom, falling on the floor, and crying, "God, if you're there, *help* me!" She came to realize that God was there, but she was the one who had to make herself available. She joined a Bible study group and sought time for meditation, even if it was just stealing time away from the kids for a forty-five-minute bubble bath.

Then she met and married James Baker. He was a high-powered Houston attorney and a widower with four children. They moved into his house, which had only three bedrooms, so some of the seven children had to sleep on the landing. The adjustment was difficult, especially since one of her new step-sons was making her stepmother role very difficult.

She gathered strength from daily devotionals before the morning hubbub of carpools and classes. "It's very important to take a quiet time to get centered and ask God to guide me through the day, so I can stay centered. There were so many things on my list, I couldn't get through it. But I wanted a time for quiet and discernment. And for God. To find what really mattered from His perspective, I listened."

While Jim worked fourteen hours in the office, she worked eighteen-hour days at home. She turned to a passage in Proverbs to help her cope with the strain of her hectic schedule: "Reverence for the Lord makes the days grow longer." That brought calm, which in turn made the hours seem longer and helped her accomplish more with her time. "You have to begin your faith all over when you are tested," she says. "There were plenty of times when I wondered if God was there. You just do those baby steps and keep growing . . . and then you leap and dance."

However, when we met Susan Baker she wasn't feeling like leaping or dancing. She had a cold and was visibly chilled. She had been standing for a long time in the winter wind at an out-door dedication ceremony for ThanksGiving Square. Tall and strikingly attractive, she pulled her wool cape closely around her for warmth as she talked, but remained gracious and giving with her time. There was a certain reserve to her bearing, but a sense of kindness came through.

She revealed that the problems with the rebellious son were eventually worked out. And four years after they married, the Bakers had another child, Mary Bonner Baker. "My life was wholly consumed by those eight people," she recalled. Jim's steadily growing political influence helped him land the job as campaign director for George Bush's presidential primary campaign in 1980. That experience led to his being named chief of staff and Secretary of the Treasury in the Reagan administration. When his longtime friend George Bush was elected president, Jim Baker was appointed Secretary of State.

Uprooted from Texas, Susan had to adjust to another new role in Washington, D.C. Her older children were on their own. Mary Bonner was attending school. And Susan was lonely for her husband. "Once again, my heart felt deserted. So I looked to God for answers. What should I do? What could I do?" She sought guidance in quiet time. She prayed. She listened. And felt moved to reach out to others.

As she recalls, "I found other women in Washington who also needed company for the same reason: their husbands were in office. We started meeting and thinking of things we could do to help other people." She was drawn to the idea of helping the homeless. So she founded the National Alliance to End Homelessness. She also teamed up with Tipper Gore, the wife of then-Senator Al Gore, to protest raunchy lyrics in rock music.

"I'm one of those people who had to be pushed out," she admits. "In retrospect, I'm glad I was forced to do things like being involved with the homeless and the music issue. Taking stands and having to speak out in public has been a challenge for me," she said, because it was hard to move from a lifetime of being in a supporting role to being in the spotlight, speaking publicly about private views. Still, she learned to speak at a lectern and do media interviews. She hosted coffees for hundreds of wives of foreign diplomats. She persuaded officials to donate leftover food from inaugural parties and embassy receptions to the homeless. She arranged for surplus food from military commissaries to go to the poor.

But the most difficult adjustment she had to make was living in the fishbowl of Washington. She became angry and frustrated reading negative news stories about her husband. The worst came, she says, when one of their sons was arrested on a marijuana charge. Though she makes no excuses for her son, she thought it was unfair that this was treated like a major news story on TV, in capital newspapers and national newsmagazines. She went ballistic: "If he had not been the son of the chief of staff of the White House, it wouldn't even have made the county weekly. Families give up a great deal in public life. And it is particularly hard on kids. For several days I stomped around and was so angry I couldn't do anything."

Once again, she had to retreat and pray for guidance. It didn't happen overnight, but eventually, she says, she learned to forgive the press and began praying *for* members of the media. Today, she still prays for members of the media to be sensitive to families. She prays that there will be more people in journalism who are less cynical.

As we talked, she revealed without hesitation that she was about to turn sixty and had thirteen grandchildren, with another on the way. Her strawberry blond hair is now more gray, and in a black cocktail dress and pearls, she presents an elegant figure at fund-raising speeches. She looks you straight in the eye with clear blue eyes as she talks, as if to signal, "I have

> "Never be afraid to sit awhile and think."
> —LORRAINE HANSBERRY, PLAYWRIGHT

coped with eight children, two husbands, and the Washington press corps; I will survive."

The Bakers are now back home in Houston, but both travel frequently to speaking engagements and meetings. She has a full-time career rallying support for the homeless. The alliance born of her loneliness in Washington has grown to include thousands of members and has operations in every state. The once intensely private Susan Baker now crisscrosses the country, making speeches to help raise money for the homeless. And during the millenium Christmas season of 2000, she hosted an international seminar on forgiveness in Jerusalem for leaders from around the world.

To cope with her busy schedule, she has developed still more ways to find solitude. She does not give out her car phone number so that time alone can be used for thinking and praying. While she gets dressed, she listens to what she calls "praise tapes." And she retreats to her Houston garden whenever she can. "I love to putter around in jeans and dig in the dirt. It restores your soul."

Her advice to other women who may be called to begin new phases in their lives? "Relax. Reflect. Pray. They should listen to their hearts about what they want to do. What they *really* want to do. And then ask God's guidance to confirm."

What are other ways you can listen to yourself and God? Some women recommend the "palms up, palms down" exercise. Begin by placing your palms down as a symbol of your desire to let go of your concerns. Whatever is troubling you, just turn your palms down and release it. After several moments of release, turn your palms up as a symbol of your desire to receive input. Then spend your remaining moments in complete silence. Do not ask for anything. If impressions or directions or feelings come, fine. If not, fine. At the end of the quiet time, close with a thanks that you have at least had this time to yourself.

> "Certain springs are tapped only when we are alone. . . . Women need solitude in order to find again the true essence of themselves, that firm strand which will be the indispensable center of a whole web of human relationships."
> —ANNE MORROW LINDBERGH, WRITER

Others like to focus on one word as a way of shutting out persistent worries of the day. For example, pick a word or phrase that carries a peaceful or happy connotation for you, perhaps hope, or home, or health. You may need to try several before finding a good fit. Focusing on the centering word helps bring you back to a calm place in your mind when you find your mind wandering back to problems. This is a common meditation technique. You will find as you try different ways of using quiet time that there are subtle differences between solitude, reflection, and meditation. Roughly defined, solitude may mean just peaceful time without interruptions. Reflection is more of an evaluation of events in your life, advice from others, opportunities for change. Meditation is a conscious effort to let your unconscious thoughts surface.

Sarah Ban Breathnach (pronounced *braw-knock*) relied on a variety of meditation and motivation techniques as she put her life back together at midlife. Back in 1991, she was a busy writer, wife, and mother. She was a columnist for the *Washington Post* Writers Group and an expert on Victorian fashion, design, and manners. Her husband, Edward Sharpe, was a Commerce Department attorney and mayor of Takoma Park,

Maryland. She loved shopping with their preteen daughter, Kate. It added up to a full day. But not to a fulfilling life.

Her moment of reckoning with her lifestyle came when she was hit on the head by a ceiling tile that fell in a restaurant. As a result, she lost parts of her memory, she couldn't taste food, she couldn't play her beloved piano. During the next two years of recovery, she had to learn to read and listen to music all over again. She was, at times, deeply discouraged. To propel herself forward, she sat down at her dining room table one day and began compiling a list of one hundred things for which she could feel grateful. Number one, as you might expect, was health.

The list grew into the idea for a book about being grateful for the simple things in life and finding a more satisfying way to live. Her book was not an immediate success. It was rejected by thirty publishers. An editor persuaded her to reconfigure the book into bite-sized motivational essays, 365 daily readings in all. The result was *Simple Abundance: A Daybook of Comfort and Joy,* which became a *New York Times* best-seller, with three million copies sold!

If Steven Covey and Peter Drucker were the gurus for businessmen in the 1990s, then Sarah Ban Breathnach became the muse for women. Her primary prescription was keeping a "gratitude journal" to list five things that you're grateful for every day. But her reoccurring leitmotif is the need for solitude. Using her own practices as examples, she instructs her readers to stop the clock, relax, and meditate.

For starters, she suggests women create a sacred place where they can meditate in peace. She composed a homemade meditation table in her bedroom. She covered the table with a small white tablecloth, then placed some favorite objects on it: a lithograph of an angel, a print of the Madonna and Child, a gold-framed mirror, photos of her family and pets, a blue-and-white china vase that was a wedding present, and a potpourri bowl. Sarah says she can sit at the table and lean back on the foot of her bed, alone in her own space.

Sometimes she simply gets back in bed with a hot cup of tea to find solitude. The procedure need not be elaborate, she says. Just turn on the answering machine so calls don't interrupt. She often spends an hour "going within" to write in her journal, pray, or create a collage of dreams that she'd like to make happen. Then she plans her day. She also recommends simply sitting in silence, listening attentively, waiting expectantly. She suggests starting with a half hour in the morning and another before going to bed, or whatever time you can snatch. If this is a new practice in your life, just try for ten to fifteen minutes.

As she puts it, "Meditation helps. So do long walks, soaks in scented bubble baths . . . smiling at everyone we meet, being more gentle with ourselves, watching a sunrise or sunset, petting an animal, playing with a child, having some small pleasure to look forward to every day, being grateful."

Her own reconstructed life has brought incredible material success. In turn, she demonstrates her gratitude by donating 10 percent to charity. One year, that translated to $250,000 for the House of Ruth, Habitat for Humanity, and the Pediatric Aids Foundation. But her new abundance has not excluded her from difficulties. She is now swamped with demands for her time and advice. She receives so many requests for speeches, interviews, advice, etc., that she has to have seven assistants. She receives more than five hundred letters a week. Finding time for solitude is more challenging now.

When her marriage fell apart, she applied her own advice to herself and grew stronger. The post-*Abundance* Sarah is more poised and has become more comfortable being in front of a TV camera. There's an impish curl to her smile. You can sense that she speaks from experience when she now advises other women to set boundaries and not worry so much about pleasing others. She says, "For every 'yes,' I say a 'no.' I try to block out two hours each day for myself. You have to cherish and protect what's important in life."

She has several favorite ways of meditating. One is the "golden mirror meditation." She imagines a large-framed mirror and fills the reflection with dream scenes of what she'd like to see happen. Or she gazes into the flame of a candle. Sometimes she concentrates on a sacred word in a centering prayer or goes on a walking meditation. She suggests that for women who want to know how to start meditating, it's important to go to a quiet place. Get comfortable. Close your eyes. Enjoy the silence.

She said it was heartening to her as she faced a new round of changes herself, to discover that her basic advice for others of solitude, simplicity and gratitude had proven true once again. "They really work no matter what your circumstances are. In this past year, I was pulled ten thousand different directions. I felt like a hamster in a cage in an R&D project," she said. "If God can do this for me, he can do it for anybody."

When we talked, she seemed awed by the emotional outpouring from readers of her new book, *Something More*. Women from around the country had told her that even though they might be happily married and have healthy children, there was a void at the center of their soul. They said they felt a longing that there was something more for them to do, but they didn't know how to get there. Those feelings are a "divine discontent," she says. She believes that such discontents are the soul longing for communion and connection. Why? Usually because of self-loathing, not being pretty enough or slim enough or courageous enough. Or because of nagging feelings of betrayal, "that you haven't lived up to your potential or your dreams. Or marital indifference, which kills marriages

"Learn to get in touch with the silence within yourself, and know that everything in this life has a purpose."
—ELISABETH KÜBLER-ROSS, PHYSICIAN

in a slow death." When she pulled out of her own despair after her accident and divorce, she said, "I was a stronger, more passionate, wiser woman."

Still, she expressed reluctance at being held up as a role model for other women. She said it has become somewhat of a burden to be considered an adviser for the millions of women who bought her first book. She insists she wants to be considered a friend, but not a guru. "The irony of fame and celebrity is that the more you become well-known and people feel they know you, the more your body of true intimates becomes smaller. You have to become more private. And that zone keeps shrinking and shrinking. A lot of women think my life is perfect, that I never get angry and cry and get upset, but I'm human and I do," she revealed.

She said to her surprise, when she gained good fortune and success, she went through the same pattern as with loss. As she put it, "You go through shock and denial and bargaining. And what you are bargaining for is to get back your life. Success has been very different than I expected," she admitted. "What I am trying to do now is redefine success for myself. Creating boundaries, finding a balance, being very responsible to my audience and very caring of myself. If you get back to basics and find those still, quiet moments where you can be with God, then you can find repose of the soul."

No matter what age you are, it's very meaningful to find a place for *you* to show up. Susan Baker and Sarah Ban

> "It is in solitude that we discover that being is more important than having and that we are worth more than the result of our efforts. In solitude we discover that our life is not a possession to be defended, but a gift to be shared."
> —HENRI H. M. NOUWEN, THEOLOGIAN

Breathnach suggest that moments of solitude away from the "madding crowds" create an opportunity to refill your soul. You will be reenergized and ready to take on the world again. Without it, your soul continues to be depleted. What will it take for you to clear time for solitude? What are the barriers you can remove? Try laying out a time chart that shows how you want to spend the weeks ahead, blocking time in advance for things you would like to do, rather than letting daily events crowd them out.

Can you free yourself from the "doing" of life, to "be" in the quiet moments of solitude?

If so, how will you do it?

Where could you establish your "sacred place?"

Will you allow yourself an opportunity for a relationship with God? This would be a relationship that renews rather than uses, one that loves unconditionally, and one that fills you up with that love. What will you do to claim that relationship?

Chapter Six

Get Good Advice

"All of us, at certain moments of our lives, need to take advice and to receive help from other people."
—ALEXIS CARREL, "REFLECTIONS ON LIFE"

Much of our adult lives are spent searching for what we are made for. If you seem to be going in circles, it is possible that you may need to consult a professional to help you sort through your difficulties or gain the skills you need to start anew. Sometimes you simply may need to hear an expert's opinion that you actually can do what you would like to.

The experience of Maggie Klee Lichtenberg is a good example. Work and family had consumed Maggie's life until she hit fifty-three. By then she was divorced and had two grown children in their twenties. She had spent twenty years in the publishing business and was marketing director at a company in Boston. Then one day in 1995, when she got home from work, she looked at herself in the mirror on the closet door. She could see the toll her job had taken and she asked herself, "So this is it?" Suddenly the discontent that had been brewing for a year to two came together. She thought, "Okay, I'm successful. I'm making a lot of money. I'm well-known in my field. Is this it?" That awakened an openness to question if there should be another step in her life. And if so, what was it?

That discontent was still on her mind when she had an epiphany of sorts during a vacation in the Southwest. "I was in front of those magnificent mountains. To get over the stress of my job, I would go to Canyon Ranch. They take wonderful care of you there. You get refreshed and renewed. I would go there to hike, do the gym, massages, and all those wonderful things. Fabulous. The third time I was there, I took a walking meditation class at sunset, right on the edge of the national forest. At sunset, I looked at those mountains and I was just absolutely overwhelmed, taken in by the beauty of what I saw. I felt a beckoning, a really powerful thing. I looked at the mountains and I said, 'This is such magnificence! I want to live closer to nature!' I didn't understand what it was all about then, but I felt the pull of nature after thirty years of living in cities. I had been around nature when I grew up in Connecticut and I was not unhappy with the city, but I felt this great longing to be back in touch with nature. I looked at those mountains and thought, 'I've got to consider this. How could I change my life? How could I possibly do it? I'd really love to live in a place like this.'"

That evening she went to an after-dinner program that she had signed up for. The speaker, Jeff Raim, was billed as a coach. It turned out he was not a sports coach, as she thought, but a business and spiritual coach. It resonated with her when he said, "If you really want to do it, there is a way to follow your heart. There are practical ways to put your life together so you can really respond to what is urging you from within. Somehow you can put a new life together." She sensed that he could help her. So she signed up for advice.

Through their sessions, she came to realize that she had closed herself off from just about everything but work. "I was working away, getting well known, totally in a work mode, with no spiritual depth." Her parents were Jewish, but they had backed away from their religion because it was difficult for Jews to get a job in the town where they lived during the Depression. They changed their name and kept a low profile. "So I had no religious upbringing altogether. I always suspected there was more going on than the one-dimensional plane that we acknowledge, but it never really came to me until late in life," she said.

She also was encouraged by her counselor to get in touch with her intuition, to think about what she really wanted to do. He told her to listen to her impulses, try them out, entertain them. "If something comes into your mind more than once," she says, "it may really be a message for you to think about it. If it's coming back into your mind again and again, it's worth taking really seriously rather than brush it off." Her coach helped her work on letting her creative right brain have more focus than her mechanical left brain. "I had walled off my intuitive side and was strictly a businessperson," she says.

She began using meditation in the morning and after work. Once a week she visited a meditation center where people didn't "talk about what they do or what their business card says." She found herself becoming more open to listening to herself through quiet time. "This really has been a process of learning to listen to myself. It continues to this day. I have to remind myself to be present to the moment that is going on and to hear it. So every morning I spend quiet time by myself." She meditates, writes in a journal, sits with silence, or listens to music that is soothing. She may do some yoga exercises, a calming and stretching routine. Or a combination of techniques, whatever seems to help her start the day off well-grounded. "It's self-care," she says. "Until you can put yourself first, no matter where you are, no matter how old your children are, you are missing an opportunity for self-development. You have to give yourself permission to take care of yourself. It can be five minutes. It doesn't have to be a half hour. You just have to put yourself first once a day to get centered. Then you have so much more to give everybody else."

Maggie said she is grateful today that she was unhappy enough three years ago to be motivated to change. "Otherwise, I don't know how I would have done it. I had a very fortunate thing going on in many ways. But my wonderful job of six years went sour in the seventh year. I was really fed up with the situation at my job. I thought how long am I going to put up with this? What am I going to do next? It opened the space for me to say, 'How can I make this into an opportunity?' The message I was hearing from inside was, 'You don't belong here anymore.' But there was no blaming anyone. It was simply time to move on."

At first, she found the prospect of leaving very scary. How could she give up such a good job? How could she give up her medical benefits? How could she give up her wonderful condominium? What would she do instead? "What happened over time was that my values changed," she says now. "I realized my values shifted from material focus to another kind of focus. I was developing new values. When you ask people what is the most important thing to them about working, they may say money first. But then ask them, 'What do you really feel is abundance? Prosperity?' And they usually come up with a figure. But I started asking myself, what was enough money? What was true prosperity? For me, true prosperity was just as much about having enough time, enough space, enough community, enough health, enough freedom."

Thanks to the prodding from her conscience and her coach, Maggie decided that she was ready to get off the "more" tread-mill, which required ever increasing levels of exertion without relief, without joy, without peace. If this was success, why didn't she feel great?

The weekly discussions with her advisor helped her confront the fear of "letting go." She didn't know how everything would turn out, she says, but she did know she was gaining the confidence from her sessions to try. Bouncing around the options with her coach, she decided she was best suited to start a business and work for herself. She cautioned that many women cannot take such a risk without some financial reserves. She had some resources, she said, "because one of the things about working in a tough business is that money gets deposited to your account and you hardly have time to enjoy it. It's really crazy. So I had saved money. I could go try something. I could give myself enough time to do that."

It was still a scary prospect, she admits, but she told herself she could always get a job again, she should give the opportunity to herself. She would ask herself, "If I don't do this now, when? After retirement? My children were on their own. I had ended a long-term relationship a year before, so I could make the move easier."

Her coach provided the breakthrough with a simple suggestion. Like many women of her generation, she needed an authoritative figure to give her permission to step outside the lines. She was still complaining about work and debating a move, when her coach said to her, very softly, in a neutral voice, "You could take the initiative."

"That's all he said. I realized I could do that. I could choose my life," she remembered. So Maggie approached her boss with a proposal. She would stay on the job long enough to help with the transition. In return for her help, the supervisor would agree to give her a severance package. The supervisor, who had been dreading having to deal with her discontent, was relieved. It was a win-win for both. Maggie walked out with a nine-month pay cushion.

She moved to Santa Fe and studied through an Internet course to become—surprise—a business coach. She now has a waiting list of clients who sound her out about their business and personal decisions. The beauty of the change is that she now feels as if she is helping someone with her expertise, not just making a buck. She encourages her clients to seek balance in their lives, not just work, work, work and to never let up. That means scheduling vacations and learning how to say no to demands on their time that sap their energy. She often instructs them to say "No, thank you," at least once a day. "You just have to say 'I'm sorry, I can't do that' to put space and time back into your life. Coaching helps me work on me as well. It reminds me to slow down and take stock."

She tries to conserve time for thirty-minute walks, so she can savor the mountains that inspired her to compose a new life. Her recent spiritual growth, she revealed, has helped her understand "that I am an expression of God as much as any other human being on this earth. When I go for a walk in nature I know I am a part of that world. There is a whole peaceful feeling that I am connected. What's most important to me now is connecting with people."

Not everyone should try changing jobs and locations all at once, she advises. "If you are not happy with the life you have or want more out of life, that may not mean total change. There is no right way to do it. We are all unique individuals. It's really up to you to ask yourself, deep down, is this right for me? Hopefully, most of us will make decisions that are sensible. And there is a gut-sense component that helps you say 'yes' or 'no.'

> "For every one of us that succeeds, it's because there's somebody there to show you the way out."
> —OPRAH WINFREY

It's your life. If you don't want to be eighty-five and say, 'I wish I'd tried such and such,' or 'I wish I had only given twenty or thirty years to my job,' then it's important to get in touch with your inner voice and choose." As Maggie learned, when you are beginning a journey in unfamiliar territory, it's wise to find a guide. A trained observer can look at your situation more dispassionately than you can. And when your decision involves a spouse, a counselor could be a saving referee.

A marriage counselor helped Becky Briggs and her husband sort through a midlife crisis together. It proved a transforming experience for both of them. She gained the courage to resume a singing career part-time and her husband gained new respect for her needs.

Like many women, Becky was trying so hard to be "perfect"—as a wife, as a mom, as a daughter—that she neglected her own aspirations as an individual. Finally, when her unchanneled frustration threatened her marriage, she turned to a counselor. Her story is a reminder that when you hear yourself crying for help—take the next step. Get help.

Becky had been brought up to be a "good girl" and she earnestly tried to fulfill everyone's expectations. She was one of six children from a conservative Christian family in northern Virginia. As a believer, she found it challenging to fit in with the high school idea of fun in the rebellious 1960s. She loved being with her friends—but was not a party animal. In college, she auditioned for a Christian rock group and started singing with one of the first evangelical rock music groups, the Sons of Thunder. The group was a precursor to the Amy Grant style of "crossover" pop spiritual music that became popular a decade later. "It was the best of both worlds," she remembers now. "I got to boogie, but with a message."

After graduation from the College of William and Mary, she started a teaching career. But then she met and married Mac Briggs. He was tall and broad-shouldered. He had ambitions to make it big in the business world. They moved to Bethlehem, Pennsylvania, to pursue the American dream of home, success, and family. They had their first baby before their first anniversary. And then had four more, a total of three daughters and twin boys. Both had wanted a big family. She was from a large family and said her mom was one of her heroes. "It was chaotic and crazy, but we wanted it crazy."

However, when the kids grew out of the cute and controllable stage and into the assertive adolescent stage, she started having a midlife crisis. She had loved being a stay-at-home mom and was grateful that Mac's business was doing so well that she didn't have to work outside the home. She was intent on becoming the perfect mother, the kind who stages backyard festivals with Kool-Aid and homemade cookies. Then, as the children became more challenging to handle, she began to notice how much Mac wasn't there. He was a hard-charger at work all week, putting in long hours, so he liked to relax on the golf course occasionally. That meant she was left with the home and family responsibilities most of the time. Parenting was becoming complicated and she missed being able to share the details and decision-making with him. She tried to bring up family issues with him, with little success. So she worried to herself that her sense of frustration meant that she was not going to be as good a mother as her mother. Now the anxiety she felt about her role as mother was beginning to impact her role as wife.

"In my enthusiasm to be like my mother and my enthusiasm for Mac and the kids, I hadn't carved out time for me. That didn't seem like the Christian thing to do, it seemed selfish," she admitted five years later. She was programmed with a million "should" messages, but didn't know what to do about the frustration she was feeling. She hit her lowest point, she said, after a shouting match with one of her daughters. They had been fighting when she dropped her daughter off at a dance lesson. She put her head down on the steering wheel of the car and sobbed. "What a mess! How could I have reacted so immaturely, as immaturely as my daughter did," she said. When she got home, she got down on her knees and prayed for help. She told herself that her frustration had to be about something else, something more than struggling to have a perfect home. She was crying and desperate. "I was asking myself: What is the matter with me? My children are healthy. My husband has a good job. We have great vacations. So buck up. But the gnawing feeling wouldn't be quieted. I knew I had to move out of the box I had placed myself in."

About that time, she heard Catholic theologian Henry Nouwen speak at a seminar for couples called "The Foundation." He spoke on making time for God to talk to you. Not with a plan, just sitting in his presence, with nothing to do but be who you are. "I had been so busy. As he said, that's like being on the outside of a wheel—you go up and down and around all the time. If you are centered, you are in the hub of the wheel. It doesn't take as much energy." She read some of his books and gained more insight into what she was doing. She became less results-oriented, less intent on making her children perfect. She put more focus on her quiet time with God. And remarkable things began to happen. She found the courage to stay with the issues she had brought up with her husband. She told him she needed to regroup and not be the performance-oriented wife. She felt they needed to give God the opportunity to do something new with them.

So she went first to a minister and to a counselor. Then she and Mac started going to the counselor together and separately. Working with the counselor allowed her to think something without "should" in it. She was encouraged to think about who she really was, and what she really thought and felt. "I hadn't taken time to do that," she admitted.

Her unhappiness had caused her husband to search his role as well. He poured out his concerns about their strained situation like never before in prayer. He began expressing his feelings to her more directly. And they were able to come closer together. It was a more honest relationship as they learned to be frank with one another and to listen to one another.

Having to articulate her wants in counseling also helped her realize that she wanted to use her musical talent more. "It was my only marketable skill. I felt a need to make money of my own." So she auditioned for a job singing in a club. Her children were somewhat embarrassed. Her friends kidded her that she was a "lounge lizard." But she enjoyed singing pop music, Whitney Houston's kind of contemporary ballads. "It was perfect because I could work on weekends when Mac could be home with the kids," she said. "Because I was out of the house, the kids had to relate to him."

She still spent weekdays running errands and carpooling in a jogging suit—but then popped into a cocktail dress to sing on

the weekend. She felt gratified
that she could use her talents
and earned some money for it.
"I was glad I gave myself permission to do something out-

> "All adventures, especially into new
> territory, are scary."
> —SALLY RIDE, ASTRONAUT

side the box. It was great. I was at the right season of my life
for it," she said.

At forty-seven, Becky Briggs seemed at ease with her decisions. In a few years, her sons would be out of high school and
she would have to face the issue of what to do as an "empty
nester." But after talking to her, I sensed that she now had the
confidence to work through such decisions with her husband.
And knows how to get help if she needs it.

It took some soul-searching, but Joan Konner has learned to
listen to trusted advisors as well as her conscience. Because
she then dared to take paths not customarily taken, she has
become a role model of integrity and intelligence.

- At a time when there were few women in network news,
  she produced groundbreaking television documentaries at
  NBC News about radioactive waste, marijuana use in the
  1970s, sexual politics, and Cold War foreign policy.

- She produced Bill Moyers's *Journal* series on public television and collaborated with Moyers to produce *Joseph
  Campbell and the Power of Myth* for PBS, a program
  that still has a large, devoted following around the
  world.

The change points in her life, as she took on those challenges, were crises of conscience that propelled her from one

orbit to another. Tackling controversy was the last thing on Joan Weiner's mind when she married at the age of eighteen. She raced through Sarah Lawrence College in three years because she had promised her parents she would finish college if she could marry Jacob Konner. They quickly had two children. Perhaps because she was so young, she was discontent with domestic life. The problem was not the children; she doted on her daughters. The problem was how suffocating her life was without creative stimulation.

She didn't know what exactly she wanted to do, but she wanted to work, to use her head as much as her heart. She liked to write; she had been writing poems and essays at home. To give you an idea of her restless intellect, this is a woman for whom quoting Immanuel Kant, Aristotle, Confucius, Mortimer Adler, and George Orwell to make a point is as easy as blinking.

So when her children were old enough to be in school most of the day, she decided to "do something." She felt cut off from the ideas that she was thinking about. Yet Joan felt ashamed that she wanted to work. This was the 1950s, she recalls, "when women didn't work outside the home unless they *had* to." Society did not recognize career women at the time, so she felt guilty that she wanted more than home life. "If you were discontent in those days, you were considered neurotic," she remembers. "It was an insult to your husband if you wanted to work and an insult to those who had to work."

So she sought professional help to deal with the guilt she felt in not following the prescribed social script of the times for women who were middle-class and educated. Her psychiatrist reassured her, "I think you can work if you want to." Looking back four decades later, she mused, "It seems I needed that kind of permission from some authority figure in order not to think of myself as neurotic, or a bad mother, or altogether crazy, which I did anyway, and even worse—disobedient to the social order."

She took his advice and took the plunge. She went back to school to get the skills she needed to get a writing job. At twenty-nine, she entered the Columbia Graduate School of Journalism. "I felt comfortable at school," she says now. "I was at home with the class work and the intellectual involvement. Of course, I had no idea how hard the new working life would be. Even so, I never regretted the decision, even in the darkest nights of the soul which any thinking journalist suffers and certainly every mother suffers, no matter what course she follows," she says.

She went to work for the *Bergen Record* in Hackensack, New Jersey, just as Betty Friedan's first book came out celebrating women as beings with a destiny of their own. She began as a novice reporter and started perfecting her skills at finding meaningful stories and putting them together. She was assigned to write for the newspaper's "women's pages," which was customary for female reporters at the time. As her talent was recognized, she quickly was promoted to writing editorials and columns. Soon she was asked to be a guest on a PBS public affairs program. After her third guest appearance, the producer said, "I'm leaving, would you like to try producing?" So for two years, she produced and hosted the show. At forty she moved into hard news at WNBC-TV and went on to produce documentaries at the NBC network, becoming one of the few female producers at that level. Though she won just about every award in broadcasting for her writing and producing, she discovered there was no avenue for executive growth for women at the network. She noticed the male editors and producers were being promoted to supervisory positions, but it was "unthinkable" to elevate the women beyond certain levels. She told a corporate supervisor that she was ready to move into the decision-making area at NBC News "because I know I can do the job and you know." As she remembers, he put his feet up on the desk and told her, "There's nothing to doing this job, it's getting the job that's tough." In other words, you had to be a member of the club and it was an all-male club.

Her frustration reached a breaking point when a new vice president was named for documentaries, a job she would have liked. In one of his first acts, he failed to support her almost completed documentary on radioactive waste, which was scheduled to air in two weeks. It was controversial, but it was years ahead of its time in terms of raising concerns about radioactive contamination. The documentary would have died on the proverbial cutting room floor, she says, had not the president of the news division stepped in. The program was broadcast, but she still was incensed by the disregard of the new VP. She left NBC, she explains, because after twelve years "I got tired of other people making decisions for me that I knew I was capable of making."

Besides, she had an offer to become an executive public affairs producer at PBS, which included producing *The Dick Cavett Show*. She was encouraged by a friend, Bernie Weisberger, who was a historian and college teacher. He had helped her gain confidence in her professional life and advised her to leave without regret since she had another offer. She did.

She had been learning to take more control of her life since going through a horrific period of bereavement. Both of her parents and her sister died within a short period of time in 1969. First her mother was diagnosed with a brain tumor. Nine months later she died. Two weeks later her father died of a split aorta. Then five months later her sister Iris died. "I was flattened," Joan admits. "I used to say to myself, 'You've got to get out of bed. Things will get worse if you don't.' Then I would worry that things would get worse if I did get up." Somehow, she forced herself to "get up and put one foot down in front of the other."

"In retrospect, that seems to have unleashed some super strength and resolve, to change what I needed and wanted to change. It was as if those multiple, unrelated, and untimely deaths—I used to call it my private holocaust—propelled me somehow, to do what I had up until then been afraid to do," she remembers. She had wanted to divorce her husband for a long time, but didn't find the courage until she came out of her family crisis. "It seemed that things couldn't be worse, and might, in fact, be better," she said. She had new freedom. Her inheritance from her parents gave her the financial independence to go on her own.

Her subsequent years at PBS were triumphant ones and the programs she produced were particularly fulfilling. She describes working with Moyers as her "peak experience." Their relationship, she says, was "synergistic, symbiotic." As she puts it, "I felt as if I were growing and learning," yet his sensibility was such that she never felt "submerged by him." Instead, she felt enlarged by their work together.

During that time, she had been serving as a trustee at the Columbia Graduate School of Journalism, so she was aware of internal problems. A search for a new dean had dragged into a second year because it was a "job that nobody wanted." They turned to Joan to straighten things out. She was reluctant. She didn't need the aggravation. She was on a roll at PBS. But Moyers told her, "You need to move with your own voice. You've got to do it. It's such an important institution."

So she took the challenging fork in the road in 1988 and stayed eight and a half years as dean. Thanks to her prodigious fund-raising and intellectual prodding, the graduate school was rebuilt. Walls were painted that had been peeling for years. Computers were added. Scholarships were increased. When she stepped down, they dedicated the newly refurbished first floor as "Joan Konner Alumni/ae Hall."

In 1999, she was sixty-eight, happily married and planning new documentaries. Looking back at the decisions she made at critical junctures, she mentions that Joseph Campbell said that when you are on your right path, it's as if "invisible hands are helping." And in her case, she says, "Uncannily, that often turns out to be true. You almost feel propelled at times, then you know you're going the right way." But she said if she had not been reinforced at crucial junctures by her psychiatrist, she might not have pursued the same paths. Would she advise others today to consider professional help? "Absolutely," she said, adding, that of course, the practitioner would need to be someone well qualified and reliable. "It's unfortunate that for a time getting such professional help was stigmatized," she said, "but the fact is it was very helpful to me at certain crisis points in my life. It made the difference."

"Character is the bridge between our beliefs and our behavior. Character is the glue of personality, the connective tissue that makes a person whole, integrated, a person of integrity."
—JOAN KONNER, JOURNALIST

Though they came to their decisions from different situations, Maggie, Becky, and Joan each put aside their pride at critical moments to ask for help. Maggie needed to sort through her discontent. Becky needed the freedom in her marriage to express her talent. Joan needed the validation that it was not neurotic to work when you didn't "have to." Very often others can see through your problems better than you can. Or you may need the advice of someone with particular skills in the area you want to go.

Ironically, Kay (Katherine) Graham grew up in a privileged world of wealth, but did not know much about making money. When she found herself confronted with that challenge at midlife, she discovered she needed financial advice from the best of the brightest, because she was starting at the very top. Her story truly is the kind of dramatic turnaround that movies are made of. (If they made a movie about her, they would have to get someone like Katharine Hepburn to capture her steely charm.) As it was, they did make a movie, *All the President's Men*, about one of the gutsy decisions she made, the decision to print the scandalous machinations of the Nixon administration in the *Washington Post*.

She was an unlikely heroine. Kay Meyer grew up a shy child of affluence, with homes in Washington, D.C., and New York, and private lessons in riding and French. She studied journalism at the University of Chicago and tested her talents in San Francisco for a while. But when she married the brilliant young lawyer Philip Graham, she put any career thoughts aside. It was Phil who went to work transforming her family's newspaper into an influential journal, because that would have been an unthinkable mission for a woman at the time. Then when he committed suicide in 1963, she suddenly found herself with a major newspaper to run. She had devoted herself to raising their three children and being the ideal wife of a publisher. Now she was president of a company that operated not only the *Wash-*

ington Post, but *Newsweek* magazine and television stations across the country.

She was woefully unprepared for the task. As she later explained in her autobiography, *Personal History,* she had adopted the assumption of many of her generation that women were intellectually inferior to men, that they were not capable of governing, leading, managing anything but their homes and their children. "Once married," she wrote, "we were confined to running houses, providing a smooth atmosphere, dealing with children, supporting our husbands. Pretty soon this kind of thinking—indeed this kind of life—took its toll: most of us became somehow inferior. We grew less able to keep up with what was happening in the world. In groups we remained largely silent, unable to participate in conversations and discussions." She observed that women of that time also traditionally suffered from an exaggerated desire to please. She said that syndrome was so instilled in women of her generation that it inhibited her behavior for many years. At the time, she didn't realize what was happening, but she was unable to make decisions that might displease those around her. She admitted that for years most of the directives she issued ended with the phrase "if it's all right with you." If she thought she had done anything to make someone unhappy, she'd agonize. "The end result of all this was that many of us, by middle age, arrived at the state we were trying most to avoid: we bored our husbands, who had done their fair share in helping reduce us to this condition, and they wandered off to younger, greener pastures," she wrote.

When she took her husband's place at the helm of the publishing company, she was the only woman at that lofty position in the country. At her own company, there were no women within four levels of her. She was alone at the top. A photo of a meeting of the Associated Press board of directors in 1975 told the story: Katharine Graham is sitting at a huge meeting table, the only woman with twenty-two men in suits and ties. "If you were a woman in those days and head of an organization, people were entirely unused to you and didn't know what to make of you. They thought I was nuts," she said years later. While speaking to the American Society of Newspaper Editors in 1998, she revealed that when she became publisher, she literally did not know how to use a secretary, much less manage a business. "I had no idea what profitability was appropriate, what we should be looking for, striving for, how we should spend it." She had been peripherally aware of what her father and husband did at the paper, but she said that was like the difference between "watching somebody swim and swimming. It was helpful to be very close to my father and husband, but when I was thrown in, then it was an entirely different thing."

She had to learn, she said, which advisers to depend on, how to use advice, and who was appropriate to ask for advice. When she first went to work, she relied on corporate attorney Fritz Beebe and bluffed her way through meetings for several years, still tentative about asserting herself. When he died of cancer, she felt all alone as head of the company. But that same year, investor Warren Buffet bought into the company. Her friends warned her, "Don't go near him, he means no good. He's dangerous. He might take you over." But she had inherited from her father an ability to look people over. She studied the few articles that had been written about Buffet at the time. She called people in Omaha, Nebraska, where he ran his phenomenally successful Berkshire Hathaway investment firm. She checked him out with a friend at ABC-TV, who told her that he'd love to have Warren Buffet on his board, but that Buffet wanted to be on her *Washington Post* board. Mrs. Graham was taken by surprise. She did not even know she could ask people to join the board.

But once she looked Buffet over, she brought him on the board and he became her business coach. He told her right away, she said, "These are the things you should know about what kinds of businesses these are and what these businesses are worth." He would arrive at board meetings with the public statements of at least ten other companies and go over them with her. He would tell her, "This is a good company. . . . This is a cash-intensive business. . . ." Once, she recalled with a laugh, he pointed to a photo of a youngster in a stroller on the back of the Disney company annual statement and said, "This is you after your tenth annual report."

During those early years, Wall Street was as nervous about her leadership abilities as she was. To reassure investors, she came up with a public pronouncement: "Excellence and profitability go hand in hand." She admitted years later, "Really that was to show I was interested in profitability." She was learning that you had to be profitable in order to have the money to spend to become a great newspaper. That became particularly evident after she hired Ben Bradlee as editor, because he was eager to spend as much money as she would give him for good reporters and editors. They became a great team: Buffet the financial guru, Mrs. Graham the classy matriarch, Bradlee the editor with bravado. All of their resources came into play when the decision was made in 1971 to publish the "Pentagon Papers," a classified history of the United States' muddled decision-making in the Vietnam War. At the time, the Washington Post Company was about to go public with its stock. Just as the newspaper needed to impress investors with its potential, the government was threatening a civil suit and possible criminal charges if the secret papers were published. Mrs. Graham boldly gave the go-ahead.

It's difficult to imagine the insecure widow of a decade before defying the Justice Department. But Mrs. Graham had learned her lessons very well. Another crisis of conscience occurred soon after, whether to print the investigative stories based on an anonymous source known only as "Deep Throat." The stories implicated President Nixon in shadowy misdeeds. The revelations would move the country closer to a constitutional crisis. The *Post* was losing advertising over the controversy, but once again Mrs. Graham didn't flinch. She proved as tough as any of the men around her—or tougher, because she had more to lose than anyone.

Once I asked her at a reception for editors who she relied on most during those difficult years when she made that transition to publisher, who did she turn to, who was always there for her during those difficult times? "Warren," she said without hesitation. "Warren Buffet." In her biography she explained that Buffet was always accessible when she needed advice—"like having a personal business psychiatrist." He tended to downplay his contribution, once explaining that she had been looking at herself through a distorted mirror, like those in a carnival fun house. He saw his role as providing her a reflection without the distortions. He jokingly compared himself to an orangutan in a room with a smart person: The smart person tests his or her ideas on the orangutan, who merely sits there eating a banana, and at the end of the sessions, the smart person comes away smarter.

Graham agreed that after talking to him, she had a better idea of what she was saying. Because she was smart enough to

> "He [Warren Buffet] once told me that someone in a Dale Carnegie course had said to him, 'Just remember: We're not going to teach you how to keep your knees from knocking. All we're going to do is teach you to talk while your knees knock.'"
> —KATHARINE GRAHAM, FROM HER AUTOBIOGRAPHY *PERSONAL HISTORY*

seek advice and act on what she learned, history was made and a great institution was strengthened. If you had purchased just five shares of *Washington Post* stock when she took over, by the time she turned control over to her son Don Graham several decades later, you would have had 1,200 shares worth $630,000.

As Katharine Graham moved into her eighties, she continued to confound convention. She proved publishers can write by collecting a Pulitzer Prize for her autobiography. She risked her personal safety by hosting banned author Salman Rushdie in her home when the skittish White House would not. And yes, she was still talking things over with Warren Buffet, but by this time, no doubt, giving as good as she got.

As women, we can usually find resources for everyone but ourselves. It is hard to ask for help, to admit failure, or to admit doubt. To create an intentional second half, you may need various advisers. Allow yourself to partner with someone about *your* issues. This may be a professional person or it may be a good and honest friend who has helpful knowledge.

In the meantime ask yourself: What are the top three things you have always wished you could do?

For each area, determine what you can do on your own, and where you need help.

Identify the top ten list of self-resources:

- Doctor, dentist, optometrist for handling health issues

- Financial advisor or CPA for addressing budget issues

> "You gain strength, courage and confidence by every experience in which you really stop to look fear in the face. . . . You must do the thing which you think you cannot do."
> —ELEANOR ROOSEVELT

- Pastor or spiritual advisor for assisting with spiritual growth

- Coach for personal and/or professional development

- Community college courses on special interests

- Exercise classes for getting fit

- Counselor or psychiatrist for the more serious relationship issues

- Travel agent for planning time to get away

- Trusted librarian or bookstore to recommend new learning experiences

- Masseuse and manicurist for body therapy

Just as a business leader would seek counsel from a savvy lawyer or accountant, you would be smart to seek expertise wherever you may need it. Then when it comes time to act, you will feel more sure of yourself.

Chapter Seven

Know the Life You Can Afford

"What kind of price tag can you put on your life?"
—SUZE ORMAN, FINANCIAL ADVISOR

No matter whether it's your job, home or office, it's important to remember you are the CEO of your life. By the time you reach midlife, you should know how much money you need to live on and how long and how hard you want to work. It's important to take stock and plan appropriately to live life on *your* terms:

- Know how much it would cost to live the new life you want. If your dreams don't match your budget, develop a plan to cut or add as need be.

- Draw on the best financial advice you can find. Ask smart people what they do. Read financial advice books. Take a community college course to learn money-managing skills.

- Detach yourself from the single-minded pursuit of money. Pursue excellence or quality or service instead and the money often will take care of itself.

Like everything in life, change has a price. Changing lifestyles usually will require a financial adjustment. What is key is facing the realities of what resources you have and what you want to do and how you want to live.

The blessing for women at the beginning of this new century is that they have more financial flexibility than women at the beginning of the twentieth century had. As recently as the 1970s, women in many states still couldn't hold bank accounts or businesses in their own names if they were married. They couldn't work in blue-collar occupations like construction or truck driving. They couldn't reach the top ranks of elite professions like banking and law where they could accrue wealth. Today they can. There are still such things as glass ceilings and pink ghettos, and women who are forced by necessity to work at low-wage jobs, but there are more open doors than ever before.

That means women today can choose to keep breaking barriers . . . start the business of their dreams . . . decide to take a more satisfying but low-paying job . . . or take a "time-out" sabbatical to take stock. Whereas our mothers' generation had a very linear life, where they kept on doing the same thing out of necessity, today's generation is learning you can check in and out of the job market to suit your quality of life. At the same time, today's women are learning that we shouldn't measure our self-worth by our salaries or the kind of homes we live in. What we should strive for is finding fulfillment and meaning in how we live, not by the zeroes on that check.

Too often women defer financial decisions to their husbands or are so preoccupied trying to earn money that they don't learn how to make their money work for them. But if you want to change your life, you need to be financially literate. And the stark reality is you may need to pay your own way out of necessity, not choice. Here are some interesting statistics:

- Women on average live seven years longer than men.

- Fifty-two percent of marriages end in divorce.

- The average age of women when they are widowed is fifty-eight.

- Seventy-three percent of women die single (either unmarried, widowed, or divorced).

- Women earn 25 percent less than men.

- Women are out of the workforce an average of eleven and a half years versus sixteen months for men.

- During an average forty-year career, being out of the workforce just seven years cuts your retirement income in half.

- Women outnumber men in lower-paying part-time jobs.

- Forty-one percent of women over twenty-five have not begun saving for retirement, compared to 32 percent of men.

A super example of a woman who learned the price of a better life is Cynthia Gonzalez. She grew up in the South Texas border town of McAllen and came from a line of intrepid women—her grandmother had been widowed, but saw to it that her eight children graduated from high school, no easy feat in the Depression in the Rio Grande Valley, one of the poorest areas of the state.

Cynthia's mother also was widowed—her husband was killed in a car accident when Cynthia was six. Still, her mother baked goods to sell out of her house and went to work as a nurse. She bought her own house and cars—"those things women were not supposed to do on their own," Cynthia recalls. And she made sure her children got a good education, driving them herself to a "white school" until they could take buses. She believed the best inheritance a parent can give a child is education—*"La mejor herencia que un padre de puede dejar a sus hijos es la education."*

True to that, Cynthia earned her bachelor's degree from the University of Texas with honors. While she was in college, she got a job in the mail room at an insurance company, to help make ends meet. After graduation she went to work with Southwestern Bell, where she steadily moved up the ranks. But she balked at taking promotions that meant leaving Texas and her family. ("It probably hurt my career. Everything has a price.") So she switched to AT&T and became, in San Antonio, the first woman manager for the company. When she moved to Dallas, she quickly became a popular figure in the civic scene. She was selected for the prestigious Dallas Assembly leadership group and the board of the Dallas Urban League. Gov. Ann Richards named her a regent of a state university. She was a rising star. And she looked it. With her luxuriant dark hair, she favored styles like bright red blazers and was a standout in any crowd.

But in December of 1997, AT&T decided to lay off thousands of employees nationwide as part of a corporate restructuring. As a top manager, Cynthia was supposed to explain the generous early retirement package to her employees. She wound up convincing herself that it was too good a deal to pass up. She was not unhappy at AT&T. She was only fifty years old. But she had begun thinking about the value of time versus money since her mother had died a few years before. As she explained, "I can't replace the quality time I lost with my mother during the years when my career was my family. I had met with a financial planner who told me I could be a millionaire at sixty-one. But I started asking myself, 'Who am I working for? So what if I hang another plaque on my wall? Who cares?'"

She had decided that time was the real currency of the nineties. She pointed out that in Italy, people take two months' vacation and in Mexico they take two hours for lunch. "The world laughs at us," she said. "Because the family is still important to them. It's important here, but we shortchange it."

Americans, she said, are too wrapped up in their "work ID." She confessed that when she first considered retiring, she couldn't imagine what she would say if people asked, "What do you do?" Could she really say, "I'm an early retiree"? "But that's part of the problem," she said. "We've allowed people to do it to us. Sadly, we do measure ourselves by our paycheck. We're more than that. It's the old way of thinking. When women went into the workplace in big numbers, there were no role models, so we took the male model. We emulated the breadwinner model of making the paycheck the main goal. But over time, that's not entirely satisfying."

She began reading financial books and analyzing her lifestyle just as she would a business account at work. She pored over *The 9 Steps to Financial Freedom* by Suze Orman. She read *Die Broke* by Stephen M. Pollan. She read *The Millionaire Next Door* by Thomas J. Stanley and William D. Danko. She even took a course in Denver and became a certified financial planner. She gained new insights about putting her money to work *for* her. She learned how to save smart and how to spend smart. She got a grip on her money rather than the other way around.

The bottom line is you must bank for change. Once Cynthia had determined her financial parameters, she decided to take the early retirement package AT&T was offering. She figured she could pay herself from her investments about what a teacher would make and live on that. Any income from a future job could be a bonus. But first, she would take time off to decide what to do next. Volunteer work? Teaching in the inner city? Politics?

For the first time in her adult life, she had nothing to do. She had started work right after high school and had kept a frantic pace since then. So during her first months away from AT&T, she did things she had neglected while she was working. She traveled. She paid more attention to her spiritual life. She started an exercise program. And she sewed. "My friends laughed because I hadn't sewn in twenty-four years," she said. "But I sewed a dust ruffle for my bedroom, and a shower curtain and two pillow shams. I felt so proud of myself. It felt so good to take a little project from start to finish."

After eight months, she realized she needed to decide "what next?" She chose not to teach because the corporate work style was so engrained in her that she could not imagine being in a classroom all day, without the freedom to go to lunch with friends or to the daytime board meetings of the many charities she still supported. So she decided to take a job with a real estate company, knowing that she did not want to make it a second career. "There's a different attitude when it's a job, not a career. I used to postpone the personal because the career was more important. Now I don't want any more long-term commitments—every twelve to eighteen months I plan to reassess what I'm doing.

"So many of the women who forged the way during the breakthroughs of the sixties and seventies have been programmed that we have to work and that our self-worth is based on a job title. Those are little boxes we put ourselves in. But what do we measure now? Our paycheck or our happiness? There may have been options before, but we may not have felt we had the right to them. Or were not willing to go there. How do we define who we are? We do have options. First you have to decide, what am I willing to live on?"

She's right. You must decide for yourself how much is enough. That's the question of the hour as baby boomers look up at midlife and find themselves working harder and harder for material things that end up cluttering their life. In this time of sustained prosperity, we seem to have lost a sense of enoughness. What is enough money to live on? What is enough time off? What is enough time with your friends and family? What is enough achievement? What is the right balance?

At fifty-two, Cynthia says she now appreciates that women work for different reasons at different stages of their lives. "I was so hung up on myself and moving up and things," she says with a laugh. "I don't blame anyone but myself. But as we get into our wisdom years, we start to learn the value of time and friends. You can't put a price tag on that."

If you want to change your career, you need to have a plan that reflects where you are and where you want to go. Marion Asnes, senior editor at *Money* magazine, advises women to start by learning how to save in a serious way. That means you must live on less than what you actually earn so you can build retirement assets. Begin by writing a budget. It doesn't have to be an intimidating spreadsheet; just get an index card and write down what you pay for rent, your car payment, and a couple of things you cannot do without, like heat and phone. That'll give you a rough idea what you're dealing with. The second step is to create an emergency fund. You'll need a little cash put aside if the car breaks or the TV fizzles. Ms. Asnes suggests keeping three months' living expenses on hand. If you are a homemaker, she recommends you start a retirement or "lifechange" fund as early as you can. Start thinking of yourself as a "home CEO." Insist that part of your family budget include retirement money set aside for you. You can put up to $2,000 a year in your homemaker IRA. Start making core investments, perhaps starting with an indexed fund, which is a diverse portfolio. As you gain more confidence and capital, hire a financial planner or consult with a stockbroker so you can take the risks that lead to the greatest rewards.

Remember the chances are more likely that you will have to support yourself than not—an estimated 70 percent of women will find themselves solely responsible for their well-being during midlife, perhaps with another person, a child or parent, to support as well. And chances are you will need to support yourself for a longer time than you might think—women who are fifty years old in the year 2000 and in good health can expect to live as long as ninety-two by some calculations.

Buddy Ozanne, a financial planner in Dallas, says the first thing he tells women who have been divorced or widowed is not to be afraid. Whatever scenario they work out, he explains, they can get by, even if it takes some financial or attitude adjustments. "People give way too much emphasis to money in the first place," he says. "It's not going to be the end of the world if they have to change their lifestyle or even if they have to go to work."

Personal finance writer Pamela Yip also has these suggestions for specific groups of women:

- **For the newly divorced woman:** Divorce can be financially
  draining for husband and wife, but hardest on the
  woman. The average woman's standard of living falls by
  10 percent after a divorce, but can drop as much as 45
  percent, according to the National Center for Women and
  Retirement Research at Long Island University. Long
  term, the effects can be even more challenging. Women
  need to establish as much financial independence as possible after a divorce and the first place to start is with the
  divorce agreement, which includes child custody and support arrangements and alimony, if you are receiving or
  paying any; and how assets will be divided between you
  and your husband. If you can afford it, hire a financial
  planner specializing in divorce issues to work with your
  attorney. The planner can work with the attorney to cal-
  culate exactly how much you're entitled to in the divorce
  in order to meet your financial needs. After the legal
  process is over and you start focusing on a job, find a
  company with the best benefits for you and your kids.
  And because many divorced women are playing catch-up
  in saving for their retirement, look for a company that
  offers a generous match on your 401(k) contributions. If
  you haven't already, make sure you buy a generous
  amount of disability and life insurance because you will
  no longer have a second income as a backup. In your
  budgeting, account for the increased amount of money
  you'll spend for health insurance if you were covered
  under your husband's policy. This is crucial: if you are get-

ting alimony or child support, your divorce pact should require your husband to have enough disability and life insurance of his own to cover those payments. Obviously, you and your children should be the beneficiaries of the life insurance. As for property, don't give up a share of your husband's retirement funds in exchange for the family home unless you already have a fat nest egg yourself and you can afford to maintain the house.

- **For the married woman who wants to control some money of her own:** Open a bank account in your own name and start saving. That includes a checking account, savings account, and retirement account. Get a credit card in your name, not your husband's, and start using it to establish credit on your own. Start shifting money into your own investment portfolio. You can begin learning and gain confidence by forming an investment club with several friends so you can pool knowledge.

- **For the woman who wants to establish her own business:** Hook up with a woman's business network in your city such as the National Association of Women Business Owners (1-202-205-6410; www.nawbo.org) or contact the U.S. Small Business Administration in your town (1-800-827-5722; www.sba.gov). The SBA can give you a good checklist of questions you should ask before getting started:

  - What would be the nature of this business?
  - What services or products would I sell?
  - Is my idea practical and will it fill a need?
  - Have you identified the market? And the competition?

- Are you prepared to be an entrepreneur? Could you meet the operating requirements?
- Can you prepare a realistic business plan and project the start-up costs, monthly statement, and three-year projection?
- What are your goals?

You will need to consult with a competent accountant or attorney to decide whether you want a sole proprietorship, the most common arrangement, or want to form a partnership or corporation.

If you've always wanted to start a business of your own, you're in good company. About 38 percent of small businesses today are owned by women, more than at any time in U.S. history. In contrast, in 1972, women owned less than 5 percent of all businesses. Now's the best time to jump in, but first you should get your financial act together.

Wanda Brice says she only had a rudimentary business plan when she started her first computer programming business in 1978. She was only thirty-four and there were few female contemporaries to share advice. She was a single mom with a special needs son, so she was determined to succeed. And she did. In fact, she did well enough not to need the line of credit her older brother offered. But by the time she started another business in 1993, providing computer personnel for corporations, she had learned enough to realize she had been more lucky than organized the first time, so she came up with a textbook business plan. She now has a formula for other women thinking about beginning a business of their own:

- Whatever revenues they project the first year, they should cut in half in their plan.
- Whatever expenses they project, they should double in the plan.
- Whatever you hope you can make in one year, make it two years in your plan.

She advises, "You'd be amazed at the things that will come up that you have no control over. No matter how good your idea or how good you are at doing what you do, you have to manage your money or you won't succeed. It's that simple."

- **For the career woman who wants to downsize:** Meet with a financial adviser to determine whether you have enough money put away so you can afford to work for less pay or volunteer for a nonprofit. One simple test is to figure 5 to 6 percent of your total retirement savings and determine if you could live on that for a year. If not, you need to save more. And since women outlive men, it is important that you don't outlive your money. Be sure to account for adequate health insurance.

There's no great mystery to having enough money to do what you want. It always boils down to this discipline: spend less than you make and put the excess to work for you. Unfortunately, the U.S. savings rate dipped below 0 percent in 2000, so this apparently is hard for many Americans to do. But a good rule of thumb if you are in a business that is subject to sudden dislocations, or if you want to be able to bail out quickly, then you should have three to six months' equivalent of your living expenses saved up in case you have to make a quick change. If

> "I own my life. And only mine. And so
> I shall appreciate my person. And so I
> shall make proper use of myself."
> —RUTH BEEBE HILL, NOVELIST

in the process of developing a financial plan, you lower your spending expectations and are less materialistic, so much the better. "That's where an almost spiritual dimension comes in," Ozanne says, "when you build your discipline about money into your philosophy of life."

More women are searching for a new work philosophy. Cynthia Gonzalez is not alone in her reevaluation of the corporate grind. When the international search firm Korn Ferry surveyed executive women in the 1990s, they discovered few who wanted to stay in their current jobs until retirement. Three-quarters said they wanted to opt out before age sixty-five. In contrast, the most comparable survey of executive men found only 30 percent wanted to leave their jobs. Employment experts agree that more women than men have been leaving the corporate world. The departures are part of a trend becoming known as "stepping out." More women are taking time out, starting their own businesses, or working in public service.

Why? Frustration with office politics. Fatigue from the competitive pressure. The pain of restructuring. Some are exhausted from juggling family demands. But often, the women want more balance in their lives. First they worry if they can afford to leave the executive suite. Then they wonder if they can afford *not* to.

Karol Emmerich is the kind of executive who is giving up the corporate grind for philanthropic work. She had been an MBA cover girl. In 1969, she was one of four women in a class of three hundred at Stanford Business School. Her husband, whom she had met at Northwestern University, enrolled the next year. They took a course in life planning together. Their dream plan was to make enough money to support a family and have time for social service. As graduates of the 1960s, when young people were inspired by "ask not what your country can do for you, ask what you can do for your country," they both felt drawn to helping others.

But life didn't exactly follow their idealistic plan. She graduated in the top 10 percent of her class. But she hit a wall of job rejections. Nearly a hundred companies snubbed her. Those were the days when no one wanted to hire a woman. Finally she got an offer from the Bank of America and became the first woman loan officer in the national division. A year later, her husband graduated, and even though he was not in the top 10 percent, he had job offers from every major city in the country. They wanted to return to their midwestern roots, so she joined Dayton Hudson's treasury department in Minneapolis as a finance analyst. She was promoted every couple of years. And before long, she was an officer of the company. When she became pregnant with their first child, one boss tried to fire her. But another wanted her to come back after her pregnancy, so he promoted her to treasurer. By the time she was in her early thirties, she was a corporate vice president, one of the highest officers in a $20 billion company. She was responsible for all the financial activities, investing employee savings and pension plans, accounting, and acquisitions. She was identified in *Working Woman* magazine as a member of "the Breakthrough Generation"—one of seventy-three female executives who were "ready to run corporate America."

But as she admits, the MBA fairy-tale career had two sides. Karol still liked social service and tried to satisfy her yearning to help others through volunteering and contributing, but she wished she could do more. And as the economy faltered in the early nineties, the corporate games became less fun. She explained how corporate contractions brought out the worst in people in a 1997 speech called "Why I Left When I Was at the Top/What's Worth the Rest of Your Life." As she viewed the corporate pressure-cooker from inside:

- People weren't valued or respected, and they certainly weren't loved.

- Key executives ruled by fear and intimidation, criticizing people in front of their peers and subordinates.

- Disagreement was not tolerated. Blame was thrown around. The net result was an organization that behaved like a dysfunctional family.

This led to still poorer earnings, which fed the downward spiral of behavior. The pressure, she said, produced three distinct groups of people in the workplace: a small percentage who had integrity, courage, and authenticity; a small percentage who were awful to work with all of the time; and a vast majority who blew with the wind to hang on to their jobs. "In good times they could be pretty admirable," she said, "but regressed when the going got tough."

Still, she hung on, because she had invested almost twenty years of her life with the company. When she raised the issue of company morale with the corporate shrink, he said the company was probably better than most. Judging from the horror stories from her friends, she decided maybe that was right. But when her boss of nineteen years retired, she found herself having to please three new bosses. It took its toll. She felt exhausted. "I felt like I was eighty years old," she recalls. "I could barely get through the week and couldn't imagine how I'd ever live until the normal retirement age."

So she asked to take six weeks off. She spent most of the time designing and planting a large botanical garden at home. Digging and ruminating in the garden eight to ten hours a day, she began to feel more confident and at peace. She started writing her dream goals on Post-it notes and put them all over the wall. They included helping people. Being a mentor and encourager. She dreamed of turning the property adjacent to her home into a garden and conference center where people could be motivated to help others. She saw herself as a catalyst, spark plug, and equipper rather than a numbers-cruncher. But she struggled with what she would be giving up if she bailed out. First was money.

"I always thought that the main thing I was good at was making money for God and cheerfully giving it to His work. My job paid very well and we gave away an amount equal to my take-home pay. Leaving my job would mean walking away from compensation plans worth millions at retirement and therefore walking way from the ability to give that way. In fact, I anticipated that a job change would take my income level to *zero*," she said.

Her husband was also quite concerned. They both thrived in a dual career marriage, knowing that one of them always had the flexibility to leave a bad job situation to do something different. In fact, her income had enabled her husband to leave a highly successful job at one point to start his own company. Having two incomes was an insurance policy they were both used to having in place. And she says, "He was also worried that what I was feeling might be temporary." Then, too, she worried she would be giving up respect. What would she put on her business card? Like Cynthia Gonzalez, Karol worried what would she say when people asked, "What do you do?" She recalls, "Although I was sure I would be doing a lot, the word 'do' just didn't seem to be descriptive of my new life. It would be a lot easier if they would just ask: 'Tell me about yourself.' "

No money, no power, no respect. She felt as if she were jumping off a cliff. But a friend reminded her, "Look whose arms you're jumping into." She felt in her heart that God would be there for her. It would be just her God, her family, a few friends, and her garden for the rest of her life. Not bad, she thought. When she resigned in 1993 at the age of forty-four, she told local business reporters, "I'm not dropping out of business. I'm just dropping out of having a boss and having to deal with somebody else's agenda." She started putting her "dream Post-it" plans into action. And discovered she had not paid the financial price she feared. She had anticipated going from a big income to zero. But soon after her resignation, she was asked to join two well-paying corporate boards, one of which granted generous stock options. In the first two and a half years after she left Dayton Hudson, she made nearly 75 percent of what she would have made there.

Ask yourself if you could live on 75 percent of what you currently make. Or less? Would the downsizing be worth it if you gained a new quality of life? Karol found that giving up her title did not mean giving up respect. She found that when people asked her to join corporate boards they wanted her expertise and her character, not her title. Plus, she no longer felt old. She had new energy and ideas. In short, everything she thought she was giving up came back in abundance. The best part was that she now had time for her garden and faith. She also began a new roster of projects:

- She designed a course for the business school at the University of St. Thomas in St. Paul that included making team playing work, how to mediate and negotiate, how to manage diversity, how to resolve conflict, and how to handle change. She called it "Street Smarts 101."

- She volunteered to chair the major gifts segment of the United Way campaign.

- She helped organize a national talent bank of business and professional volunteers to assist religious nonprofits with their planning, finance, and other management problems.

- She worked with a group of Twin Cities businesswomen to develop a matchmaking service to help local companies find qualified female directors.

- She launched a nonprofit consulting firm called the Paraclete (Greek for "advocate") Group to work on such issues as women, work, faith, philanthropy, and volunteerism.

When we talked in 1998, Karol was more convinced than ever that she did the right thing. As a consultant, she said she is seeing more and more women make the same decision. She theorized that part of the reason is that "mind work" doesn't "engage enough of who we are as people. For centuries most work required physical effort and produced a tangible product. People had something to show for their effort. What I have are

Lucite paperweights from debt deals I was involved in and lots of paper files. Survival in previous times was also an ever-present issue and it required establishing strong relationships with others. Mind work requires none of these and as a result it doesn't tap into the inner core of who most of us are. It reminds me of a science fiction show I saw where bodiless heads in jars were hooked up to computers by wires. The heads could think and talk, and therefore do work. You'd be surprised how often that was my image of myself at work."

She pointed out that by the late 1990s, there were some 33 million Americans between the ages of forty-six and fifty-five. At that age, there generally is a reassessment of life up to that point. But for baby boomers, the midlife reckoning may seem more acute because they are the first generation in the new knowledge society; their jobs, as well as their lives, are much more stressful in two-worker families; they have more affluence and therefore more choices; and their values were shaped in the late 1960s and early 1970s, a time of idealism and change. She says, "I think women are expressing their frustration more openly now because women are more introspective. They look at the games and say, 'What's the point?' They may continue to do increasing-production things, but do it in a way that is more consistent with their value system."

She pointed to a *Fortune* article from 1995 called "Fed Up" that reported women are leaving corporate America in droves to start their own companies, change careers, and take jobs at nonprofits. Some three hundred career women were inter-viewed, ages thirty-five to forty-nine, with a median salary of $60,000. Almost all were managers or executives. Eighty-seven percent said they had or were seriously considering a major change in their lives. Thirty-three percent said they were depressed, 40 percent felt trapped. Karol bridled at the suggestion that some interpret that exodus to say women can't take corporate pressure. "It's not that women can't take it, but they choose not to," she said. "Life's too short."

Let's hope that business leaders out there somewhere are listening to what disaffected, middle-aged employees like Cynthia Gonzalez and Karol Emmerich are saying with their departures. If they do not, they may have a greater shock coming with the "Gen X" workforce. These new workers in their twenties and early thirties are not bound to tradition and are no respecters of "that's the way it's always been done." They value their free time and independence more than a far-off pension. They would just as soon go as stay. Companies that are adding concierges to handle errands for stressed-out employees (dry cleaning, theater tickets) may find that's not enough. Companies that want to keep talent and loyalty may have to stretch to find new ways to make employees feel appreciated as human beings, or else the employees are likely look elsewhere for personal fulfillment and meaning in their lives.

In the meantime, more women may seek a more holistic lifestyle as Cynthia Gonzalez and Karol Emmerich did. To do that, you have to right-size if not down-size your finances. You should assess what you're doing with your financial life whether you change directions or not. When money worries us, we enjoy our work less. It drains energy away from us. When you spend the time it takes to educate yourself about your finances and have them organized and in order, life lightens and becomes more manageable. Energy levels increase and you become more productive than you thought possible.

Answer the following questions to assess your financial flexibility:

1. What does financial independence mean for you?

   - How much money is enough?
   - How much operating capital do you need for your life?
   - What size reserve cache (safe from plunder) will allow you to feel comfortable?
   - How will you go about funding your daily needs while having a reserve of assets that make money for your future?

2. How will you get the financial advice you need?

   - What role models educate you about handling your finances?
   - What one thing can you learn from each of them about money?
   - What does your financial plan look like?
   - If your plan is nonexistent, who will teach you how to have one?
   - If you have begun making a plan, what will stand in the way of completing it?

3. Is your life defined by how you make your money or how much money you make?

   - What are the primary outcomes you desire from your work?
   - Do your role models want to build a financial empire and reputation? Or do they work because they love it and because their success is in having other people reach success? Which style suits you?
   - If someone asked you, "Who are you?" would you describe yourself as the career title you possess? Or

would you describe yourself as what you contribute to the world?

"Don't be afraid your life will end; be afraid it will never begin."
—GRACE HANSEN, NOVELIST AND POET

4. The biggest question is: Is your financial life running you, or are you running your financial life? You can decide.

Chapter Eight

Don't Let Life Wear You Down

"If I were asked to give what I consider the single most useful bit of advice for all humanity, it would be this: Expect trouble as an inevitable part of life, and when it comes, hold your head up high, look it squarely in the eye and say, 'I will be bigger than you. You cannot defeat me.' Then repeat to yourself the most comforting of all words, 'This too shall pass.'"

—ANN LANDERS, COLUMNIST

You may think it is too late to start again. You may feel tired of trying. Used up. The idea of living thirty more years may make you groan. You may even be asking, "Start something new? Now? Are you *kidding?*" But this is exactly when you should. Reach deep down inside yourself for the gumption to start again. Too often women in the prime of their life give up on their dreams. They settle for the hum-drum just when they may actually be more free to improvise than ever before in their lives. They settle for the familiar feel of routine, simply marking time, even though that becomes depressing. It's almost like sleepwalking, where every day is pretty much like the next, because change seems like too far to go. But when you are feeling beaten down by life it is precisely then when you should scrape up the courage to try something different.

You are not alone. By the age of forty, everyone has seen loss or deep disappointment of some kind. Those heartbreaks are the laundry marks of time. So quit having a pity party for yourself. Start accepting that you are not the only one who has had problems and move on. Consider the experience of Donna Sanson. When we talked, she was fifty-eight and had survived widowhood and a devastating financial situation.

She worked first as a schoolteacher and later as a manager in a department store while her two children were growing up in Charleston, South Carolina. She and her husband separated when their children went on to college. "I moved out the week before Hurricane Hugo hit," she recalls. "So I sat in darkness for twenty-eight days. It was the first time in my life I had been alone. I told God then that if I could do that, I could do anything."

She left Charleston, her home for twenty-five years, to take a job in Columbus, Mississippi, as the administrator of a school nutrition program. When her sister had called to tell her about the job, she said at first, "You must be nuts." She had no experience in the field of nutrition, but she thought, "I'm not going to lose anything, I might as well apply." She got the job over another finalist who had thirty-one years' experience. Once you witness her can-do style, you can understand why. It was a helpful transitional job at first. She was able to buy her own little house. She began the healing process of becoming a whole person again. But the work environment deteriorated under a new superintendent. Turnover was constant. Morale was miserable. "They were not kind to people there," she said. She began praying for a way to get out of the situation. She had given up her familiar life in Charleston to move to Columbus. "What do I do now?" she asked herself. "I'm fifty-something years old. Where do I go now? I felt very trapped. I didn't want to start over again at my age."

Then one day, she went with her son to have lunch in the Mississippi Delta area. They ate at a charming restaurant with a gift shop. As she started to relax in the cheerful ambience, the seed was planted in her heart that she could start a restaurant of her own. "I had not one dime. No retirement. Nothing. But I couldn't let go of the idea," she recalled with a trace of wonder in her voice. "I've had four seemingly unrelated careers. The first three are what God did to get me to the point of doing this. But if you had told me ten years ago this was what I would be doing today, I would have screamed and run in the other direction."

It took her three years from the time she first started talking about the restaurant until the day she opened for business in 1996. Her brother, who is a CPA and an attorney, helped her draft a business plan. She found a building to lease in a crime-ridden part of town called Catfish Alley. It was the kind of area you were told not to venture into. A disco was next door where police reported drug use, prostitution, killings. The building had holes in the ceiling and mold dripping off the walls. But she saw it transformed with bright colors on the tables. And that's the way it is today.

"Sometimes I had to walk two steps backward and sometimes five forward," she remembers, "but I kept on walking." She went to five bank presidents seeking a loan before she found one willing to bank on her. She didn't have any collateral or a penny of her own to put up. But she had a vision to pursue. "People seemed to come from nowhere that wanted to put in money or wanted to work for minimum wage. God would put them in my path and it would be the answer to prayer. By human standards everybody said, 'There's no way you can do this.' And there were times when I would try to go through a door that turned out to be the wrong one and I got slammed in the face. But I would just try another door."

She opened for business "with that horrible disco" still open and succeeded anyway. She named the restaurant the Front Door because she was sure the fellow who owned the building would buy the adjacent building, which she intended to lease for an expansion called the Back Door. She put a scripture reading over the door: Zachariah 4:6—"Not by might, not by power, but by the spirit."

Sure enough, her faith and positive thinking paid off. The restaurant was a success from the first day. The owner was encouraged to buy the adjacent building. She added not only the Back Door expansion, but a patio as well. Her daring renovation started the transformation of the rest of the Catfish Alley area. New businesses began coming in. Apartments were added. Today her story of urban and personal renewal has been profiled on National Public Radio.

The secret of her success? "I make everything from scratch. We have a different soup every day. We have wonderful deli sandwiches. The Mennonite community makes the bread. We have wonderful salads. It's real high-quality, simple but good food. Homemade desserts like turtle fudge pie with caramel. Almond delight with toasted almonds. They're decadent. They're wonderful." She doesn't serve alcohol and doesn't allow smoking. She features local products in the gift store, stuffed animals, jewelry, baskets, pottery, stationery. She never has to advertise for help because word-of-mouth brings a steady stream of would-be employees.

Visit the restaurant and you can expect to find Donna, with

her short auburn hair and glasses, energetically tending to customers. Because she knows from experience what it is like to work in an unhappy environment, Donna says her mission is to make her restaurant a place where people are treated well, both employees and customers. "I like to think that every single person has had a little bit better day because they came into this business."

Thanks to that people-sensitive attitude, Donna now is in a good position to pay off her five-year loan and may finally realize some profit herself. As she put it, "We've been successful since the day we opened our door. I knew we would be. Everything I have is in this building. The most important thing is to touch hundreds of lives every day. It makes me feel happy every day. I can get up feeling miserable and have arthritis so bad I can hardly get up out of bed. But after the first few customers, it doesn't matter. When we're all dead and gone, nothing will matter except the people we have touched in a positive way. Otherwise, what did I do with my life that was significant? My children certainly. But it's the people you touch, ultimately, that's all that matters."

She said friends still ask her what it was that made her think she could start a restaurant with no experience in one of the worst parts of town. "If I had not had a burning passion in my heart and I had not believed—through prayer and reading and listening—that this is what God wanted me to do and where he wanted me to be, then never in a million years would I have had the courage to do this. When you are my age you can't afford to make mistakes. So I put everything I had and didn't have in here. I have learned to trust that inner spirit of God in me." Even if she doesn't make a lot of money, she says she is gratified that "marriages have been healed sitting at these tables . . . prayer groups have been formed . . . special relationships have been formed . . . employee after employee has been touched."

"We have to grow, we have to move forward, to learn and evolve, add to our dictionary of life."
—JANET LEIGH, ACTRESS

Clearly her faith has been a big part of her transition, but she said she now tells others that whatever their faith, whatever they believe directs their life, they should follow through when they feel an urge to pursue a new dream. "You shouldn't ignore what your heart is telling you to do," she says.

And she's right. Who has not been disappointed in some way—whether marriage, money, status, work, people. Make peace with your past and your problems. Look around—you never see someone who is blatantly negative, cynical, or pessimistic come back from a setback. Even if you have to fake it for a while, start taking positive steps and saying positive things to yourself. Over time, either you will start to believe it yourself or good things will come along to change your outlook. Most often those good things will come from reaching out to other people.

Houston family therapist Anne Grizzle was used to giving other people advice rather than needing it herself. She had prided herself on juggling all her roles: wife, mother, sister, psychologist, writer, volunteer. Then she found herself relocated from New York to Houston with her husband, an executive at Continental Airlines. They were welcomed to Houston by a hurricane. Their newly purchased "historic" home was full of fleas and without air-conditioning in what seemed like a Calcutta summer. It was then that she discovered she was unexpectedly pregnant with number three. "Although this may sound like only a small speed bump on my otherwise smooth road, a more apt analogy for me was that of one last ball thrown into a juggler's act, which upsets the whole routine and brings every-thing crashing to the ground. I was out of control, my limits passed, sick and depressed," she later wrote.

She had hoped to find a promised land in Houston. Instead she felt as if she were wandering around in circles in the desert. She was still struggling to adjust when she learned her identical twin sister had breast cancer. They discovered the cancer while she was in the hospital giving birth to her first child. Anne went to her sister's side, to help care for the baby. Doctors advised Anne that her own risk of cancer was 100 percent, due to a family genetic propensity for the illness. So she opted for a pro-phylactic radical mastectomy. Once again, her hopes for a well-ordered life were derailed. But she now says that the experience showed her she needed a stronger foundation. "When one area of your life comes crashing down, it gives you permission to learn to live within limits and choose more carefully," she said. While hospitalized, forced to stay in bed, unable to move, she discovered the freedom from "doing" and from gaining praise for productivity. As she lay dependent, she came to appreciate others rather than seek to be appreciated. As she wrote, "I learned to hear love from family, friends and God, not for all I did, but rather just for me."

She had been a poster girl for overachieving: salutatorian of her high school class, a graduate of Harvard University. She went on to earn a master's degree in social work from Columbia University. She worked six years in Harlem Family Hospital, trying to prevent foster care placement by treating families holistically. She went into private practice and wrote a book,

Mother Love, Mother Hate, while in her early thirties. She was active in her church and her young children's school. In short, she was busy, busy, busy.

But after her jolting series of crises, she changed approaches. "I hit my limits," she admits. "In the process, I looked at the juggling routine I was in and shifted paradigms. In the process of slowing down, I have grown deeply, a depth that is in the long run more fruitful." She dropped activities that did not have deep meaning to her. Her theme now is "braiding" the interlocking events into her life rather than juggling. For example, at the urging of a Trappist monk acquaintance, she helped start a mission for the homeless in Amistad, Bolivia. He had felt called to minister to the Quechua Indians there, who were without water and health care. He asked his friends in North America to help him provide for sixty orphans in the Bolivian village. She said yes. While that might seem like picking up another juggling ball, she says it actually has given her the excuse to drop less relevant things. She says it was a hands-on way to communicate with the poor and get to know them as friends, not just write checks. She "braided" the mission project into her life by helping one of her sons develop a junior sports Olympics for the Quechua youngsters as his Eagle Boy Scout project. All three of her sons—ages fifteen, twelve, and seven at that time—pitched in. "We got the kids in our Houston neighborhood to donate trophies," she explains. "We got prizes and ribbons and organized the competitions for them. We even had an opening ceremony in Bolivia. For many of those kids, it was the first real sports event they had ever participated in."

On Sunday afternoons, she volunteers at an inner city church in Houston. She plays guitar, helps with the church service, and serves meals. "Now when I drive by a homeless person on the street, I can look at their faces and say, 'Is that John?' In many ways, I am seeing these people for the first time. Here are people with nothing. There was a man who had been writhing in pain with a toothache. I asked him what he was grateful for. He said that he was grateful that 'Jesus didn't have to wake me up this morning.' It's like that when we visit Bolivia. You learn what's really important. That keeps me from getting in the rat race here. Especially when you are educated and successful, you can live in a rarefied atmosphere," she said. "You need to stay in contact with the rich soil of life."

To keep herself focused, she has developed the habit of a weekly "night watch" on early Saturday mornings. That means getting up at five A.M., wherever she is, to watch the sun come up and meditate. As she explained, "It's a waiting period where my soul is renewed weekly. You know the saying, 'As the watchman waits at morning, so waits my soul for thee.' I sit in my garden or anywhere I can. If I'm in a hotel, I ask for an east window so I can watch the sun come up. Waiting time is considered a waste of time by many Americans, but for me, it is a place of nourishment."

Since her prophylactic surgery, she said she feels a surge of gratitude for every day. "I am alive today. I am breathing today. I cannot take that for granted anymore. When you face cancer, you measure the number of years not from when you are born, but how many might be left until you die. When you are over the fall line, you measure differently."

When we talked again, nearly a year and a half had passed. Her oldest son had gone off to Harvard. And she had learned her twin sister was succumbing to the eight-year battle with cancer, which had come roaring back after some remission. Anne's voice grew so soft when she talked about her sister that I could barely hear her on the phone. She said her "night watch" ritual of praying and waiting for the sun to come up had become even more mean-

> "There are years that ask questions and years that answer."
> —ZORA NEALE HURSTON, WRITER

ingful to her. "A terminal illness teaches you a lot about watching and waiting," she said. "I can see where my night watch has prepared me. It has taught me to listen for God more carefully and sense his caring hand. I think it will help me as we go through the days ahead." Her sister, she said, would be leaving two children, eight and four years old. "I'm going to have some more to reflect on at night watch," she admitted, adding ever so softly, "It's going to be hard."

It was after ten P.M., the quiet part of the evening. As I hung up the phone, still feeling her words, I realized that I had only talked to this woman on a few occasions, and yet we had shared more intimate thoughts about living and dying than I had with some of my longtime friends. But perhaps that was because I had never asked them the same questions. Or listened so carefully.

Sometimes life forces you to change; it's up to you to make the most of it. You can get bitter or you can get better. In an economy where layoffs and downsizing have become common, many women are having to learn how to start over whether they are ready or not. Donna Drewes had been the on-air fund-raiser for WNET-TV in New York for eighteen years when the station decided to trim back its staff. She was one of those who got the bad news. The layoff presented her with an opportunity, but it felt more like a midlife crisis. She had liked doing the program voice-overs and pledge drives because it allowed her to combine her experience as a former radio news reporter and stage actress. But the pledge drives had gotten redundant. She had started feeling guilty about entreating viewers to send money when she believed the station's funds could be better managed. As she put it, "Little old ladies on fixed incomes would call in and say, 'Because you seem so nice, I am sending fifteen dollars. I know it's not much, but it's all I have this month.' And I would want to send it back to them because the station didn't need it that bad."

So when she got the news she was being laid off, she had mixed feelings: anger, relief, hurt. She had known in her heart for a few years that she needed to move on. But she hadn't been uncomfortable enough to take the plunge. The first year of the layoff was a hard time. She lost her lease on her apartment and had to move into a tiny apartment that cost as much as the previous one. A trained actress, she kept up her cheery façade in front of friends, but tears came easily over little things that wouldn't have bothered her before. She worried, Was she on a downward slide? It wasn't supposed to be this way. It wasn't fair. It was painful. Try telling someone else you've been "let go" several dozen times a week and you'll get the idea how it felt.

When her PBS job disappeared, Donna was forced to find another way to earn a living. She had tried moving into another side of the business by working on several documentaries, but it was hard to get the executives to consider her as a producer rather than on-air talent. After mulling her options, she decided to make teaching her primary income and augment that with commercial voice work. To her surprise, the teaching turned out to be much more gratifying than the work in public television. Her students, who often were learning English as a second language, loved her. They were grateful to learn from such a caring coach. And she got a charge out of giving them homework using some of the best of American literature. She was giving them the gift of words. And teaching them to appreciate good writing. At the end of the day, that felt good.

"If you turn off the TV, you can get by without it," she says. "But if you can't read and write, you've got a problem. A lot of my students are adults who weren't taught how to write in school, or adults who come back to school after raising kids. It's an interesting mix from all over the world. Teaching them how to get confident as writers is a very tough job. Just as tough as any TV job. But it's very satisfying, too, because I make a real difference in their lives. I learn from them, too. In one class I may have students from the Bahamas, Ghana, Germany, Puerto Rico, Harlem, Ohio. From all over, all different ages. They need a degree to move on with their lives, so they work very hard and are very appreciative. I had a Chinese woman in my last class that I thought would never make it. Her English was very minimal. But she wound up getting a B through sheer, hard work. I was so proud of her."

What didn't feel great, she confessed, was the fact that she made less money. And she was now an anonymous teacher, rather than a television personality. "In my heart I knew it was unhealthy to depend on the kind of appreciation I got from people who saw me on TV," she said. "It's addictive and losing that was like going through a withdrawal from any addiction. But it forced growth in me. I realize now that I was treading water at WNET. And I may have even made my departure happen in a strange way, like creating the kind of negative energy that brought it about. Down deep I knew I didn't want to be there any longer. And now I feel kind of like a good soldier who has embarked on a new thing. It's something that calls on all my resources, instead of treading water in a job that was using a tenth of my resources," she said.

After a year, she said she thought, "I'm a better person than I was. Calmer. Happier." Having passed fifty, she says, "Now I

> "Although the world is full of suffering,
> it is also full of the overcoming of it."
> —HELEN KELLER, AUTHOR

realize I have lots of options. It's a question of choosing. But I don't have to stay in a job that pays well just to get a pension. I don't have to buy my future by handicapping my present. I'm not doing that anymore."

In all our lives, there are times when we feel the effects of discouragement, rejection, or loss. Times where things just don't turn out the way we hoped. Times where life does not seem fair. During such times, we just wish someone would take care of us for a change. This is the best time of all to take care of yourself. It helps to be in meditation like Anne Grizzle's "night watch." It helps to call in friends who care about you, like Donna Sanson's church supporters. It helps to embrace "Plan B" as a potential improvement rather than a sign of failure. You have to be proactive in order to dispel the negative thoughts you may be having about your current situation.

1. Begin by clearing away the fog of sadness or anger. Avoid trying to do this alone. Ask a friend you trust completely, or a pastor, or a professional coach or counselor to help you move beyond the roadblocks you are up against.

2. Ask yourself, What do you need most right now?

3. In talking with others, or journaling, answer: What is God asking me to learn from this situation? Have I been on the right track for serving my true purpose in life? What is that track?

4. Make an inventory of the accomplishments you've had in your life. Can you recognize that your life has been successful in some ways?

5. Will the strengths that helped you be successful once before help you with a new beginning? If so, itemize those strengths. Determine how you can build on them. If not, determine what new skills you need, what is missing, and where you need to grow.

> "Hey, this little kid gets roller skates. She puts them on. She stands up and almost flops over backwards. She sticks out a foot like she's going somewhere and falls down and smacks her hand. She grabs hold of a step to get up and sticks out the other foot and slides about six inches and falls and skins her knee. And then, you know what? She brushes off the dirt and the blood and puts some spit on it and then sticks out the other foot *again*."
> —MYRA COHN LIVINGSTON, WRITER

6. What roadblocks still remain that may keep you from getting into action? Make a list of them. What will it take to remove those roadblocks? What resources do you need?

7. Whom will you allow to help you? Who will pray with you? Whom will you have a thoughtful conversation with?

8. Determine what you are willing to do once the roadblocks are removed. What are your new goals? Where will you be and what will you be doing in six months? One year?

9. What will you do this very day to be in the present moment rather than bogged down in the past? What can you do today to point yourself forward?

10. Write the words "thank you" on a little piece of paper and slip it into a pocket, wallet, or briefcase where it will remind you to be grateful for the difficulties you have survived.

Chapter Nine

Build a Circle of Support

"One's life has value so long as one attributes value to the life of others, by means of love, friendship, indignation, and compassion."

—SIMONE DE BEAUVOIR, WRITER

Too often women who are dutifully trying to please everyone don't have time left to share their concerns with their circle of friends. The frantic pace of today's lifestyles makes it more difficult to have let-your-hair-down talks with friends who are also on full-gallop schedules. But if you want to change your life, you need to exhale your pent-up frustrations with trusted friends. You need to share your long-held-in dreams with empathetic friends. You need to test your plans on friends who will tell you the truth. Friends will lift your game. Friends believe in you. As Marlene Dietrich said, "It's the friends you can call up at four A.M. that matter."

Most of the women profiled in this book said they relied on the counsel and encouragement of trusted friends when making transitions and decisions.

- Because there were so few women who had reached a Fortune 500 executive position, Karol Emmerich turned for helpful advice to male business friends who had made midlife transitions when she was wondering whether to leave her job as treasurer of Dayton Hudson Corporation.

- Elizabeth Dole regularly hosted a women's Bible study group, which shared prayer concerns in her Red Cross office, as she was pondering a run for the presidency. Likewise businesswomen Jane Russell in Tacoma and Barb Finley in Wisconsin said women in their Bible study groups helped them stay "grounded."

- Susan Baker, when struggling to adjust to her husband's long hours at the White House, bonded with the wives of other politicians and diplomats.

- Marcia Beauchamp was mentored by one of the elders in her church, who functioned as a sort of spiritual uncle while she shifted from styling hair in Oklahoma to studying theology.

Other women have found a sense of sharing with other women through book clubs, exercise partners, or lunch buddies. What you will need is a personal community of like-minded people. It's important to tell your story and to listen to other people's stories. The wisdom you seek may be aggregated in your friends. You will find that participating in activities with peers stimulates thinking and action.

Unfortunately, studies have shown that the time of life when people have the least number of friends may be when they need that shared wisdom the *most:* at middle age. According to Jan Yager, author of *Friendshifts: the Power of Friendships and How It Shapes Our Lives,* most people have more friends when they are young adults and during old age. That's due in part to the fact that those in the age bracket from forty to sixty either have children or elderly parents to tend to as well as a job and a spouse. These people take priority in our lives and our circle of friends tends to shrink for a while. As Deborah Bohren, a vice president for Empire Blue Cross and Blue Shield in New York, told the *Wall Street Journal* in March 2000, "Having drinks or dinner with a friend is taking time away from my family. You feel a little selfish."

Jobs have also become more demanding, putting a squeeze on social relationships. Americans are working longer hours and have less leisure time today than they did thirty years ago. The number of people working at least forty-nine hours a week continues to go up. These pressures are even more acute for women, who still do most of the housework in two-worker families. And when a child is sick, 83 percent of mothers stay home with the sick child, compared with 22 percent of fathers.

Meanwhile e-mail, fax machines, laptops, beepers, and cell phones have blurred the boundaries between work and home. Some people are never really ever off-duty. There was a time when the switchboard closed at five P.M. Workers went home when the factory whistle blew. Today work can follow you in the car, on the plane, and into the weekend.

Those who have had to reschedule multiple times to get together with friends for a movie or dinner know how difficult it is to connect in a 24/7 world. In earlier generations, men had weekly bowling leagues for bonding and women had bridge groups. Today's aging boomers are lucky to have time to grab a latte at Starbucks. They realize they are working harder and harder for a future they are not sure they want. Today's workers say they don't have time for restful sleep, much less to have long, thoughtful talks with friends. But that's exactly what they need. As columnist Ellen Goodman once observed, in the 1980s there was a poster

> " 'Unbosom yourself,' said Wimsey. 'Trouble shared is trouble halved.' "
> —DOROTHY SAYERS, MYSTERY WRITER

that said, "Oops, I forgot to have children." She suggested the poster for the 1990s should be, "Oops, I forgot to have a life."

Connecting with your friends can help you physically as well as psychologically. Researchers at Yale University surveyed mortality rates among ten thousand seniors with different degrees of social contact. Having friends reduced the risk of death by about 50 percent over a five-year period. This was confirmed by another large study in Alameda County, California, where researchers discovered that having friends had a bigger impact in reducing the risk of death for seniors than having a spouse. Dr. Yager concurs that neglecting friendships can pose a psychic risk. "Too many people are finding out when the marriage doesn't work or there's some family tragedy that no one's there for them."

Like many women, I had a close set of friends in high school who were much like the true friends in Rebecca Wells's *Divine Secrets of the Ya-Ya Sisterhood.* We decorated the gym together, frosted each other's hair, and stayed up all night at slumber parties with Cokes and bean dip. They have remained my touchstones, the people with whom I feel most real and natural. The problem is almost all of them live in different cities now. One of them has been close enough to keep up contact and that has been a blessing. Ann Carruth and I have been friends since the seventh grade in San Angelo, a ranching outpost in the middle of West Texas. I still remember a matching aqua sweater and skirt set she wore that year. It had a cowl neck and came all the way from Neiman Marcus in Dallas. I must confess that at the time, I wished I had the outfit and she had a wart on her nose. Still, we have gone from Beatles albums to AARP cards together.

Ann is the kind of friend who advised me which pediatrician to get when I had my first child. She's the one who planned a fortieth birthday party for me the same summer I was trying to recover from a divorce. She's the one I called for a ride when I poked a grocery bag in my eye and had to go to the emergency room. When no one else can, she can tell by looking at my face how I really feel.

When I was forty-nine and starting to get the midlife dreads, Ann gave me Sarah Ban Breathnach's delightful daybook, *Simple Abundance*. And sure enough, late one night when I was so stressed from work that I couldn't sleep, the message from the book struck home: be grateful for your blessings and be audacious in seeking your authentic role in life. That night, I followed the *Simple Abundance* advice and started making lists of things each day that I was grateful for: my two dear sons . . . my friends . . . my sister, Karen . . . my faithful secretary, Carol . . . my aging, but cozy house . . . a new *Mozart at Midnight* CD . . . my health . . . my faith . . . my hilarious parents . . . my tennis partner . . . my almost-paid-for car . . . my friend Richard, who encouraged me to try new things and promised to be "just a phone call away" . . . my friend Bill, who shared books and music . . . well, you get the idea.

When we turned fifty, Ann and I went to Paris and celebrated with champagne at the chic Pre Catalan restaurant. Each season of our friendship has had lessons, especially this autumn one. When we can find time to get together lately, it's to brainstorm about things we'd like to do now that our children have plans and credit cards of their own. Art classes? Write a Christmas book? Hike the Milford Trek in New Zealand? If only our schedules would quit getting in the way.

Over the years, it has been helpful to cultivate new friends who were juggling similar pressures in the business world. I'm in two women's groups that network and this spring I helped start a Bible study/prayer group for businesswomen in downtown Dallas. To my surprise, some of the busiest leaders in the city instantly said "yes" and started making the morning sessions at the Crescent Hotel. Precisely because they had such weighty responsibilities—managing law firms, corporations, foundations—they knew they needed to grow in their faith. Over time, they began to let down their guard and share their concerns—a child going into the hospital, a spouse trying to start a new business, problems with staffers in the office, an exhausting travel schedule. The sessions always seem to soothe the way as we go on to work.

At midlife, you come to appreciate that we are to be guides for each other. To paraphrase Kathleen Norris from *The Cloister Walk,* friends help us see something that's easy to lose sight of in our infernally busy lives: "That we exist for each other, and when we're at low ebb, sometimes just to see the goodness radiating from another can be all we need in order to rediscover it in ourselves."

We may not realize it, but often we are making quilts with the threads of advice we share with each other. Because

> "My favorite nights in the world are the nights I have my girlfriends over. That is when I sleep the best, hardly a nightmare at all when my buddies are with me."
> —REBECCA WELLS, FROM *DIVINE SECRETS OF THE YA-YA SISTERHOOD*

families are so fractured today and neighbors are not as neigh-borly, we have to build artificial families with friends. It's a way of connecting. Cathy Bonner has taken "the good ole girl net-work" to new heights. She got her motivation when she was in college in the 1960s. Baby boomer women at the time were starting to challenge the status quo: Patricia Ireland, later presi-dent of the National Organization of Women (NOW), was a Delta stewardess who protested unequal benefits. Wilma Mankiller, later president of the Cherokee Nation, visited the Indians protesting at Alcatraz Island and was inspired to work for the rights of women and Indians from then on. It was a time when greater numbers of women began to reject boundaries.

Cathy had majored in education because her father told her that she would "always be able to get a job teaching." But what she really wanted to do was start a business like her dad did. So she wouldn't take "no" for an answer when banks wouldn't lend her money to start a business in her own name. When she was twenty-six she started her first company, an advertising agency, with a $400 stake from her father. She remembers with a hearty laugh, "I was too dumb to know how high the failure rate for small business was." But she was smart enough to start and sell at a profit, not one, but three successful businesses in the fields of communications, market-ing, and cable TV.

She was cheered on by a feisty group of friends during the 1970s and 1980s. These soul mates extended from Dallas, where she grew up, to Austin, where she went to school. They included future federal judge Janet Guthrie, the future governor of Texas Ann Richards, and attorney Sarah Weddington, one of the attorneys in the landmark *Roe* v. *Wade* abortion case. "Since I didn't have children, it was very important to me to have friends to boost me up and keep me going," Cathy says. She called them her "stealth network." They were survivors of the "three D's"—diets, divorce, and disaster.

They were also inspired to get involved in the women's movement, each in her own way. You might say in the 1970s, Cathy worked to change laws, then in the 1980s, she worked to change lives. In 1975 she teamed up with Sen. Kay Bailey Hutchison, who was then a state legislator from Houston, to reform rape laws in the state. As a result women were treated more fairly in the courtroom and rape was treated as a more serious assault.

Cathy and her friends formed the Texas Women's Political Caucus and together they pushed for equal credit laws so women could get loans in their own names, and they helped change the law so teachers could keep their jobs if they became pregnant. As Cathy saw that her friends could be individually successful by thinking positive collectively, it dawned on her that they should expand their mutual support system to include other women. So they formed the Foundation for Women's Resources, which she once described as a "quilting club run amok." One of the foundation's first projects was the Texas Women's History Exhibit, because Cathy is a staunch believer that women need to "appreciate their history and know that they are building on the shoulders of those who go before them."

Next, the foundation formed Leadership Texas, a statewide leadership training network for women. The idea was to embolden more women to believe they can get challenging jobs, be leaders, get things accomplished. In the next two decades, more than a thousand women would go through the training. A member of the first class became mayor of Corpus Christi and another became mayor of Lubbock after members of her Leadership Texas group made it their class project to help her get elected. No wonder one of Cathy's favorite quotes is Margaret Mead's advice, "Never doubt that a small group of thoughtful, committed citizens can change the world. Indeed, it is the only thing that ever has."

In the 1990s, Cathy jumped into public office herself. She worked to elect Ann Richards as governor and Richards then tapped her to become executive director of the Texas Department of Commerce. As the state's business advocate, she helped convince Southwestern Bell Corporation to relocate its corporate headquarters from St. Louis to San Antonio. She was at the forefront of the campaign to pass the North American Free Trade Agreement (NAFTA).

When the Richards administration ended in 1994, Cathy decided she needed a break from politics. "I looked around and decided I needed to get a life. All I did was work. So I decided to take a few years and do the things that were important to enrich me as a person." In an interview with the *Dallas Morning News,* she compared that midlife shift to the corporate women who leave business careers to spend more time with their families or do things that provide more balance in their lives. As she told a reporter, "Maybe it's a progression of maturity, where you realize that what you do is not who you are. I think it's a demographic shift and women who blazed the frontier are now wanting to regroup and take some time to be better human beings."

Yet it was not too long before she started another business—Bonner Inc., a marketing consulting firm. And

> "Instead of looking at life as a narrowing funnel, we can see it ever widening to choose the things we want to do, to take the wisdoms we've learned and create something."
> —LIZ CARPENTER, PRESS SECRETARY

she soon took on another public service project—The Women's Museum: An Institute for the Future, in Dallas, Texas. During the next four years, she pulled together a national campaign to raise $30 million to transform a historic (translation: about to tumble down) building at Fair Park into a state-of-the-art museum. Her dream was to celebrate women's accomplishments of the past as well as their potential in the future.

The idea was to tell the story of path-breaking women, to show how the lives of women today have been informed by the lives of women yesterday. "People respond to storytelling from generation to generation. Women today still need to hear stories of inspiration . . . and women today have no idea what it was like before. . . . It's been all about giving women choices."

The idea caught on. "I think it was something that was meant to be," Cathy marveled at one of our interviews in the construction office outside the museum. "All these helping hands came forward to help: We found an incredible design architect in Wendy Evans Joseph, who was senior designer for the Holocaust Museum in Washington, D.C. . . . Dealey Herndon, who restored the Texas capitol building, came on board to do the construction . . . to our surprise, big corporations said 'yes' when we asked for money. It was the right time for the right idea."

She had just come from one of the hundreds of hard-hat tours she regularly led at the museum site. Every week for the last four years, she had flown from her office in Austin to Dallas to personally show the site to prospective donors, journalists, Smithsonian museum officials, etc. With her white plastic helmet smashed down on her blond coiffure, she walked through the army of carpenters and roofers with an excitement as if she had just discovered it herself. Once I saw her give a tour in 110-

degree summer Texas weather. She stepped over wires and woodwork in high heels and a St. John knit suit, smiling gamely as beads of sweat started forming on her forehead. Surely one of the reasons she has been so successful, whether marketing reforms or products, is that she is so genuine about her enthusiasm. She always puts the project rather than herself in the spotlight. You rarely hear Cathy Bonner say the "I" word, as in "I came up with the idea for the museum," or "I founded Leadership Texas." Instead, she's great about using the "we" word and making other people feel that includes them.

Thanks to her networking, money was raised by women from El Paso to Atlanta to New Jersey. And thanks to her drive, the museum project came in early and under budget in September 2000. It now has officially joined the Smithsonian Institution affiliations program as the first national museum dedicated solely to the accomplishments of women.

Of course, there is the obligatory hall of fame, with portraits of exemplars like Susan B. Anthony, Pearl Buck, Eleanor Roosevelt, Amelia Earhart, Margaret Mead, Marian Anderson, Barbara Jordan, and Sally Ride. But visitors to the museum also will learn how women throughout history have played a civilizing role in communities, establishing libraries, hospitals, schools. They will learn that it was a woman, Mary Pennington, who invented refrigeration. That Maggie Lena Walker, an African American, was the first woman president of a bank, the Penny Savings Bank. And they'll discover the stories of other women who spoke their conscience and broke new ground, such as:

- Cockacoeske, queen of the Pamuskey tribe, who in 1677 helped settle Bacon's Rebellion, bring a century of peace to Virginia colonists and her tribe.

- Attorney Belva Lockwood, the first woman presidential candidate in 1884 and 1888.

- Emily Bissell, who in the 1920s printed the first Christmas Seals and sold them, raising $135,000 in a year to fight lung disease.

- Mitsue Endo, who in 1942 petitioned the United States to end Asian American internment during World War II and won.

- Lois Gibbs, a housewife who, in 1978, won the drive to get the federal government to clean up the toxic waste in Love Canal.

Visitors will learn that women invented the square-bottomed paper bag, the windshield wiper, and the cotton gin (Eli Whitney didn't invent it, he just got the patent, because women weren't permitted to get patents in the nineteenth century). Likewise, visitors will learn how "Mother's Clubs" became the basis for PTAs, boosting schools for generation after generation. They'll learn how the Daughters of Liberty supported the American Revolution by holding spinning bees to sell yarn and creating tea substitutes with flowers and herbs. The idea is to show how ordinary women have done extraordinary things. And to remind visitors that everyone—famous or working behind the scenes—is a shaper of the future. To complete the link to the future, there will be a computer lab, where girls can come for cyber coaching.

Not bad for an idea that literally started as a dream that Cathy Bonner had. "We should take our dreams more seriously," she advises. "Sometimes it's an idea that compels you to act."

"If you want to be listened to, you
should put in time listening."
—MARGE PIERCY, POET, NOVELIST

When she recently turned fifty, she celebrated by traveling with a Winnebago full of friends to the McDonald Observatory in rugged Big Bend territory to look up to the stars for inspiration. Her next challenge is figuring out what to do after the museum is settled. "I don't intend to do the same old thing," she told me. "I have a different perspective now. Some things don't matter as much to me as before. I don't care so much what people think. I don't suffer fools. I'm more jealous of my time. I'm more secure. I don't worry about appearances.

"My mother always said the forties were the best years, but I think it's going to be the fifties," she went on, "because I have learned that change is good. You never grow until you change. Henri Nouwen has a wonderful story about letting go of what you know to reach out for something new, like letting go of a trapeze to reach out for the catcher on the other trapeze. You have to learn to take someone else's hands and trust that it will work out. You won't grow until you do."

When you are seeking your passion, it is helpful to join with others who understand the process. It is sometimes a rocky road to shift between a nonpassion pursuit and one in sync with your feelings. What smoothes the way is a circle of friends and supporters.

1. Do you regularly schedule time with old friends or seek ways to cultivate new friends?

2. Do you have a friend who can serve as a touchstone for you at various stages of life?

3. Have you ever been in a close-knit circle of friends, sisters, or family by whom you felt supported and heard? If so, what about that worked best for you?

> "Only friends will tell you the truths you need to hear to make . . . your life bearable."
> —FRANCINE DU PLESSIX GRAY, BIOGRAPHER

4. Who do you currently have in your network with whom you could join in conversation regularly?

5. If you decided to form a small intimate group of women who would grow and support each other, who would you want to have in that group?

6. What will you do to get *your* group together right away?

7. List hobbies that could use group activity.

8. Seek out: book clubs, volunteer organizations, retreats, athletic events where you can connect with others.

Of course, the best way to have a friend is to be one. Isn't there someone you could be reaching out to?

Chapter Ten

After the Kids Leave, Launch Yourself

"We all have choices that we have made. . . . When a woman makes a choice to marry and have children, in one way, her love begins, but in another way, it stops. You build a life of details, and you just stop and stay steady so that your children can move. And when they leave, they take your life of details with them. You're expected to move on again, but you don't even remember what it was that moved you, because nobody says thanks a lot, not even yourself."

—SPOKEN BY THE CHARACTER FRANCESCA, AN IOWA HOUSEWIFE,
IN THE MOVIE *THE BRIDGES OF MADISON COUNTY*

Most of the women who are middle-aged now grew up in an era when they were taught to color neatly between the lines. The sky had to be blue. The grass had to be green. There were rules and norms. Particularly in the conformist era of the 1940s and 1950s, women took on the protective coloration of what everyone was doing around them. Unfortunately, that conventional thinking still limits many women. After their children leave home, they settle for small pursuits to fill their time. There might not be anyone telling them specifically that they *cannot* do something more ambitious, but they may be reluctant to give *themselves* permission to do something totally different.

What women need to do is recondition their outlook, reprogram themselves with positive messages. First, you must start thinking differently. Open your mind to a new pattern. Then you can take some baby steps and start reviving dormant skills or interests. Start each day by looking in the mirror and telling yourself, "I am going to try new things today." Then, as you go to sleep at night, mentally picture the change you want and expect. Visualize it clearly and attractively in your mind. Picture yourself walking through the steps. After all, you have sovereign control over what you hold in your mind. Condition your mind with the different image you want of yourself. Then you can begin to act out more venturesome thoughts.

Carolyn Shoemaker saw herself in a role that was a significant departure from the first half of her life. She reached for the stars, literally. When Carolyn Shoemaker's three children left for college, she thought, "What am I going to do with all this spare time I have?"

Those who have been there know well the piercing ache you feel when you walk into a child's empty room, catch the personal scent of clothes left behind in the closet, see the school photos on the bulletin board starting to fade. You realize that an all-important chapter of your life as a woman is over, closed, finished. Bye, Mom, don't worry, I'll call.

Life is never quite the same again.

It's quieter. And as Carolyn discovered, there's all that spare time to fill. She didn't want to go back to teaching. Three decades before, she had majored in history and business at Chico State College in California and trained to be a junior high school teacher. But after teaching seventh graders for one year, she thought, "This is not for me. Never again." It turned out she was more interested in her brother's college roommate. His name was Gene Shoemaker. They met when he came to be the best man at her brother's wedding in 1950. It was a brief meeting, but it was truly love at first sight for both of them. Gene left after her brother's wedding to return to Princeton and she reluctantly went back to teaching. They corresponded and the next summer he invited her and her mother on a two-week camping trip. It was really a way of checking her out. He wanted to see if she would be a good geologist's wife. After the first week, he asked her to marry him. When they got married, they had only seen each other a total of three weeks.

He went on to become a university professor and an eminent planetary geologist. He was chairman of the National Academy of Sciences committee that trained scientist-astronauts for the Apollo lunar program. She continued to accompany him on field trips. "It was fun to go along with someone who was a born teacher and liked to explain things. He would patiently point out to me the differences in varying shades of orange and red and indications of a different formation. . . . He loved mapping, field work, deciphering. . . . 'How did the world get this way?' He loved to explain it."

Though the whole family would go on the field trips together, raising their three children left little time for Carolyn to explore her budding interest in science. "It was a time when women did not hold a second job outside of the home. I stayed home until they were through with school and had moved out of the home, and then I wondered, 'What am I going to do now? I have all this newfound freedom!'"

She tried working in a florist shop briefly, but wasn't too keen on it. So she asked Gene if he had any ideas. She explains, "I wanted to find something that I would enjoy as much as he enjoyed geology. Because it was not only his work, it was his hobby. He was totally absorbed in it." Gene, who was a professor at Cal Tech at the time, suggested several projects that needed volunteers. She wasn't necessarily looking for money, so she signed on. One of the projects dealt with paleomagnetic work, a form of dating rocks. She had done a little bit of the lab work on field trips and it did not thrill her. One of the other projects was the search for Earth-crossing asteroids. "Those are bodies that cross the orbit of the earth and might hit us sometime," she explains. *That* piqued her interest.

She said Gene had started the asteroid program with Eleanor "Glow" Helin at the Palomar Observatory in 1973. The program had not located many asteroids by the early 1980s, and Gene felt the work needed speeding up if more was to be learned about objects that impact the Earth. She wasn't sure how she would like the task. She didn't mind studying photographic plates and films taken of the night sky to locate objects that moved. But she wasn't sure she could do telescope work. It meant she would have to stay up all night long. "I'm a morning person and until that time I had never stayed up an entire night in my life. So I had some doubts," she recalls. "Over time, as I became more and more interested in the project, I also went to the telescope and I discovered I loved that aspect as well. We still were doing rather old-fashioned astronomy at the time. It was the kind of telescope that we would load film into . . . in a dome under the stars. It was kind of nice. I found myself sitting up there, thinking 'Gee, here I am at the Palomar Observatory and I'm an observer. How can this be me?' I loved it."

She was fifty years old and she had just started a new career as an astronomer. She slid into astronomy very slowly, she says, just a few hours a time, then she discovered, "I was doing it all the time and wishing I had more hours for it." The observatory had a big roof that rolls right off, so she would have the whole sky to watch at night. Even though it was often freezing cold and tedious work, she found the hunt thrilling. As she told one interviewer, "There's nothing like discovering something new. I imagine the way it must have been for the early pioneers to climb over a mountain and find a lake . . . it's so exciting, you almost lose your mind for a moment." She described the feeling of searching the heavens as a sort of spiritual feeling, though she doesn't consider herself religious. "Let's put it this way. When you are in astronomy and feeling how big the universe is and how very distant it is, I think it adds a dimension of mystery. You have to wonder what is out there and why it is like that and is that what we call God? Or, does it have anything to do with religion and is it just a very spiritual experience in a way? Gene used to say that the whole outdoors was his church, and I know exactly what he meant."

She also discovered working with her husband on projects was enjoyable, although she felt some conflicting loyalties that even with her children gone, she should tend to the cooking and house chores. "But I didn't really want to spend the time doing all of that, not anymore," she said with a rippling laugh. "Gene was very understanding," she recalled in our conversation. "Every now and then, he would say, 'It would be nice to have a pie.' And I would say, 'Would you rather that I stay home and make a pie, or would you rather me do my work?'"

The work trumped the pie. And the hours of scanning films paid off in 1982. "The first thing I discovered that no one else had seen was an asteroid. The first asteroid was exciting, but the near-earth asteroid was *terribly* exciting. When I found that, I thought, 'What's this weird thing?' It turned out it was a group of asteroids called Amours, because their orbits come close enough to sort of kiss the orbit of the Earth, hence the name."

According to *TPO* magazine, Carolyn also discovered a Trojan asteroid, which are asteroids in swarms within 60 degrees of either side of Jupiter. She also discovered a comet in 1983 and her big breakthrough came in July 1994. Along with their colleague David Levy, the Shoemakers discovered a comet that impacted Jupiter in what many considered the astronomical "event of the century." It became known as Comet Shoemaker-Levy 9 (SL9 for short). The comet's orbit had been disturbed by the planet Jupiter until it orbited the Jovian giant instead of orbiting the Sun. In the process, it had been pulled apart into a long train of individual fragments, each of which plunged into Jupiter's atmosphere, leaving dark scars that could be seen even in amateur telescopes for some time afterward.

The event thrust all three into the science spotlight. But Carolyn was the first person on Earth to see the odd-looking trail of cometary fragments on the plates taken by Gene and David. It is perhaps what Carolyn is best known for among the general public. She concedes that SL9 was the most exciting thing she has discovered, but she said, "I think the fact that within twelve years' time I discovered thirty-two comets is the main thing I'm most proud of. I don't have time to waste." *Astronomy* magazine has called her "arguably the best in the business." In twenty years of work, she can claim credit for some eight hundred asteroids as well as the thirty-two comets. That's more than any living astronomer and just five shy of the all-time record.

Even if you don't rechart the heavens, you, too, can find something challenging to do with the second half of your life. That's not to say the child-rearing that takes up so much of the first half of a life is unimportant. It is an opus Gloria. But you can have more than one noble pursuit in your life. Like other mothers, Carolyn is proud of her three children, all educators, but she is equally proud that the work she and Gene did together triggered new interest in the fields of asteroid astronomy and comet astronomy. Their work has been particularly helpful in analyzing the mass extinctions of dinosaurs that might have been caused by comet showers and in predicting the threat to Earth from a collision with an asteroid.

And she seems pleased that her high profile has encouraged other women in science. "I think because of my age—seventy going on seventy-one—and because I have been very fortunate in my work, that many young women look up to me. I find myself looking over my shoulder thinking, 'It can't be me they're talking about. Must be someone else standing back there.' "

With her close-cropped silver hair and bangle earrings, she defies the old stereotypes of a scientist. She credits her parents with instilling the belief that "if I really wanted to do something I could do it. I've never felt that I had to conform. In fact, I tried to teach our children that you don't have to be a conformist. So long as what you are doing is right, you don't have to follow the crowd on everything. Many young people put that first, but I think it is more important to be your own person, your own individual."

She had just returned from speaking to girls at a middle school in Montana. She said she always advises young women to "take all the math, all the physics, all the chemistry that you can. You want to have something to fall back on that you might enjoy. They sort of groan when I say that, because you know girls have an attitude about math and physics in this country. But there is no sugarcoating it. To do original research, you need to know math, you need to know science. And I want them to understand that if you have it ahead of time, rather than try to get it on the job like I did, it will be a lot easier."

She said she hopes she is a role model for older women as well. "It's important for women who have raised their families to know that you can change and do something else. And you can do it successfully. You can start anytime, I think. There's nothing that says you have to start out when you are twenty-two and just graduated from college. Even Gene said it's very good to change your direction every ten years or so. Then you bring a fresh new way of looking at the area. So we should not feel so compelled to stay in the same hole and be so afraid to step out. It is very comfortable to just go along with what you know well. But it is more satisfying to try something new."

She has been learning a new lifestyle yet again since the death of her husband. He was killed in a sudden accident when they were on a field trip in Australia in 1997. He was driving and failed to see a Land Rover coming toward them as he turned a corner. He died in the crash. Carolyn suffered five fractured ribs, a fractured wrist, a dislocated shoulder, a dislocated thumb, and nerve damage in her legs.

It took a while to heal physically. She found it good emotional therapy to finish commitments they had been working on together. She helped edit a book on the solar system and published a book based on lectures Gene had given in England at Yale University. It helped her work through the loss to sift through the work of a lifetime. She said, "I guess the answer is to work very, very hard. At the same time, I've been doing things of my own. I'm learning to stand on my own two feet."

In 1999, NASA honored Gene Shoemaker's memory by placing a vial of his ashes on its Lunar Prospector spacecraft. When the probe crashed on the moon to end its mission, his

"Life is a succession of moments. To live each one is to succeed."

—CORITA KENT, WRITER

ashes were scattered on the lunar surface. So now Carolyn Shoemaker can look into the night sky and check her husband's burial spot.

Perhaps one of the greatest gifts a mother can give her daughters is to show them how to start over. Eleanor Arnold Oberwetter had been valedictorian of my high school class in the sixties and was impressive in every way: bright, articulate, friendly. In our high school annual, she was saluted for National Honor Society, French Club, Spanish Club, orchestra, Chess Club, and Math Club.

But such were the times in small towns that school counselors didn't encourage even the best and the brightest girls to think about careers that required graduate school. Years later when we filtered back for class reunions, we discovered none of the women out of our class of more than eight hundred had become a lawyer or a doctor.

Eleanor graduated with honors from the University of Texas, married a fellow member of the Young Republicans, and settled down to raise three children. Only when the children were older did she begin teaching and became a highly popular English and history instructor at the Episcopal School of Dallas. Teaching gave her time for swimming pool excursions with the kids during the summers and it was stimulating enough. She livened up the literature studies by having the students create mock newspapers with stories about King Arthur and his court. Eleven years of teaching went by, filled with station wagons and Scouts and soccer and homework.

When their children all headed off to college, she and her husband decided to call it quits. And she decided to do something she had wanted to do since those high school valedictorian days: she went to law school, at the age of fifty-three. She wasn't burned out; she loved teaching. But all that freedom beckoned. She figured she could always come back to teaching if need be. One of the ironies was that while she was preparing her law school application, she was teaching advanced placement courses and counseling students, so she was helping her students prepare their college applications while she was filling out hers.

Not surprisingly, she aced the LSAT. She scored so well she was admitted to the University of Chicago law school, ranked one of the top five in the country. With one daughter still in college in Texas, she was soon living far away in a high-rise apartment building on Lake Michigan, studying law ten hours a day, seven days a week. "It's the most awful, exciting thing I've ever done," she said. "It's soooo difficult. I love it."

She gives a lot of the credit to her daughters, one of whom is in law school herself. "They say that they became strong women because of me, but I say I got strength from them. They encouraged me every step of the way."

She was not sure what type of legal practice she would pursue when she finished—perhaps government or public interest work, perhaps teaching. She was initially least interested in practicing with a big firm, but she didn't want to rule it out. She now realizes all of those choices are possible, even at midlife.

When her friends back home heard she was leaving for law school, she said, they unanimously were supportive and then she could see a lightbulb go off in their eyes as they realized, "Oh, my gosh. I could be doing something different, too!" She now is

> "We're still not where we're going, but we're still not where we were."
> —NATASHA JOSEFOWITZ, SCHOLAR

encouraging others to at least study the options of going back to school or trying something new. "It's not like jumping off a cliff," she said. "You shouldn't create obstacles in your mind that aren't there. You can take it one step at a time. Research the costs and requirements, the deadlines for tests and applications. You don't have to make a commitment until you mail in those filing fees. I figured I could be fifty-six with a law degree or fifty-six without a law degree. It was time."

Carolyn Shoemaker's and Eleanor Oberwetter's stories are examples of how much roles for women have evolved in the last half century. Being a proud mother is not the end of the story anymore. That's because a convergence is under way of all the various roles debated for women since the 1960s. Since it has been occurring all around us, the pattern of the events may not have registered sharply. So let's look back for a moment to how we got to where we are, with grandmothers starting brand-new careers just as corporate mothers throw up their hands in exhaustion. You can trace the evolution in ten easy steps through the women who symbolized the various phases:

1. The paradigm shift started in 1963 when Betty Friedan's book *The Feminine Mystique* was published. As she later explained, there had been a one-hundred-year struggle to get the vote for women. Then the movement stalled after women got the vote in 1920. Women's energies were diverted into issues like temperance and other social work. Women started speaking up for themselves again as equal persons in all of society, not just as a man's wife, mother, sex object, daughter, or housewife, in the sixties, just as the nation was dealing with civil rights and the Vietnam War.

2. At about the same time, along came Gloria Steinem, the photogenic and witty journalist, who provided a more attractive image for women's issues. She had a knack for bumper sticker phrases like "A woman needs a man like a fish needs a bicycle." She made waves when she told Smith graduates: "Now you are becoming the men you once would have wanted to marry. But too few men are becoming the women they want to marry." Still, she made people think in new ways by raising questions such as, "If the shoe doesn't fit, must we change the foot?" She helped popularize pants suits and the honorific Ms. for women who did not want to be defined by their marital status. Her *Ms.* magazine was often predictable and unreadable, but it kept issues like the Equal Rights Amendment in the forefront and coached women on how to get credit in their name, how to press the glass ceiling, etc.

3. Yet those initial sixties feminists later lost ground with some women around the country by keeping abortion rights at the forefront of their mission. Many of those women, while they believed in equal pay and fair play, were concerned that advocating abortion conflicted with their religious faith. Then, too, those who wanted to stay home with their children resented that career women always seemed to be depicted as more glamorous or more courageous by Manhattan feminist leaders.

4. Along came people like Marabel Morgan, who championed stay-at-home moms, and encouraged wives to keep their husbands happy by greeting them at the door with nothing but Saran Wrap and a smile on. And Phyllis Schlafly, who articulately defended conservative "family" values with pearls and hair carefully in place.

5. Then there were the brainy bad girls like Germaine Greer (*The Female Eunuch*) and Erica Jong (*Fear of Flying*). And *Cosmopolitan* magazine editor Helen Gurley Browne. They tried to

prove through their lifestyles and their writing that women could enjoy sex as well as men.

6. Coming from still another direction was Naomi Wolf, who argued in *The Beauty Myth* that fashion ads and music videos and the billion-dollar beauty industry conspired to make women obsessed about their looks in order to attract men.

7. New perceptions were added by hard-edged intellectuals like Kate Millett, Susan Brownmiller, and lawyer Catherine MacKinnon, who crusaded against rape as a crime of power and aggression rather than a sex act.

8. Contrarian Camille Paglia took a different tack by defending pornography as part of the sexual personae of art and literature through the centuries.

9. Not surprisingly, by the 1990s there was a new wave of feminists like Susan Faludi, who warned that there was a "backlash" against all this uppity women stuff. The backlash ranged from blue-collar workers who harassed women on the street to right-wing preachers who denounced feminists as "witches."

10. As we cross into this new century, it appears that *all* of the women were partly right. From the thesis that women had rights . . . and the antithesis that women had responsibilities . . . has come the synthesis that women have more choices today. Though women still do not have the political or financial power of men, they now have much more freedom than before. They can choose to be stay-at-home moms without being considered mindless. They can take a crack at just about any profession. They may not have it all, but they can have *more*. And they can have it in just about any order. It's sequencing with multiple options at every step, a very modern phenomenon. Today's women have more latitude than their mothers and grandmothers to choose who they will be for a while. Which means they must be much more discerning and deliberate about those decisions.

No, that does not mean the debate over the "women's movement" is finished. Child care is not what it should be for all income levels. More could be done for flexible hours for any parent. Pay for women only averages seventy-five cents for every dollar a man makes. We now realize the birth control pill, which emancipated women from a life of endless childbearing, also encouraged men to abandon their long-term responsibilities. No-fault divorce has weakened the meaning of commitment for both sexes.

And yes, there are prices to pay for whatever the sequence—home first or work first. But the decision is made more often by the woman nowadays, rather than by an authority figure deciding for her, which was the norm forty years ago.

To bring the modern story of women full circle, Gloria Steinem got married at the age of sixty-six in the fall of 2000. She said then, "Though I've worked many years to make marriage more equal, I never expected to take advantage of it myself. I'm happy, surprised and one day will write about it, but for now, I hope this proves what feminists have always said—that feminism is about the ability to choose what's right at each time of our lives."

She was sharply criticized by some feminists and columnists for being hypocritical in saying women didn't need men to feel fulfilled in one decade and embracing matrimony in the next. But they should cut her some slack. Attraction happens. It is wise to wish all well who enter the noble institution of marriage, the second greatest leap of faith there is. Besides, her personal evolution proves a point. If your only choice in life is to say "yes" to options determined by others, as it was half a century ago, then you are not really free to choose. But if you can say "no" or "not now," then when you say "yes," it has more meaning. Gloria Steinem saying "yes" to marriage, even late in the game, brought the last four decades full circle. And when you think about it, it was a positive step. We have entered an era of "big tent feminism," where there is room for diverse approaches to self-realization for women. What's even more heartening is that so many women are now looking for ways to be useful to society, to make positive use of talents that may have been underutilized in the first half. You do not have to conform to old ways of thinking. You can make a new start at midlife. You can color your life the way you want to.

If you could add one more accomplishment, what would it be? What would you like to try? When your life has been organized around raising children (whether you are a stay-at-home mom or a working-outside-the-home mom), there is a large void when they leave. When they are launched, it's time to launch yourself to fill that void in a purposeful way. This is the time to be "at choice" about what you want to do and how you want to do it. Consider the following questions:

1. What have you discovered so far about yourself from the questions in the previous chapters? Stop and take stock a moment.

2. What have you always wanted to do but kept saying about it, "I'll do that when the kids leave home"?

3. As you spend some time collecting data about the possibilities, what is the one thing that keeps being the most attractive? Is there a way to try it on for size?

4. Would you be willing to get together with women who have the same need for life design to brainstorm possibilities? If so, who will you invite and how will you make that happen?

5. What woman (women) can you have as a mentor through this transition time?

> "I have met brave women who are exploring the outer edge of human possibility, with no history to guide them, and with a courage to make themselves vulnerable that I find moving beyond words."
> —GLORIA STEINEM, JOURNALIST

6. In thinking long term, what will you share with younger women about your "life after the kids leave" journey? What would you like them to know about this experience?

7. Do you think your path has been shaped by changes in the role of women in recent decades? Can you see new opportunities for yourself?

8. What steps could you take, one at a time, to get your second wind?

Chapter Eleven

Coordinate with Your Spouse

"To have and to hold from this day forward, for better for worse, for richer for poorer, in sickness and in health, to love and to cherish, till death do us part."

—*THE BOOK OF COMMON PRAYER* (1928)

Going through a midlife experience, changing directions, seeking a more significant life, does not mean you have to junk everything from the first part of your life, such as your husband. You don't have to go it alone to find a more meaningful path, although some do. You may very well find that there's a more fulfilling second act ahead for both you *and* your spouse. Just remember that the arrow of time only points one way: forward. If you keep moving forward to new experiences and can share them with your mate, that's twice as good. You may discover that a spouse can be a wonderful copilot.

Many women come to realize as they reach the prime of life that the first half of their life was a training process. However, what the training will ultimately lead to is rarely apparent at the time. It's only later that you may be able to see that your experiences came around full circle and that you used lessons from the first half for a different kind of relationship with your spouse in the second half.

Tacoma housewife Jane Russell learned that raising four children was like being a "flexible systems engineer." It prepared her for the rigors of corporate life. And a globe-trotting lifestyle she had never imagined possible. For most of her adult life, she tried to be the perfect mother like June Cleaver or Harriet Nelson. She did lots of volunteer work and juggled all the family needs while her husband, George, turned his grandfather's mutual fund company into a powerhouse pension consulting firm. "A lot of us were the sort of moms who are supposed to raise the super kids. And the dads were supposed to build the business. It was pretty typical fifties stuff. We didn't know any better—we had a great time."

Yet they also had to deal with tragedy. The Russells' fifth child, a son, was stillborn and she took it hard. But she learned that life moves on and you have to pick yourself up and move on with it. "Life's disappointments are there for a reason. It certainly taught me how to deal with other people when they go through that kind of loss. Because people were so wonderful to me and it made such a difference."

She thought her productive years were over when their youngest daughter went off to college and she was faced with an empty nest. Then her husband asked her to help research a new building for his firm, Frank Russell Company. "I didn't think I would fit in because I didn't have a degree and had been at home all those years. Finally I realized I had a lot more skills than I thought I had." She realized she had learned many management skills with her busy family: "I was surprised how they transferred when I went into the business world. Crisis management: You have a crisis in the family, you have to go on intuition and common sense and make something happen. Time management: You have to be able to move by task. People management: You have to be able to motivate people who don't want to get motivated. All that transfers to the work-place."

Her people skills paid off in her first assignment because she interviewed employees in every department to find out what changes they would recommend for the new building. Her husband was so pleased with the worker-sensitive plans for the building that he asked her to take on other duties. Soon she was supervising the personnel department.

But she says candidly that the first year was "perfectly awful." She explains, "It was a shock and not terribly well received by a lot of people, first because I was the founder's wife." Executives with MBAs and PhDs were skeptical that a homemaker could help shape the world's largest pension fund consulting company. She was viewed simply as George's wife. She was not so sure herself that she was up to the job. "My problem was with confidence. If more women can just get in there and do it and give themselves six months or a year before they judge themselves, they'll find they have a lot more skills than they think they do. Staying at home, you learn to have a can-do attitude. If one thing doesn't work out, you have to figure out something else. That's very helpful in the workplace."

It took some time and some lumps, but she proved the critics wrong. Jane Russell is now credited with bringing "soul" to the business world in the form of sensible, sensitive human relations practices. She was the architect of the company's pioneering people programs like ethics training, sabbaticals, and wellness education.

The company now has clients around the world and 1,300 associates. Yet it still has a family feel, thanks to the human touch that Jane Russell brought to the corporate culture. Turnover is minimal. The company has been named by *Wash-*

ington CEO magazine several times as one of the state's best companies to work for. It's typical for her to receive grateful feedback from employees for the company's outpouring of support during an illness or death in the family.

She jokes that it was George's fault that she got into the people side of the business. "I learned not to ride with him to work and suggest something. I told him one day, 'You should have an education and training department.' He said, 'Good idea. What are you going to do about it?'" But she admits that he turned out to be a wonderful mentor. "He said he would help me and he did."

There have been difficulties—the first time she had to tell him "no" at work was hard on both of them. When he wanted to know what was going on in some areas, she refused to tell him if the information was part of a confidential conversation with employees. She considered it a matter of integrity and refused to budge. He learned to accept that. For her part, she had to learn to "let things drop and not fuss about them."

She tells him teasingly that he is a "visionary and a stubborn mule." He brags that she is an "awesome people person." They have been married forty-five years and have been through "three or four stages" together, she says. "Each one is richer and better and we have gotten better at communicating honestly with each other. It's like playing tennis. You have to practice to be good at it." For example, they learned to put the cares of the day behind them by saying a prayer together before they go to bed.

They like working together, she says, because driving to work together gives them time to talk. She made a breakfast deal with him: "If I was going to get in the car the same time as he was, he could not be out there sitting in the car and honking the horn. He agreed to bring me breakfast while I got dressed, so we got out the door together."

Keeping up with her high-energy husband, a fitness fanatic who has climbed Mt. Rainier twice, can be rigorous. Once when we talked, she was recovering in Phoenix from a sinus infection that she contracted during their strenuous travel schedule. "It's certainly not a vacation trip being married to a tornado," she sighed. Their travels took them around the world seven times in six months the previous year. With offices in Australia, Tokyo, Hong Kong, London, Zurich, and Paris, they are often on the go. They ended up having to schedule "sunshine days" when they would not work. Often that meant just a couple of days a month for themselves. When I spoke to her last, yet another phase in her life was on the way: She and her husband had decided to sell their company. Both will remain on contract for two years, but they plan to shift their focus to a family foundation, which they want to direct with their four children. "I am suddenly feeling that the corporate time of life is behind me now and it's time to move on," she said.

Several weeks later she sent a copy of a commencement speech that she and George gave together at Pacific Lutheran University. As usual, they took turns speaking, going back and forth like a Burns and Allen routine, with George supplying the facts and Jane supplying the tender touch. It seemed a perfect example of their partnership, one that she probably never would have envisioned back when she was driving carpools and cooking Sunday dinners.

Here are some healthy examples in their story for other couples to note:

- Learn to respect each other's talents—one may be the navigator, one the mechanic; both roles are important.

- Set aside times to talk about plans, even if it's in the car.

> "Grow old along with me.
> The best is yet to be."
> —ROBERT BROWNING, POET

- Know what your mission is. In their case, to grow a business in a people-friendly way.

- Know your expectations of each other. Don't assume you are always on the same page.

- Learn to respect boundaries. Be up-front about what you will *not* do.

- Try to put aside differences at the end of the day so you will still be partners in the morning.

If you are one of those who has loved and lost in marriage before, take heart. Our endings can be turned into beginnings. Sometimes what seems like a setback may only be a rehearsal for the real thing. Like many women, Barbara Findley learned that the end of a first marriage is not necessarily the end of hope for an enduring partnership. She had been married four years when her husband announced one day that he didn't love her anymore. When they had married, it had seemed the thing to do. But there was a separateness in their life together. She was a hardworking junior high teacher. He was an aspiring attorney. He never went to church with her and they grew apart before she fully realized it. So in some ways, the divorce was under-standable, but no less painful.

Those who have experienced divorce, or who have been close to women whose spouses opted out, know how difficult it is to recover from the hurt. Lawyers say they were "poured out" when they lose a court judgement. That seems to capture the feeling of loss in divorce—you feel poured out, empty. No matter what the circumstances, it takes time to heal.

She thought it would take a long time to meet someone new, but six months after her divorce was final, she met John Findley, a handsome, dark-haired businessman who was six years older than her. They dated two years and then got married.

For several years, she continued teaching. The students called her "Frau Findley." She sponsored the German Club and one Easter break she took fifty students to Germany. She liked the kids and they liked her. And when she chaperoned the dances, John would come with her. After four years of marriage, they talked about having children. She was in her midthirties and her biological clock was ticking along. But he already had a son from his first marriage. He didn't want more children. She thought, "That's fine, I will be happy to have him and be a step-mom." But she came to realize his son already had a mom. So she brought the issue up again and he agreed this time. Tests showed they couldn't have children. They tried in vitro fertilization, but it didn't work. "We decided this is where we draw the line. It wasn't meant to be. We moved on."

So once again, Barbara went through a grieving process, this time giving up the idea of motherhood. She decided to take a sabbatical to think her life through. During her sabbatical, she began thinking she might not want to go back to full-time teaching. This was a new season in her life. When she was teaching, it was hard to keep up her Bible study. It became more and more important to her not only to learn about her faith, but to have a group that was like a second family. She could bounce ideas off of them.

Besides, being home on sabbatical gave her more time with John. And they both liked that. He told her he liked having her at home. Before, they had divided the duties at home. In 1995, he decided the family business—making adhesive labels—needed outside investors to grow. Then they were faced with a positive problem: what to do with the money they made from stock sales?

"There was no question it was going into a foundation," she said. "The company was grown with gifts God gave to John and because of God's grace. This was a way to give back to Him. Every single share went back into the foundation," she says. That meant they poured several million dollars into a foundation called Vines and Branches, which gives grants to inner-city projects. One involved converting a duplex into an elderly care facility. Another resulted in after-school study halls for low-income children.

They also began an operating foundation to run a pastor's retreat at a lake. They were drawn to that idea after a real estate friend came to them and offered a lake property. It had six bedrooms and six baths. Cedars of Nemahbin was the name. It needed a lot of work, but Barbara loved it. It seemed perfect for a retreat site. She remembered a Harville Hendriks motivational tape in which he said, "If I were a man of means, I would run a pastor's retreat house." The opportunity to buy the lake house came before they had decided to sell their company, so they weren't quite prepared financially. They told themselves, "If the offer closes, God will show us how to pay for it." A year later they started remodeling. When it opened in May 1997, it was quickly booked up by ministers who needed a quiet place to "refill their well." They stocked the house with audiotapes, videotapes, and maps for nature walks. During the first three years of operation, some 1,800 pastors and couples would renew their faith at the Findleys' lake house.

Meanwhile, during the transition period when new management was being installed at his company, John read Bob Buford's book, *Halftime*. He felt 90 percent of the message about finding a more meaningful life applied to him. So he left his job with the restructured company and went to work full-time for the foundation. Barbara started working part-time there as well. It is a small, simple organization. There are only three members of the foundation board, with one outside member. Barbara says it is less complicated to move into foundation work than you might think; and a small foundation can be started with as little as $10,000.

These days she divides her time between working for the foundation and as an administrative assistant at her church. She also has been pastor of the women's ministries for eight years. And she later started volunteering for the Rescue Mission in Milwaukee one day a week. She admits with a laugh that now, as a volunteer, she is as busy as she was when she taught. She is, she reveals, the kind of person who has alphabetical spice racks. "I can be compulsive," she said. "I like to get everything tip-top."

But in conversation, she seemed relaxed, soft-spoken, almost shy. With her gold-frame glasses, short brown hair, and simple jewelry, she has an unpretentious manner. She seemed well-grounded; mature. When we first talked, she was forty-five. She said she realizes that there are more seasonal changes ahead of her. "I don't know what those will be," she said. "I'm sure there's something else the Lord wants me to do that I'm not aware of yet. I think I know how to be more open to it now. Ten to twenty years ago, I never would have dreamed I would have the opportunity to give money away. My father was a blue-collar worker. I had to take out a loan to go to college. It shows you God can do anything."

Like many women, Barb Findley learned that faith can

heal. And provide new strength. As she discovered, the answer for her as an individual was to work more closely with her mate. That shared purpose gave her the wholeness she had been seeking for a long time.

D uring times when people make major shifts in their lives, they sometimes leave their spouses in their wake. What is energizing to one partner may seem threatening to the other. Unless you want to grow apart instead of together,

"Let woman then go on—not asking favors, but claiming as a right the removal of all hindrances to her elevation in the scale of being—let her receive encouragement for the proper cultivation of all her powers, so that she may enter profitably into the active business of life. . . . Then in the marriage union, the independence of the husband and wife will be equal, their dependence mutual, and their obligations reciprocal."
—LUCRETIA MOTT (1849),
ABOLITIONIST, FEMINIST

there should be a conscious effort to communicate and brainstorm together. It is amazing how helpful that helpmate can be if you include him in the loop.

Is your relationship good enough to dream together about the next phase of life? If not, are you willing to do what it takes to build the relationship to that level?

Are you aware of what he wants to do in his second half? Does this match with what you want to do (e.g., he wants to retire and fish a lot and you want to start a new business)? If not, how will you combine this for the greater good?

How will you broach the subject of having a relationship where you can talk about such things? What should the guiding principles of this type of communication be?

What resources will you draw on to help both of you grow closer together?

It should be encouraging to know that there are so many

couples who are starting to make "halftime" transitions together that new programs are being developed to coach them. Bob Shank was a successful executive with a large mechanical company in Orange County, California, when he started devoting more time to speaking to businessmen about transforming their lives. The demand from businessmen who wanted direction at midlife proved so great that Bob created a full-time program for men at halftime called "The Masters Program." His wife, Cheri, operates a parallel program for the wives. The idea is to mentor "priority living" so the couples can grow together in the next phase of life rather than apart.

"Our passion is to help couples find how to work together, to find compatible strengths and talents so they can do something significant in the third quarter," Cheri said. She advises the women if they can't see what their gifts are, to ask friends what they think their talents might be. Sometimes friends truly can see us better than we do. They encourage the couples to not be afraid to probe their feelings. And to not be afraid to try anything once. In the process, they put the couples through some tough questions:

Does their second half feel more like survival than success?

Has their marriage aged like fine wine or a used car?

Is Monday morning, when they start their week's work, the best day of the week or the worst?

How would they answer the question, "One of these days, I plan to . . ."?

Those questions might be a good start for your own

> "Life is to be lived. If you have to support yourself, you had bloody well better find some way that is going to be interesting. And you don't do that by sitting around wondering about yourself."
> —KATHARINE HEPBURN, ACTRESS

journey. If the two of you have been thinking about what you might do "someday," what are you waiting for?

Even if your midlife plans as a couple are derailed somehow by divorce or a death, having once made a new start can help you later when you must start again alone. Cass Peterson and her husband, Ward Sinclair, were both reporters at the *Washington Post* when they decided to chuck the city life to cultivate a dream farm in southern Pennsylvania. He was the agriculture correspondent and she was an environmental writer, bright, gutsy, and curious about many subjects.

A colleague who knew them both at the *Post* recalls how Cass was always planting things, like marigolds and strawberries. When she and Ward moved in together, they immediately had most of the yard tilled into a garden. To get more land to grow, they bought the "dream farm" in Pennsylvania, which they called the "Flickerville Mountain Farm and Groundhog Ranch."

They worked out a deal so they could work four-day weeks at the newspaper in Washington, D.C., giving them three days at the farm in Pennsylvania. They tailored their organically grown crops to satisfy customers: striped tomatoes, asparagus, zucchini, petit pois, and radicchio. After commuting for several years they shifted to farming full-time. Their friends in the city asked them constantly, "Don't you miss the city? Don't you feel isolated out here? Don't you miss the *Washington Post*?" They replied, "Well, no."

Her husband loved standing at the end of the day at the top of a hill where he could look at the whole panorama of their farm, just as the slant of the sun was turning everything golden. And he would shout, "I love this farm!" That pretty much captured the fullness of heart they felt, even though it was hard work, even though she had to get up at 4:30 in the morning to squeeze in some freelance work, even though, sometimes, crops failed. It was theirs.

Then in the fall of 1994 Ward started feeling "kind of crummy." The doctor thought it was irritable bowel syndrome. But by February, a CAT scan showed it was pancreatic cancer. He died two weeks later at the age of sixty-one. Cass worked the farm by herself after that, continuing her writing at the same time. She felt she needed to stay at the farm. She felt there was healing in the earth.

After a half dozen years of working the land with a helper, she decided in 2000 to sell the farm and go back to writing full-time. Looking back at their "dream farm," she told me, "I'm glad we did it. I would do it again. People thought it took courage to leave the *Post*. They kept asking, 'What will you do without health insurance?' But if you make a life change one time, it is very easy to do it another time. You know you can do it."

She was turning fifty and facing a new life. But thanks to Ward, she said she knows better now how to turn a dream into a life. And she has a deeper appreciation of time. "When your husband is diagnosed and two weeks later is dead, it really changes your perception of time," she said as she prepared to move to Morris County, New Jersey. "Nothing is anywhere close as valuable as time. And we're all equal in that regard. We all get the same amount of hours in a day. It's just a question of what you learn to do with them."

Chapter Twelve

Have a Series of Careers

"I've always tried to go a step past wherever people expected me to end up."

—BEVERLY SILLS, OPERA STAR

Back in 1850, it was rare for women to live beyond menopause. Today, most women will live at least one-third of their lives *after* menopause. Whereas their mothers probably had only one occupation in their lifetime, today's women can expect to have several careers. This is a truly liberating concept. It means that women can exercise several different facets of their talents and they can have not one, but several careers in sequence. Wife to mother to businesswoman. Corporate fast track to heart-healthy nonprofit track. Or vice versa.

The trick is to recognize that the end of one career does not mean the end of productive living. It just means it's time to try something else, something that may be completely different or something that may be a variation. True, that may seem daunting. But there are now many more role models of women who retired from one role, but were not ready to fade away. One of the most high-profile examples of a woman who changed direction without missing a beat is opera legend Beverly Sills. There are few contemporary figures who truly have "charisma" and Beverly Sills is one of them.

When I walked into her cozily cluttered office in Lincoln Center, I immediately felt the warmth that radiated from the stately lady who rose from her desk to greet me. All you can see for a few minutes is that photogenic smile and a mass of reddish-blond hair. You'd never imagine that she could be seventy-plus years old, because she certainly doesn't look it. Or act it. The woman exudes life.

She was delighted that I had brought along some of her favorite caramel candies from Neiman Marcus, which she promptly opened and offered to share. She was in a good mood. And for good reason. The *New York Times* had trumpeted the news that morning: Beverly Sills had just recruited a whopping $25 million donation to Lincoln Center for the Performing Arts, where she is chairman of the board. It was a record donation. And that evening she was going to the season premiere of the New York Philharmonic, one of Lincoln Center's star tenants. It was a triumphant day for Beverly Sills. But she was enjoying it with the grace of someone who has known heartbreak as well as triumph.

You may know the outlines of the Beverly Sills story, but not the personal struggles that she learned to mask with the foot-light smile. She was born Belle Miriam Silverman in Brooklyn in 1929. The name "Bubbles" was given to her by the doctor who delivered her because she had a bubble of saliva in her mouth. Most people later assumed it was from her outgoing personality, because she quickly proved a talented little charmer. She won the Miss Beautiful Baby contest when she was three and was performing regularly on radio by the time she was six. She had America humming the "Rinso White" commercial's jingle at a time when other girls were skipping rope. Yet her real love was opera and her immigrant parents stretched so she could study with one of New York's premier voice teachers, Estelle Liebling. As a result, "Bubbles" Sills retired the first time at the age of twelve—she left radio to pursue opera more seriously.

However, she was not an overnight star in the opera world. She had to work in clubs to make ends meet. Touring cross-country was rigorous. She had to audition numerous times before finally landing a position with the New York City Opera in 1955. Though she had a number of critically acclaimed performances, most notably as Baby in the New York premiere of *The Ballad of Baby Doe,* she was not established as a superstar diva until her performance as Cleopatra in *Julius Caesar* in 1966. By then, she was thirty-seven. And life had taught her lessons that meant she didn't have to act when she sang about pain.

She had married wealthy Cleveland newspaperman Peter Greenough in the mid-1950s. Her family initially was skeptical about the match—he was twelve years older and not Jewish. But he has remained the leading man of her life. For a time, she commuted back and forth to New York performances while struggling to be accepted as stepmom to his three children in Cleveland. When she moved to Cleveland in the late 1950s, it was a shock learning to manage a twenty-five–room house with three maids and a laundress. During the day the maids wore pink or green uniforms; at night their uniforms were black-and-white. "My most arduous household chore was finding things for them to do," she recalls. Two of the maids were openly rooting for Peter's ex-wife to return, so Beverly showed them the door. She felt isolated and lonely because Cleveland society was not welcoming.

But it was her husband's home, so she stayed and turned her attention to having children. She gave birth to a daughter and then a son, who both had special needs that demanded great attention. Their daughter Meredith ("Muffy") was found to be profoundly deaf and would never hear her mother sing. Their son Peter Jr. ("Bucky") was diagnosed as autistic. She put her career on hold while she devoted all her time to her children. She did not return to the stage until the mid-1960s. With special schooling, Muffy went on to achieve a career as a technical artist in New York. But Bucky's condition ultimately required institutional care and heart-wrenching separation.

Beverly became so depressed at one point that her husband pushed her to go back to work. The performances became therapy for her. As she wrote in her autobiography, "I could escape from whomever Beverly Sills was and become somebody else. I left all my troubles outside. All my worries about the kids, everything, went out. And when I walked out, I was Manon, I was in Paris. No question about it, when it was over, I came down with a thud. No question about that. But four days later, I could go back in there."

Audiences discovered her soul had become as magnificent as her voice. Her voice hadn't changed, but *she* had. She became one of the most important coloratura sopranos in the United States. She was well into her forties when she reached the pinnacle of opera success. But unfortunately, there was more trauma. She had to abruptly cancel a performance in Dallas to have surgery for ovarian cancer. A year later, she made her long-overdue debut at the Metropolitan Opera and was greeted with an eighteen-minute ovation. She was a well-seasoned forty-six, still beautiful and a very convincing actress.

"Nobody escapes this world untouched," she told interviewers. "I've often said that I don't consider myself a happy woman, I consider myself a cheerful woman. There's a difference. A happy woman has no cares at all; a cheerful woman has cares and learns to ignore that. When these blows were dealt me, I made the decision to be happy in life, and then

> "I think it's the end of progress if you stand still and think of what you've done in the past. I keep on."
> —LESLIE CARON, ACTRESS

you don't cry anymore." As she explained, the way she stopped feeling sorry for herself and her children was to "put on a happy face. The public part of me became extra cheery; my innermost feelings were nobody's business but my own."

To her credit, she did not rest on her rave reviews and made many innovative efforts to popularize opera in the United States. She appeared on Johnny Carson's late-night show and even did a duet with Miss Piggy on *The Muppet Show*. Still, time and her voice were running out. She decided to retire from her singing career just as she turned fifty. And immediately began a challenging new career. She became the manager of the company that had been her home base for two decades, the New York City Opera.

To her surprise, she discovered the company was in debt to the tune of $5 million. She got another unexpected blow when the company's costume warehouse burned to the ground with ten thousand costumes. And she discovered there were plenty of critics who didn't think a singer, especially a woman singer, was up to the job of manager. "There was a great deal of skepticism whether somebody who was a Miss America superstar opera singer the night before could step into running a company that was so much in debt. I think they dealt with me in a way they would not deal with a man. Everything they reported about me was exaggerated. I would come to a press conference to announce the season and they would describe my cashmere dress and gold jewelry and fur coat! Well, the press conference was held *inside* a building, so there was no need to even put on a fur coat even if I had done that," she told me.

"And I don't wear jewelry," she added, holding up her hands to demonstrate. "When I go out tonight, yes, I'll put on my jewelry; then I should. But that was the kind of thing they would exaggerate. At the beginning, there I was, going to the office at eight A.M. and not leaving until half past eleven after the performance. And there actually were people who would stop my secretary and say, 'Does she really come into the office every day?' Those are the kinds of questions that *never* would have been asked of a man," she said, her temper rising at the memory.

Undaunted, she plunged on with the moxie of one of her stage heroines. She charmed money from donors to pay debts. She had an ear for new talent. She introduced "supertitles" so audiences could follow the action without a libretto. She cut prices so blue-collar fans could attend more performances. By the time she retired yet again, at the age of sixty, the company had a surplus of $3 million. She had proven that a diva could run the show.

However, that retirement was short-lived as well. Within a few years, she had accepted another tall order: chair of Lincoln Center, presiding over a cultural empire that included not only the Metropolitan Opera, but the Philharmonic, the New York State Theater, the Julliard School, and the American Ballet Theater.

She brought her prodigious fund-raising ability to the cultural center, personally raising as much as $16 million a year. But she also brought her considerable audience instincts and intellect—after all, the lady does have an IQ of 155 and speaks fluent Italian and French. Once again, she pushed to broaden the arts audiences, expanding free public events in the summers where people in sandals and jeans could attend. Somehow she also found the time to serve on the boards of Time-Warner, Macy's, and American Express. And as chairwoman of the March of Dimes, she frequently traveled around the country for speaking engagements, helping raise money to prevent birth defects.

Looking back at her series of careers during our interview, she mused that not long ago she had met at lunch a very famous prima donna who was retired. One of the other guests said, "How are you spending your time?" to the prima donna. Beverly listened in, thinking the former singer would say "I teach" or somesuch. Instead, the prima donna said, "I stay at home all day and listen to my records and I cry." Recalling the moment, Beverly added in a soft voice, "I feel very grateful that I never stayed an ex-anything. I moved on. And I am very happy about that."

She graciously but firmly declined to give any advice for other women who might be struggling with new chapters in their lives. But she did observe that at various times, women all have to define how to balance their marriages, their children, and their personal goals. "There is one word that comes into our vocabulary as women. And you have to define it differently for each one of us. And that word is *all*. How do you have it all? I do some lectures and people always ask, 'How do you have it all?' First, you have to define 'all.' If you finally come to your own definition of what all is, you have to realize that somebody has to pay a price for that all," she said. In her own life, that meant at times stopping her career to tend to her children. At other times, it meant being apart from her children while she performed. Or later, being away from her husband while she worked long hours. There was no perfect, painless answer.

Today, she speaks from the sanguine perspective of one who has outlived or outsucceeded many of her critics. "I feel I've paid my dues," she admitted. "When you reach this stage, you have more self-confidence, you've lived a lot and things fit into perspective more simply. I mean you suddenly realize that you can't let little things bother you or let little people bother you. Because in the grand scheme of things, there are so many important things that need to be fixed or enjoyed or adjusted to, that you can't let others bother you. I don't aggravate myself over small things or small people like I did when I was young. There were people who used to make me very angry—now I feel very sorry for them. It's a genuine change. Having reached seventy, I realize that because of their smallness, those people are missing some of the great wonderful things that life has to offer. It's like Auntie Mame would say, 'Life is a feast and so many sons of bitches are starving to death.' I think a lot of that rubbed off on me. I try to enjoy life."

Her Jewish faith, she conceded, has become more important to her over the years. "I rely on it more," she said. But she explains, "I certainly don't need a temple to worship in. I'm not attracted to ceremonies. I think one practices one's religion by how one behaves toward one's fellow creatures. The rest of it doesn't matter. . . . I believe in God, but I've never been religious in the sense that I think you have to go into a building, whether it's a synagogue, church, mosque, or cathedral, to pray. I don't believe God is interested in real estate."

When her husband, who was eighty-two when we talked, became seriously ill the year before, she said she shook her fist up to heaven and vowed, "I'm not going to give up!" Then she told him, "You may have trouble walking and talking, but this is not going to be a permanent fixture in our lives. I didn't plan on this and I am not going to accept it."

If there is a theme from her life that translates for other women, it is that attitude of "I won't be defeated." One anecdote from her autobiography is a fitting summation. Back when she was struggling to save the City Opera, a friend gave her a plant that she placed on a little wooden stand in her office. Within a week, it died. That bothered her. One of its leaves was still green, so she clipped it off and planted it. "I took very good care of that leaf," she wrote. "I watered it every day, and left it under a lamp at night—I made sure everyone knew that lamp had to stay on at night. I then pasted the headline of a newspaper article about me across the bottom of the pot." The headline read, " 'I won't be defeated'— Beverly Sills's indomitable spirit is infusing new life into the New York City Opera."

Everyone who worked in the dingy basement office thought she had lost her mind over the leaf. But pretty soon they all started coming to water it. She remembered, "I know this will strike you as a little crazy, but everybody really started rooting for that little leaf to live. I don't know how long we kept it up, but one morning, when I walked in, another little shoot had come up through the earth. A couple of days later another one appeared and then another after that. Eventually that leaf became a lovely, healthy plant, that's alive and well in my basement office. You don't have to tell me how dumb it was for a group of intelligent people to identify with a leaf, but we did. That leaf survived. The New York City Opera would survive. It *had* to. I wouldn't *allow* our company to die."

That's the spirit. Not everyone is born with Beverly Sills's

> "I'm not going to limit myself just because people won't accept the fact that I can do something else."
> —DOLLY PARTON, SINGER-SONGWRITER

remarkable talent. But everyone can learn from her feisty example. If you are approaching a new phase in life, you might ask yourself how you can leverage what you've done in the past to make the next career even more meaningful.

Is there a resource person in your field who could offer advice on how to make a wise choice with your next steps?

How will your next career reflect your true passion? List the gifts that you feel you haven't used yet or could use in a different way.

Can you combine both profit and nonprofit community pursuits?

Where can you make the most impact on the lives of others while using your strengths and talents?

If you are holding back on taking action, ask yourself why.

Sooner or later you realize that life really is yours for the taking and those commercials about going for the gusto are right. Nelda Cain certainly did. If her life were a country-western song, it might be, "I'm Gonna Rent Out My House, So I Can Sing Out My Heart." She's living proof that you can change your scenery and your career when you are old enough to be a grandmother.

When Nelda was forty-eight, she was working as a real estate broker and doing counseling at a women's center part-time. Mostly she was marking the time until her son and his wife had a first child, so she could enjoy being a grandmother. But her son, who had only been married a year, told her, "Mother, get a life!" It made her realize that she was just waiting for "the next stage." As she put it, "It dawned on me how ridiculous that was." The irony was that she used to counsel many women who weren't sure what to do at midlife. She mused, "If I were sitting in my office then hearing what I was saying, I would probably say, '*What* has happened to my *imagination?*' "

Not long after the exchange with her son, she was at a dinner party with friends who were talking about what they would do if they could do anything for fun. Nelda confessed that if she could lease her house, she would move to Nashville and "get big hair and a big bust and sing." Everyone laughed. But one of the executives at the table offered to recommend her house to a Swedish couple that was moving to Dallas and looking for a place to live. Nelda didn't think much about it until a real estate broker called and said the couple wanted to look at her house. They loved it. And the next thing Nelda knew, she was moving to Nashville.

She had sung as a young child and she sang as a "warm-up" act for entertainers like Ike and Tina Turner while she was a senior at North Texas University in Denton. But by then, she already had a young son and she decided that going to school, student teaching, mothering, and singing was too much to do at the same time. She graduated from college one night and quit professional singing the next night. After that, she only sang for fun, at friends' weddings or family gatherings.

Until she decided to follow her dream to Nashville. "I moved there not knowing a single person," she recalls with her rippling laugh. "I had never even *been* to Nashville! I thought, 'I must be having a nervous breakdown and nobody will tell me. Why won't my friends intervene here?' " But she went anyway to the mecca of country-western music and rented a one-bedroom apartment across the street from Vanderbilt University. She wanted to record a compact disc, but she didn't know any music producers. Then the phone rang. It was a friend who used to help her with her counseling practice. "What on earth are you doing?" he wanted to know. Once she explained, he offered to contact a priest he knew in Nashville, who in turn knew a record producer who was originally from Texas. The producer's name was J. Gary Smith. Smith agreed to go to lunch with her solely as a courtesy. She was nervous, but they hit it off pretty well. Then he told her, "Nelda, I'm going to be perfectly honest. You are too old for this business. That's all there is to it. They are getting their talent these days out of day care. You're too old."

Her heart sank, but she didn't even have a house to go home to anymore, so she pressed on and asked him to give her a chance. He told her at least six more times during lunch that she was too old. But that only convinced her that he would be a perfect choice to be her producer because he was honest.

She was still trying to persuade him, when a man walked up to their table at the restaurant. To her surprise, he told the record producer, "You're sure in good company" and complimented her on her singing, saying she could "charm a crowd." She recognized the man as a musician who had played drums at a birthday party back in Texas for her brother-in-law, where she had sung. She was taken aback by his interruption, but decided to turn it to her advantage if she could. She told the producer, "Now, Gary, I have just one question for you. I don't know a single person in this city. That guy coming over here and saying that has to be a God deal. Are you going to say 'no' to God?"

He laughed, but said he still thought she was too old to begin a recording career. So she tried again. She figured he was about the same age as she was, so she suggested, "I tell you what. Let's meet on Friday and have lunch again. You go home and ask your wife if *she* thinks I'm too old." Sure enough, he asked his wife, Ginger, that night if she thought Nelda was too middle-aged. No, she told him, "You need to help her." So he relented. When he told another producer that he had taken Nelda on as a client, he confessed, "I don't know what I'm going to do with her, but you just can't say 'no' to Nelda."

For the next year, he worked with her on selecting appropriate songs and musicians. Her voice was best suited to standards such as "It Had to Be You" and "Ain't Misbehavin'." Her voice didn't really have a country-western twang, so they added a steel guitar and a fiddle to make the album sound quasi-country. When they finally got to the recording studio, the band included Reba McIntyre's keyboard player and Garth Brooks's fiddle player. As they started the session, one of the musicians interrupted to chide her through the earphones, "Nelda, honey, try to stay in the beat," as if she were a total novice. She ribbed him back: "What beat?" That broke the ice and the musicians started warming to her moxie. "I think they all loved my courage for just jumping in there and trying it," she recalls. "By the time we finished, we were all having a ball."

She remembers leaving the studio after recording everything multiple times and getting a call from her sister Nancy in Dallas. "How did it go?" her sister asked. Nelda's voice broke as she realized that singing with such talented musicians was what she really had wanted to do all her life. She told her sister, "If I die in my sleep tonight, I wouldn't take anything for this day. It was *that* much fun."

The CD was dubbed *Raising Cain*. In the music video that her friends helped her make, Nelda says, "I think part of the fun was when somebody would say it would be impossible to do, especially the music industry people, who would say, 'This is totally impossible at your age,' then that just inspired me that much more and I became that much more determined. Because I thought, '*Impossible?* This is hardly impossible.' Anything is possible, including a singing grandmother."

The video shows her dolled up in evening clothes as well as down home in jeans and a white blouse. Blond and petite (five feet two inches, counting hair), she is not the traditional image of a grandmother. And yes, she looks as if she is having a ball. She explains, as she is shown on the video kidding around with the studio musicians, "Laughing is part of my deal. If you can't have fun, then what is this life about?"

When her album was released in 1999, she was featured as "Artist of the Week" on Broadcast.com and *Nashville Lifestyle* magazine did a profile story on her. The fact that she had the gumption to make her dream come true has had a ripple effect. Emboldened by her example, several of her closest friends decided to follow through on their wishful thinking. One would-be writer started writing articles for a community newspaper. Another friend, who is a college professor, made the music video for her.

"It was a huge event in all our lives," says Judy Kelley, who teaches at the University of Dallas. "We all felt a real sense of victory because she didn't just *talk* about it, she did it."

Nelda was further emboldened to buy a house in Colorado. "I had to go to Nashville to figure out I could leave Dallas after living there most of my life," she said. Now she lives near Aspen, next door to the former keyboard player from Three Dog Night. Offers to sing were pouring in before she had time to unpack her moving boxes.

But true to her commitment to continue helping other women, she is dedicating a portion of the proceeds from her CD to the Susan G. Komen Foundation to

"The beginning is always today."
—MARY WOLLSTONECRAFT SHELLEY, AUTHOR

prevent breast cancer. And she is using her "singing grand-mother" story for motivational speeches to inspire other women. Twice-divorced, she is empathetic with women who have seen disappointment in life.

She has learned from her own ups and downs that "we learn a lot more from our failures than from our successes." And she learned from the women she counseled that the ones who were able to heal hurts and make real change in their lives were those "who had the ability ultimately to let go of injuries, injustices, self-destructive relationships, and simply to imagine in full color, a better way."

He advice to other women is to "be one with God and ask that you will be given courage and direction. Be realistic—I had no illusion of hitting the top of the charts—but do it. Do it for your heart and because it's fun and it *will* be rewarding. It's important to get in touch with that inner voice and do something here that is really your life's work. Maybe it's the second half of your life's work, but still it's as powerful as the first time. It's just with a little more perspective, a little more maturity, and, at least what I've found, a lot richer."

Then with typical irreverence, she added a closing thought: "I didn't want the most boring stories in the rest home."

Chapter Thirteen

Don't Be Afraid of Failure

"When we can begin to take our failures nonseriously, it means we are ceasing to be afraid of them. It is of immense importance to learn to laugh at ourselves."

—KATHERINE MANSFIELD, WRITER

One of the advantages of middle age is that you can look back and see your mistakes as part of a process. You learn to recognize them as course corrections. You learn to laugh at yourself. It helps if you can say, "Wow, that mistake was a *beaut!*" just like you can sail through a bad weather day by saying, "Isn't this a *wonderfully grim* day?" instead of grumping and grousing. It's better to make some healthy mistakes rather than living in continual fear of making a mistake or continual regret of having made one. Who among us has not failed at tasks, at relationships? Admit it, then absorb it or file it. Keep on.

What is your definition of failure? If it means the end of the world, does that definition work for you and is it really the end?

Is your problem that you can't get over something, or is your problem that you won't? Can you make peace with your past? Are you replaying a tape that makes you feel miserable all over again? Can you forgive, if not forget?

Are you still seeking perfection, or are you able to see perfection in every day?

It would be helpful to write down all your failures as well as the good that may have come out of them. Seeing how things turned out even though you expected the worst may provide a different perspective.

Linda Ellerbee is living proof that you can outlive your mistakes and dare to try something new. When we first met, it was 1972 and we both worked for the Associated Press in Dallas. She had just been hired to write the overnight radio news and I was supposed to train her. We were both in our twenties and were the only women in the bureau, so it was natural for us to become buddies. We both had grown up in the complacent fifties in Texas, and went off to college in the early sixties just before the "Me Generation" rebelled. We had been brought up in a culture that seems quaintly tame by today's standards: The big movies included *Gigi* and *The Sound of Music*. Folk singing groups like The New Christy Minstrel were in. Girls wore madras wraparound skirts, Bass Weejun loafers, white blouses with Peter Pan collars and a circle pin, known by the euphemism of the "virginity pin." If you pinned it on the "wrong" side of your blouse, it meant you had "put out." That was something nice girls didn't do.

It's instructive to look at how much things have changed since then because that was the culture that the huge block of women who are now in their fifties grew up in. It was a time when coeds were expected to follow the rules, which included not wearing slacks or shorts to class. On many campuses, girls had to wear a raincoat to cover up their legs on their way to gym class. Sororities taught young pledges that it was unladylike to snub out your cigarette yourself, so you were supposed to hand it to your date to extinguish. And if you got caught kissing with too much enthusiasm on the dorm steps after a date, you might be cited by the dorm mother for O.D.A.—Obvious Display of Affection. It was commonly joked that the reason most women were on campus was to get their Mrs. Degree.

Linda Jane Smith's irreverent spirit began to break through at Vanderbilt University, as seen in some of the cartoons she drew for the student magazine. One showed an ugly woman standing in front of one of those machines that gives out quarters in exchange for dollar bills with a sign on it: "CHANGE— ONE DOLLAR." The quote balloon coming out of the woman's mouth says, "I've spent $18 and I haven't changed a bit!"

Linda quit college after two years, inspired by the "Make Love Not War" spirit of the "Age of Aquarius" times. The music had changed to Rolling Stones and Jefferson Airplane. She let her hair grow. She put on an old army jacket and marched in peace protests. Sang at love-ins. Lived in a commune. Talked about revolution. Wore tie-dyed fashions. Ate organic brown rice. Acquired a husband named Veselka and a young daughter named Vanessa and a young son named Joshua.

She became a writer when they were living in Alaska because she needed money to support her children. She was fired from her job at a radio station in Juneau over what she described as a "personality conflict" with the manager. Translation: She had a tendency to say what she really thought, which in later years would turn out to be an asset. She got work telling someone else what to say, writing speeches for the majority leader of the Senate.

When her marriage fell apart, she needed to start over. She

missed her folks in Texas, so she started searching for jobs in the Southwest. That led her to the AP in Dallas. She was desperate to do well because her kids and her furniture were on their way in a few weeks.

I was struck by her warmth, talent, and sense of humor. During one of our dinner breaks, we discovered we had a friend in common, a newspaper reporter named Allan Frank, who had become a buddy of Linda's in Alaska. Later that night she got bored on the overnight shift and decided to write him a letter saying we had met. She used one of the AP's new word processors to write him a note. It was teasing, intimate, and *very* irreverent about the AP management. What she didn't know was that when she printed out the letter, a copy was still in the computer's memory. So the letter went out with the Associated Press news of the day the next morning to news organizations all over the Southwest. In fact, it was at the very top of the news report because it did not have a file number. As fate would have it, the chief of the AP southwestern bureau was at the NASA press center in Houston that day, showing off the new computer system to a group of editors. Imagine his surprise as he read Linda's chatty, salty note. He immediately called her at home where she was asleep, having worked all night, and informed her she was fired. He told her not to bother picking up her belongings, they would be shipped to her.

She cried for days and went to her mother's home in Houston, mortified with embarrassment. She felt like a total failure. But by then, calls were starting to come in to the AP bureau from editors who had seen the letter. They recognized how terrifically talented the mischievous writer was. Even rival UPI called with a job offer. But the call that clicked with Linda was from KHOU-TV, the CBS affiliate in Houston. The news director talked her into trying TV news. She didn't even own a TV. But the pay was twice what AP paid.

With her typical resilience, Linda threw herself into the new assignment. She proved a natural at TV writing, so of course she was made an anchor (where she read other people's writing). She was a natural at that, too. And she married a fellow TV journalist with a name that she then made famous—Ellerbee. She moved rapidly up the network ladder as a political reporter, then coanchored and cowrote three news shows, including *NBC News Overnight* with Lloyd Dobbins. It became a late-night cult classic of tongue-in-cheek truth telling.

Along the way, there were other marriages that didn't work out, constant battles with the network bureaucracy, and some mistakes that almost eclipsed the legendary AP letter. Like the time she wrote a news brief about a tragic airline collision on the runway in Tenerife. She ended her report with what she thought was a poignant line about 576 people whose vacations had ended in death. What she didn't know was that the news brief interrupted a made-for-TV movie called *Flight to the Holocaust,* a saga about a plane crash. And adding insult to injury, the commercial that followed her news brief featured actor Karl Malden telling viewers that the worst thing that could happen to them on their vacation was to lose their traveler's checks. The next day, a newspaper columnist suggested she consider another line of work.

She was understandably nervous when she later was assigned to coanchor a segment with legendary journalist David Brinkley. But he advised her not to worry, all they could do was fire her. And of course, having been fired from Alaska to Texas by then, she had learned that sometimes a pink slip just means another interesting beginning.

She had a knack for getting into trouble but she also had an indomitable spirit, what used to be called spunk. No wonder they later modeled the quick-witted TV character Murphy Brown after her. She was good at making sport of her own foibles and survived the network high-wire act until she was forty-two. That was ancient by network standards of the time. (In her book *And So It Goes,* she points out that when Barbara Walters was fifty, she was considered the grand old dame of TV. In contrast, when Dan Rather was fifty, he was considered the young man who replaced Walter Cronkite.)

Though she was the picture of unblinking composure on the air, her life off the air was frequently interrupted by storms. Between the ages of twenty and forty, Ellerbee married and divorced four times. Between the ages of forty and fifty, she checked into the Betty Ford clinic to get help with a drinking problem. It was a soul-searching process. She learned to understand herself, forgive herself, accept herself mistakes and all. She learned to be sincere with others, not just clever. She now understood that her wit had been a lifelong defense mechanism to mask her shyness. Despite her surface bravado, she says it took until midlife for her to be able to say both out loud and to herself, "You are good at what you do."

Then, just as she was getting back on her feet, she discovered she had breast cancer. Now she had to deal with her own mortality. She had to marshall all her strength and faith and gutsy humor. She later joked that when her daughter, Vanessa, first saw her naked after her double mastectomy, she said, "Oh, Mama, you look just like Buddha, but without the wisdom." Her motto became, "When the going gets tough, the tough lighten up."

Today Linda Ellerbee has found professional maturity at

midlife—she now produces quality shows for television with her company, Lucky Duck Productions. She's made thoughtful documentaries on women in Congress, breast cancer, and teenaged sex. And she has found personal stability—her business partner is Rolfe Tessem, who has also been her partner in life since the mid-1980s. When I called to catch up with her, I noticed the throaty laugh was still there, but hers is now the seasoned voice of experience, a worldly mixture of Simone Signoret and Ann Richards. She explained that for many years, she had thought it would be wonderful to start her own production company and only do projects she loved. She wanted to sell programs to the networks instead of being their salaried employee. It is instructive that what finally propelled her out of her network job was not one of the big mistakes she always thought would mean her exit, but a small matter. Frustrated by the meddling of an annoying producer, she thought, "I'm outa here." Like the experience of many other women, it was a tipping point, an "Ah ha!" moment when she realized it was time to do what she *really* wanted to do.

Comfortably into her fifties, she added a new chapter to her story: children's book author. Her series of *Get Real: Girl Reporter* books follows the exploits of two sixth-graders who are coeditors of the school paper. One is perky and wants to cover school dances. The other one has a mouth that always gets her in trouble and wants to cover city council. You can guess which one is autobiographical. Linda says her goal is to provide "daring" role models for today's young girls, noting that when she was growing up she was inspired by Jo March in Louisa May Alcott's novel *Little Women* and the Nancy Drew detective novels. So in a way, she is passing her moxie down to another generation of young girls—who are sure to need it someday.

She says that looking back has shown her that "sometimes things really do get better. The last half of my life is the most wonderful. I found the man of my dreams in my forties. And I didn't even know it. He was simply an old friend. Now I have work I love. I am blessed to see the world through new eyes. And I don't have to follow strangers down the hall with a microphone!"

She counts the years since her mastectomy and says, "I am grateful for every day. I know it sounds corny, but I still do a lot of work in this area and a lot of women call me who have just been diagnosed with cancer. I'm very grateful because every year I'm alive is a year I get."

She has changed her life so she has more time for her family—she takes off early on Fridays to go to their home in upstate New York, and comes in late on Mondays. She also makes more time for beauty in her life. If she goes to Austin for a shoot, she schedules an extra day to go hiking. "I often go to the woods," she said. "It's a huge change in midlife. Growing up in Houston, my family didn't hike and didn't camp. The climate didn't encourage it. After I got breast cancer, I decided to take good care of my body and started walking in the Catskills. When I was twenty minutes out in the woods, then I knew as clear as anything that I was meant to be there and it was waiting for me. One of the biggest gifts of my midlife change was discovering the huge enjoyment of backpacking and paddling. It settles my soul. It keeps me in touch with God and nature and reminds me in a very big way of a sense of proportion. It's hard to hang on to your anxieties when you are standing in the middle of the woods."

So the lady who once roller-skated through NBC headquarters in Rockefeller Center has learned to hike through her prob-

> "Success and failure are both greatly overrated. But failure gives you a whole lot more to talk about."
> —HILDEGARD KNEF, ACTRESS

lems. And travels all over the country giving speeches to encourage other women. What advice does she give to a friend struggling to change? "I listen to them. Smile at them. Give them the Nike slogan: Just do it. You've got to be passionate. It's more important in midlife than before. To get it later in life, you have to seek it and inject it. You can't expect a passion for living to just come like when you're eighteen, but it is there for the having. Really it is."

Linda learned that as you get older, you must consciously choose change from time to time rather than simply letting it happen to you. She learned that change is a form of hope, because to risk change, you must believe in tomorrow. Particularly after a setback, you need to believe that tomorrow might be better. Don't worry if you don't have all the answers today. Just bluff and move forward. Most of the other people are making it up as they go along, too.

Keep in mind that only 10 percent of life is what happens to you; 90 percent is what you do with it. That means making the best of your goofs as well as your successes. Just ask Verla Gillmor. She made one of the biggest career mistakes of her life by drinking a Coca-Cola.

She was riding high as a public relations executive with Hill and Knowlton, the biggest PR company in the world, whose clients included Pepsi. She had just helped launch a major outreach effort—the Pepsi School Challenge. Pepsi was offering $2,000 college scholarships to students in inner city schools if they would maintain a C average and not drop out. Verla had to stay up all night to get the last-minute changes to the press kits completed, but the launch at a Detroit high school went well, balloon drop and all. The *Wall Street Journal* covered the announcement and an appearance was scored on *Good Morning America*. The company was pleased and the head of the firm sent her a huge flower arrangement. "This is going to secure my future," she thought to herself. "I did good."

The next day she was told to accompany the president of Pepsi Central to a TV interview. She was bone tired and feeling ill and she asked if they could find someone else. But she was told she had to go. It was very important. So there she was in the "green room," waiting with the regional president and feeling as if she were going to throw up. There was no ladies' room on that floor. No water fountain nearby. But there was a Coke machine in the green room, full of Coca-Colas, which Pepsi employees are not supposed to drink. She cajoled the executive to please grant her an exception. She would just have a sip and take a couple of pills and destroy the evidence. But just as she got her hands around the verboten beverage, the host of the TV show walked in. The first words out of his mouth were, "Hey, that's rich! How often do you get to see a Pepsi spokesperson holding a Coke can?"

The ride home in the limousine was icy. The next day, Verla got a call from the chief of the Pepsi account in New York. "What did you do? How could you be so stupid?" She had been taken off the account. Twenty-four hours before, she had been a rising star. Now she was a pariah.

She felt as if God were trying to send her a message, but she wasn't quite sure *what*. After all, she had seen job changes before in the brutal world of radio and television, but they usually had been to her advantage. She had worked for several networks as a radio news anchor and reporter in Chicago. She had found success in public relations, working with Fortune 500 companies and celebrities. She couldn't let the Coke incident derail her forward progress. And she didn't want to look like a failure.

So she blocked out the Coke debacle and steamed on. But increasingly, she had the nagging feeling that she was not in control of her life. At one point, for example, she was hit by a drunk on the freeway. Her car was totaled and she was taken to the hospital in an ambulance. No bones were broken, but she was sent home to rest for at least a week. One arm was in a sling and she had to use a cane.

Nonetheless, she received a call saying that she was needed back at work immediately. The *Chicago Tribune* was planning a page one story in the business section. Because, at the time, she was trying to get some publicity for a Midwest health care company, she was asked to help the newspaper's medical editor with the story. They stroked her ego. It was her baby. It needed her special touch. "Well, if I must, I must," she thought. She was covered with bandages, so she looked like a patient herself as she walked the *Tribune* medical editor through a hospital. Again, she got the feeling that something was wrong with the picture, but wasn't sure what the message was. She was afraid to insist on boundaries on her time because she didn't want to risk her advancement.

Then there was the time the head of her department resigned and took several key people with him. They asked her to take the job and she declined. It wasn't a post that played to any of her strengths and it would strain all of her weaknesses. She was told she had to take the position, at least on an acting basis, or it would count against her when the time for promotions came. So, once again, she was compliant and swallowed her reservations. But after ninety days, no effort had been made to fill the positions. She and her coworkers, who were working twelve-hour days to compensate for the vacancies, were doing such a good job, the managers decided to delay filling the positions to save money. Improving the bottom line would look good for a merger.

"I felt defeated. I felt trapped," she recalls in speeches today. "I felt like I was being pushed on by the need to look like I had it all together. I had to have it all together. I had to be in control. What's the old line—never let them see you sweat? What would it look like if I couldn't manage this crisis? I am a crisis consultant. What would it look like if Verla the overachieving, hard-charging person somehow didn't make it work once? One of the reasons I had never let something fall apart was not that I was so smart, but just because I couldn't stand the humiliation of failing and so I pushed myself to unreasonable extremes." But she realized she wasn't living her life anymore. "My boss was living my life, my family, my friends, my circumstances, needing approval, not acknowledging my limitations, being afraid of failure."

She said she knows from her mentoring work with other women that they have stifled some of the same concerns about failing: "Maybe it's a lifestyle that dictates that you keep the job you are in because you would have to move to a different neighborhood, a less fancy house. Or not drive a late-model car. Maybe people that are your colleagues might think you're not as smart as you were, because gosh, you're not living up to your potential. They might say, 'She's decided to cut back, she's given up!' "

She began to realize that the trouble with the popular concept of the American Dream, which now requires a two-paycheck family, is that people think the trappings of success will give their life significance. Or at least some security or control. It dawned on her that a backlash was developing and she was part of it. "There is an epidemic of discontent from people who have sacrificed whole careers and they're awakened to the fact, 'Is this what I get for sacrificing my family, my health, my friends?'"

She kept on with her marathon lists of things to do, working on the premise that being busy was next best to happy "because at least you're productive." But she still felt unsettled about the dehumanizing aspects of her work. She felt she was losing her way, if not her soul. So, at her husband's urging, she took a six-month sabbatical, to get her bearings and get rested. She went on a forty-day cross-country trip, traveling six thousand miles through fourteen states, keeping a journal about the people she met. She came back enthused with the idea of turning their stories into a book. But midway through that process, her husband left.

She was devastated. Her marriage had failed. She went on working, now a single mom, still struggling with the feeling that she couldn't make her life behave. She had to deal with a series of medical problems—skin cancer, shingles, and shoulder surgery—but survived. Then, at fifty-four, she finally got the message. If she couldn't control her life, she could control herself. She would turn her setbacks into something positive. She would limit her work as a public relations consultant so she could spend more time doing what she loved most: writing and motivating others to deepen their faith. She would take what she learned from her "wilderness period" and write a book. She would take what she learned from her searching and counsel others.

Today she is a popular motivational speaker and is a contributing editor for a magazine called *Today's Christian Woman*. She also freelances for publications like the *Chicago Tribune* and works as a part-time radio anchor. She is a small group leader in the Executive Women's Ministry of Willow Creek Church, one of the fastest-growing churches in the country. Her new book, *Reality Check*, will be published in 2001.

When we talked, she sounded happy. She has an engaging sense of humor and a quick way with words, with a polish gained from years of radio work. "I realize now I had lost all sense of who I was under all the layers of 'shoulds' and 'oughts.' I was Our Lady of Perpetual Responsibility, doing what everybody expected of me. I'll never forget one Thanksgiving when I got a call and had to leave dinner because a client, *Kraft*, needed something. I'll never forget the look on my daughter Lisa's face. I don't ever want to be like that again."

She realized she had pressed herself forward out of fear of failure, fear of being criticized, not meeting expectations, not being a success. She was afraid to say "no." Then she realized what she really needed was to say "yes" to herself. "My life is totally changed," she says. "Do all my friends understand that? No. Do I feel comfortable all the time? No. Do I feel more at peace and exactly where I am supposed to be? Yes, yes, yes."

Changing your life to something that gives you a better sense of purpose is not easy, she warned. "It's not like you go singing on down the yellow brick road. Change will cost you something. But it costs you something to do what you're doing now. It cost me something to get out of bed and go to that hospital for an interview."

She compares the churning of her life to the use of a farm implement called the deep ripper: "It looks like a medieval torture device. It has three-foot-long spikes on it on a big cylinder. If a field is barren and no longer producing like it is supposed to, sometimes that's because a hardpan has developed below the surface. That can be about two feet down below the ground. It is a layer of dirt, but it is like rock, because over the years, it has hardened. The churning of the harvesting doesn't go down deep enough to break up the deeper ground, so nutrients and water can't go in either direction. So the field becomes barren. The only way to resurrect it, to bring it back to life, is to use the device called a deep ripper to go three feet down, destroy the hardpan, so the roots can grow, rejuvenating the field. Farmers say you can't tell from the surface that the hardening is there or that anything is wrong. But there have been times my heart has gotten dry and hard and got the deep gripper. I didn't particularly care for it, but it was the only way to break through the hardness of my life."

That's a vivid image, but it brings home the point. You know you have the right attitude when you treat mistakes as something to learn from, a teaching moment, not a life sentence as a loser. Today a failure is not a Scarlet Letter—Dick Morris lost his job as a political consultant for President Clinton, but became a TV news commentator. Chuck Colson and Jeb Magruder served prison sentences as a result of the Watergate scandal, but found new meaning with personal ministries. Donna Rice went from a tabloid exposé of her fling with Sen. Gary Hart to a new career campaigning against child pornography on the Internet. You can lose a job or a spouse or even a reputation and start over.

What can you find in Linda's or Verla's stories that might apply to your life?

How could you change how you view your failures and mistakes in the future? Do you see them as shameful setbacks or learning opportunities? Would you say that you are able to "roll with the punches?" Can you laugh at your problems?

Practice breathing out all the hurt you may feel from a disappointment; breathe in the fresh air you will need to start clean. Before you go to sleep make a list of constructive things you will do to make a fresh start. Include some way to be outside where you can feel close to nature.

Be positive. Tell yourself that you are made out of rubber and that you will bounce back after disappointment, not break. You may not get what you expected, but you are more likely to get something better if you get back in the game.

Keep in mind that the teenaged Ella Fitzgerald wanted to be a doctor until one fateful night in 1934 at the Opera House in Harlem. It was "Amateur Night," when members of the audience could go onstage to perform. If they won enough applause, they might be invited back to perform another night for pay. Miss Fitzgerald went on stage intending to dance, but her legs wouldn't move. She was paralyzed with stage fright. As the audience started to laugh at her, she knew she had to do something. The presenter is supposed to have said, "Okay, correction, folks. Miss Fitzgerald has changed her mind. She's not gonna dance, she's gonna sing." So she started singing songs she had memorized from her mother's records. She won the $25 first prize. And a singing legend was launched. Later composers such as Ira Gershwin would say they never realized how good their songs really were until they heard them sung by the incomparable Ella.

So what sometimes looks like a mistake may merely be a message that you should be doing something else with your life. Often people look to the synchronicity of events in their life—

"The only people who never fail are those who never try."
—ILKA CHASE, ACTRESS AND WRITER

an old friend calls with a better job offer just when you need more money—as an omen that they are on the right track. But when events seem to conspire against us, emotional responses often keep us from recognizing that it may be a message to try Plan B. If you don't make the best choice today, it's okay. Tomorrow you can make another choice. Keep in mind that there is a difference between having a plan and having a purpose in life. It is up to us to find our purpose. That might take several plans.

Chapter Fourteen

Strengthen Your Spiritual Foundation

"A woman can do anything. She can be traditionally feminine and that's all right; she can work, she can stay at home; she can be aggressive, she can be passive, she can be any way she wants with a man. But whenever there are the kinds of choices there are today, unless you have some solid base, life can be frightening."

—BARBARA WALTERS, TV JOURNALIST

The word *spirituality* often is misconstrued as an other-worldly matter, with mystic images of sitar music and incense, or heavenly clouds and chubby angels. In truth, spirituality is about how to live in *this* world. It's interesting to note that the search for God by both conventional and unconventional means has increased dramatically in the last ten years. Just walk into any bookstore and look in the "Religion/ Spirituality" section. What used to be sparse is now filled with books on all sorts of spiritual matters. Our culture is undergoing a spiritual quest. In the prime of their lives, many women discover that having a spiritual foundation gives them the fortitude to deal with life. They realize that time is growing dear and they need to spend their time on things that are of real value. If the mundane world is about me-me-me, strive-strive-strive, buy-

buy-buy, then the spiritual world is about internal wealth. A spiritual foundation helps you live well with those around you. It teaches you how to live a life of integrity and purpose. It teaches you how to find serenity, and even joy, in the chaos of living. It can be buoyant stuff. It can make midlife the prime of life.

Like many women searching for a new mission, Alma Powell discovered that faith can bring you out of yourself and into a better relationship with the world. When I flew to Washington, D.C., in 1997 to interview her, I thought I would discover why she didn't want her husband, Gen. Colin Powell, to run for president of the United States. And I did. But to my surprise, I also got a lesson on how to pray from her and an example of quiet faith in action.

We met at the America's Promise office in Alexandria, Virginia, where her husband was directing a nationwide effort to help young people at risk. The general's wife walked in right on time, dressed in a taupe pants suit that made her look casual and classy at the same time. She has a lovely, but wary, smile. One of the first things you notice are her gray-green eyes. She locks her gaze straight into yours, as if to read your trustworthiness.

To understand her compelling mixture of fragility and quiet character, you have to look back to where Alma Johnson Powell came from. Now past sixty, her story begins in the Deep South. Her father was principal of a black high school in Birmingham, Alabama, and her mother taught primary school. Her effort to make a way for herself could not have been easy. For a young woman of color, there were painful realities in the 1940s and 1950s. She attended the same Baptist church where four girls were later killed in an infamous racist bombing. Years later, her voice would crack in interviews as she remembered those days, saying, "We must remember where we have been." Not surprisingly, Alma was a good student and dreamed of attending the University of Alabama, but she ended up attending Fisk University, where black students were welcome. She graduated at nineteen and left the South for Boston, where she administered hearing tests.

Her departure from the South proved provident. While she was working in Boston, she met Colin Powell on a blind date. They quickly got married before he shipped out to Vietnam. While he was away, Alma moved back in with her parents in Birmingham. She wrote him letters of love and comfort, never mentioning the civil rights struggles at home that forced her father to sit up nights with a shotgun on his lap. Her father guarded the family while her husband guarded the country.

Even as her husband advanced in the military, there was no escape from the race issue. As newlyweds in the 1960s, the Powells discovered that the only adequate housing for married officers at Fort Bragg, North Carolina, was for whites only. They had to move in with white friends and sleep in their sons' bunk beds. When their white friends went to play miniature golf or to get a Coke, the Powells had to stay behind.

All those slights over the years left scars, and even today, Alma Powell seems to visibly shrink when the subject of racism comes up. She prefers not to dwell on the past and revealed that when her husband was Chairman of the Joint Chiefs of Staff, she quit giving interviews altogether, because the questions about race would leave her emotionally spent. Knowing that background, it's understandable how Alma Powell would not welcome the loss of privacy that would come with a White House tour of duty; how she might worry about mean-spirited racial threats to her husband and family.

When asked if she regrets that many people blame her for

her husband's decision not to run for president in 1996, she smiled a mischievous smile. "No, I'm perfectly willing to take the blame," she said unflinchingly. "I don't feel guilty about that at all. Not at all." She added, "In a way, it made me the envy of many women. They said, 'At least your husband listens to you.' But I didn't make him say no, because I didn't have to. He is not a politician. He says as much. You have to have a passion to run. We had the advantage of seeing the presidency up close. We lived closely to two presidents. We served with five presidents. So we've seen up close what the life is. It is *not* glamorous. You are responsible for the world. You are responsible for the health of the country. It is a tremendous burden. The family has to take a backseat. And it's hard on them. The public scrutiny of a public figure is so intrusive."

Even though General Powell kept saying, no, no, no to a presidential bid, he remained one of the top prospects in the polls well into 1999. Which meant the Powells could not comfortably do things in public, like go to restaurants and movies. "You'd be amazed how intrusive people can be," she said. "It's no fun when you go with him. You have to hold yourself in tight because people are looking at you. They don't recognize me so much, but they do him." She described herself as a "reserved" person, but explained that it is not out of coldness, but insecurity. "It reflects a lack of confidence," she admitted, "So you hold back a little."

She had always been more comfortable operating behind the scenes. For more than thirty years, her primary role was as a dutiful military wife. She made a conscious decision not to work outside the home after she married, explaining, "When Colin came along and when children came along, that was my job. For the rest of my life, my life was determined by my husband's job.

That was true in every marriage at that time, but it was especially true in the military. You have responsibilities that go along with his."

She raised their three children while he was posted overseas, twice to Vietnam and once to Korea. She provided a safe harbor for him to come home to. And in his absence, she taught their son how to throw a baseball. "The worst thing was putting together the Christmas toys," she remembered. "After you take them to church, after midnight services, and put them to bed and tuck them in, you have to go back downstairs and put together their toys all night. I remember the hardest one was a bowling alley."

Anticipating that her husband probably would not be at hand, she volunteered at the base hospital so she would have a good relationship with the doctors who would deliver her children. And later she helped in the base library as a way of coping with depression. Then, when his military career was over, she said, "in a way, mine was, too." He had to decide what he would do next and so did she. "At different times in our lives, you have to reinvent yourself. You have to ask yourself, Who am I now?" she said.

Her first thought, after having moved twenty-two times in the military, was simply to stay at home and have a house that belonged to her for the first time. So, she says, "I got fat and decided I didn't want to do anything. I thought, I like doing housework, so I'll just stick close to home. It didn't take long before I decided I really didn't like that. It's OK, in small doses. So I tried charity work. It didn't fit. It needs to be done, but I hate balls. I made a decision not to go to balls again. And I am not a lady who lunches. So once again, I had to ask myself, What is it you want to do?

"A lot of people asked me to help with their volunteer projects. It was overwhelming at first. They were all good causes," she recalled. Since it had been revealed in *Newsweek* that she had taken medication for depression, she said she received many requests to become a national spokesperson for depression. However, she explains, "I decided I should not be the poster child for depression. It is a personal thing, very personal. I received lots of letters from people who had been depressed. And I answered every one. I was touched by their sharing. And I shared with them. But I didn't feel it was appropriate for me to try to represent everyone. You have to keep some parts of yourself private."

She turned to prayer to get guidance on what to do with the rest of her life. "The answer came very easily," she said. She should put her shyness aside and volunteer full-time. Her first career had been helping her family. Her second career would be helping others. She asked herself what causes were the most important to her. And the answer was: the Best Friends program to prevent teenage pregnancy and the Kennedy Center for the Performing Arts.

Her distinctive gray-green eyes lit up as she described her volunteer work. She dropped the guarded reserve of the general's wife who must always watch what she says. She explained she wanted to work with the Best Friends mentoring program "because their work is *so* important. We have to stem the tide of teenage pregnancy for the sake of our society. We have to give the tools to cope to these young girls. Americans are so conflicted about sex. In the 1960s we said everybody go out and have a good time. Now we have to deal with it. The next generation, we have to teach responsibility." Her concern was heightened by the fact that one in three births in the country are to unmarried mothers. Those unwed teen mothers are more likely to seek welfare and their children are more likely to be ill, suffer abuse, or become teenage parents themselves.

The hands-on approach she applies to the Best Friends program she also applies to her position on the Kennedy Center board. A theater major, she delights in reading stories to children as part of the center's outreach efforts.

As she grew more confident about her public speaking, she started traveling around the country to raise money for other volunteer programs, like the "I Have a Dream" scholarship program for inner-city students. The woman who was reluctant to leave her house now is often at a podium miles from home. Yet she still keeps much of her volunteer work quiet. When her husband was on the stage in Philadelphia for a national volunteerism summit, Mrs. Powell was working behind the scenes, cleaning up a schoolyard without fanfare. Few people know she invites inner-city students to their home every summer for swim parties. She provides the refreshments while the man who directed Operation Desert Storm teaches youngsters how to swim in their pool.

She is reluctant to play up her efforts, noting that the Bible advises one to do good works quietly, not for recognition. But when she does give speeches to well-heeled audiences, she tells people frankly that those who have so much owe something to those who do not. And she tells them they can't make a difference from a distance. "You have to be right there with the people. Do something for somebody who doesn't look like you, who doesn't talk like you, who doesn't live in the same circles. You'd be surprised. They really are nice people. Like you. You don't have to be afraid to get involved. *Do* it."

She revealed in our conversation that her resolve to reach out has been further strengthened by prayer, which is woven throughout her day. "When I first wake up, I thank God for waking up . . . and before I go to sleep I say thanks for the day we have had." When a friend calls with concerns, she tells them she will pray for them. And "for somebody who is really hurting, I will call Unity. They immediately say, 'I will pray for you right now.'" And often, she said, she relies on a prayer technique, using the fingers, that she learned from a retired minister. Holding up one of her hands, she showed me:

"The first finger, the thumb, is praise for God. So you always begin by acknowledging God's greatness and love.

"The second finger, the index finger, is to give thanks. That's to remind you to give thanks for your blessings.

"The third finger, the tallest finger, is forgiveness, because this is key. That's forgiving others and asking forgiveness for yourself.

"The fourth finger is prayer requests for others.

"And the fifth, the little finger, is asking for things for yourself."

It was a touching moment and spoke worlds about the beliefs that have shaped Alma Powell's priorities in life. It was clear that her faith kept her from becoming bitter about the racial slights she has witnessed; it helped her hold her family together while her husband was overseas, and when she reached a crossroads, it was her faith that guided her to serve others. When her husband was named Secretary of State in January 2001, she was at his side, prepared to do her part.

"We are going home to many who cannot read, so, Lord, make us to be Bibles so that those who cannot read the Book Can read it in us."
—CHINESE WOMAN, AFTER LEARNING TO READ

*   *   *

There are many ways that you can use prayer to help you make transitions. When you are starting over, it helps to pray for those who may have mistreated you in the first half of your life or for those you do not like. Resentment and fear can keep you from focusing on what you need to do. Remember to give thanks for the good elements of your life, because where your thoughts go, your energy follows. That will remind you not to dwell on the negative all the time, even in your prayers. Practice the attitude of putting everything in God's hands, like a child who delivers a hopelessly snarled-up ball of twine to his parent, knowing that, somehow, the snarls will be worked out. Don't worry if you are not eloquent. Sometimes the most effective prayer is: "Help. I don't know what to do." The answer will come. You just never know who God will use to deliver the answer.

Many of the women in this book revealed that they, too, relied on their spiritual beliefs to help them work through their transitions. Their tips included:

- Set aside time to pray regularly. When Karol Emmerich was worrying whether to leave her job as treasurer of Dayton Hudson, she discovered her gardening gave her a quiet time to listen for God. She said, "At one point, I spent two to three hours a day in my garden. It's a way of worship."

- Know some prayers by heart. When the pressure is really on, Linda Ellerbee returns to the Serenity Prayer that is a staple of the substance abuse recovery programs. Originally written by Reinhold Niebuhr, it goes like this: "O God, grant me the serenity to accept the things I cannot change, courage to change the things I can, and wisdom to know the difference." Linda said she says the prayer so often she forgets that doesn't apply to everything. "When I was on the worst rapids on a Colorado raft trip and looked ahead at the bodacious, breaking stuff—twenty-five-foot-drop breaking stuff—my hands were shaking and I thought I'm going to die in this hole! So I started saying the Serenity Prayer over and over. And then it clicked in, 'This has nothing to do with this. You ought to be praying, God, don't let me die.' But it helped anyway. So I decided maybe it was all-purpose after all."

- Keep a prayer journal. Homemaker Cheri Shank needed direction to decide if she should join her husband Bob in a full-time ministry. She found it helpful to keep a special prayer journal. As she explained, "Sometimes you may think that God isn't listening or that your prayers aren't answered. But if you keep a prayer journal, you have to write your prayers out. Then there's a place where you can see the answers to those prayers, where God has met you. You can see his fingerprints in your life."

Each of these women has learned spiritual navigational skills as they changed course. You may have to try a couple of techniques to find what works for you. But the important thing is to open yourself to the possibilities that a deeper spiritual life can bring.

*   *   *

The most startling evidence of the number of women who are seeking deeper spiritual meaning to their lives in midlife is the number of women who have been pouring into American theology schools during the last decade. Women now average more than a third of the divinity students around the country. At many schools, such as Perkins School of Theology at Southern Methodist University, they account for nearly half of the students. At the same time, the age of women entering divinity schools has gone up. The typical age is now forty-two to fifty. That influx no doubt reflects the more open climate for women in organized religion, but it also seems to be an indication of a more widespread search for a spiritual connection.

Art expert Susan Barnes is a telling example. She went from the heady world of international art to a decidedly more humble pursuit: the ministry. Tall, striking, brilliant, Susan Barnes was a natural for the fastest lane in the art cosmos. She was a standout in art history at Rice University and, just after graduating, coordinated a 750-piece "Art Nouveau Belgium/France" show, which required regular commutes to Paris. She was mixing with some of the brightest lights on the world cultural scene and she was barely in her twenties. Soon Susan was working in London, cataloging the works of Rene Magritte, then pursuing graduate studies in Rome and the National Gallery of Art in Washington, D.C. She built a reputation as an expert on painter Anthony Van Dyck and became senior curator at the Dallas Museum of Art when she was barely forty. Vivacious and erudite, she was steadily in demand as a speaker and consultant on international art projects.

Yet she began to have a nagging feeling that she needed to return to church. Which surprised her enormously. She had been active in church as a young girl, but fell away in college, as many people do at that stage of life. Then in the art world, people were more likely to be talking about sculptor Henry Moore than martyr Thomas More. Like many cultural cognoscenti, she thought she was an agnostic or atheist.

But the yearning persisted, so Susan arranged to go to church with a Unitarian friend. She knew the wisecrack that "when the Unitarians pray, they say 'To Whom It May Concern,'" but the church had a certain laid-back chic that made it acceptable in some academic circles. At the last minute, the Unitarian friend canceled. Not wanting to give up on the impulse, Susan called someone she knew was a churchgoer and asked to tag along. Midway through the Episcopalian service, Susan broke down into tears with a sense of deep release. She felt she had come home—and something more. It brought her to her knees.

Only after attending church for the next few weeks was she able to admit to herself what she had *really* felt that Sunday at St. Michael's: that she should enter the ministry. She began a new life of regular churchgoing while she pondered what in the world had happened to her. She came to realize that the last twenty-five years had been like a "great wasteland" of denial. She had taken on the doubts of her learned peers and built a wall of "reason" between herself and God. She assumed God's "invisibility" was proof of his nonexistence. Over the next months she realized, "I had been searching for a long time for meaning. I didn't know I was looking for God."

The spiritual reinforcement came just in time, like the cavalry. She had to shoulder some staggering new responsibilities at the art museum. She was working day and night on a $55 million expansion, when the director resigned and she had to fill in. It was exhilarating, but exhausting. "You grow," she says dryly about those times. She was also struggling with the call to the ministry. She explains, "My ego encouraged me to strike a deal with God, to find a compromise. If I was to do God's work, perhaps I could change fields and become the administrator for another nonprofit, one involved in charity. It is normal, I suspect, to believe you are unworthy of a call to the ministry, or unequal to its demands. And humility is in order. But, like forgiveness, humility does not come naturally. Neither does submission to God's will."

She applied for an Episcopalian seminary slot and waited to see what would happen. She was accepted. We talked several times as she went through study in Austin. When we met for dinner during her first year, she fairly glowed and it wasn't just because the waiters complimented her on her French. She was enthused by her new life. As in her museum days, she looked elegant in a beige sweater and slacks, only now there was a simple silver cross at her neck. And there was that glow.

As she began explaining her decision to seek the ministry, she paused and said with an impish smile, "Just for the record, I was not debauched, I was just off-track. We fill our lives, our heads, with stuff, with noise, with activity. I did something every night at the DMA," she said. "Now I hardly go out at night. It's *marvelous.*" Her new life is filled with classes, lots of prayer time, and some art consulting that she had agreed to do before she entered the seminary. To keep herself on track, she uses centering prayers and keeps multiple journals. "We need to know what we think and we find out when we write," she says.

During study breaks, she went to Nicaragua to assist with hurricane relief and to Los Angeles to work with minority residents. She also worked one summer in the trauma center at Ben Taub Hospital in Austin. She was not sure where her new calling might take her, but she was sure she made the right choice. "This wouldn't have been right for me twenty-five years ago," she said. "But it is now. Everything I learned before was important."

What has surprised her most? That two-thirds of the students in the Austin seminary are women and many have chosen the ministry as a second career. She said, "They've learned the meaninglessness of material goods, of position, of power. The deception of it. They've felt the need to be about the essence of things, the truth." At some point in their lives, she contended, women need to ask, "Whose life is this? Who has written the script of your life? For most of us, the outline came from novels, movies, our parents' expectations. You need to identify the voices you're hearing. You may have to reject other people's intentions for us, usually our mothers. Whenever you hear a negative voice in yourself, about yourself, you need to ask where it is coming from. Recognize it and if it doesn't fit with what is in your heart, banish it."

She had several suggestions for women who might be considering a more meaningful second act:

One: "Find a community of like-minded people. There's a saying, 'Women listen each other into being.' You have to tell your story. Listen to other people's stories. We need to be sure to be mentors to others. There is so much accumulated wisdom among us."

Two: "Listen to all the ways God speaks to you, not just in church, but at all times and all places."

Three: "Trust your gut. And honor it. Don't stay in a situation that doesn't honor you. Or doesn't honor your values and ethics."

Four: "Be bold. Be confident. You can do it."

As for her, she said she now realizes that "God is writing the script. And this time, it's the real one." In her dispatches to friends from seminary, she says that her study has been like an archeological excavation of self-discovery, where she has

"None of us becomes something overnight. The preparations have been in the making for a lifetime."
—GAIL GODWIN, WRITER

had to dig through the layers of her life and confront the old masks, the old attitudes. At the same time, she has had to confront an outside world she didn't know: the poor of Latin America, the minorities of inner cities. She came to realize what a passport something as simple as skin color had been. She was learning what it meant to be powerless. She was grappling with the issue of privilege. And trying to learn what it means to be a servant leader, being a better leader by serving others.

Many others are looking for ways to integrate their spiritual beliefs into more areas of their life. According to recent reports, the merging of spirituality and work has become something of a social phenomenon. The *Harvard Business School Bulletin* devoted an entire issue in 1999 to the spirit-and-work trend. One business professor said that with Americans spending longer hours in the office, the urge to seek ways to make their jobs more meaningful is "exploding." *Business Week* did a cover story in November 1999 on the growing presence of religion in the workplace and pointed out:

- Companies such as Taco Bell, Pizza Hut, and subsidiaries of Wal-Mart stores have hired Army-style chaplains in any religious denomination requested.

- Xerox employees participate in spiritual "vision quests" in the desert to stimulate their creativity.

- The chairman of Aetna International has touted the benefits of meditation to employees.

- Some New York law firms now offer Talmud studies.

- An attorney at a Milwaukee law firm has the Muslim call to prayer programmed into his computer so he can keep the requirement of stopping for prayer five times a day.

- Workplace prayer groups are flourishing, with an estimated ten thousand nationwide.

A recent Gallup Poll found that 80 percent of Americans feel a need for spiritual growth, compared with 40 percent just four years ago. It appears that the New Age movement from the 1960s and 1970s has merged with the simplicity movement of the 1990s, into a new kind of spiritual awakening, with baby boomers leading the way as usual. Workers of all kinds are feeling a disconnect between what they believe and what they do for most of the day. They say they work such long hours that they feel separated from any sense of a larger purpose, from life itself. No wonder there are now some 850 consulting agencies promoting workplace spirituality.

In response to the discontent that is percolating in employee ranks or as an expression of their own spirituality, some executives are giving employees time for volunteer interests. Tom's of Maine, a personal hygiene company, gives workers four paid hours a month for community work. The Timberland Company gives employees forty hours a year to volunteer at a charity.

Likewise, more churches are telling members that God is not just inside the church building, that they need to look outside the walls to the needy in the community. There is a growing recognition in many faith communities that the point is not to go to church dressed well, but to spend time consoling those who are not well. That the end goal is not to read books about religion, but to read to an inner-city child. That it is not enough to pray about the poor, or even to donate clothes and money, but to do something to stop the poverty. That may mean mentoring or helping a parolee start over or providing microloans to low-income women so they can start businesses in their homes.

Liz Ellmann 41, left a high-flying Wall Street job to create a firm called SoulTenders in Seattle. It bridges the gap between the secular and the spiritual in the workplace. She helps business execs realize that everything is spiritual. One of the exercises that she encourages them to try is called the Ignatius Examen, which is named after St. Ignatius, the Catholic patron saint of spiritual exercises. It involves contemplating and answering two basic questions:

- What was your most life-giving experience at work today?

- What was your most life-draining experience at work today?

It helps to ask the questions regularly and keep a journal. Liz advises people who are "stuck" and spiritually seeking direction to try writing early in the morning when they have their cup of coffee. They are encouraged to write about what comes to mind during that early morning sense of expectation rather than merely record what they did the day before. Or, if people feel the most stuck when they are in their office, she urges them to do something radically different—take a walk in the middle of the day, or buy some pastels and start trying to draw the way they feel.

If the answer doesn't come naturally, you may have some

"And now, dear God, what can I do for you?"
—ENGLISH CHILD

journeying to do. But the important thing is that you will have begun. Even the uncertainty, the waiting, can be a constructive part of the process. The questions below may help you discover your faith needs and how to remove the barriers that prevent you from having a substantial foundation.

1. What nourishes your heart and soul?

2. What does spirituality mean to you?

3. How does your faith practice relate to that spirituality?

4. Are you teaching lessons with your life now, or learning them?

5. Do you have a relationship with God that you turn to all the time, or just in times of difficulty?

6. What does it mean to say, "Faith is what we do between experiences with God?"

7. Are you comfortable with prayer? Like Alma Powell, do you practice it every day?

8. If you formed a prayer partnership or prayer group, whom would you invite to participate?

9. What do you need most right now to enter into a life with a deep spiritual foundation?

10. If you made a contract with God, what would you include?

Chapter Fifteen

Start Small

> "Don't wait for your 'ship to come in,' and feel angry and cheated when it doesn't. Get going with something small."
> —IRENE KASSORLA, PSYCHOLOGIST

The truth is the ship doesn't make house calls. Get over it. You can find a sense of purpose without it. And you can start small if you feel more comfortable with that. Just take it a step at a time. Often by changing just a part of your life, you can reinvigorate the whole. Several years ago, I read in the newspaper about a city bus driver in New York who had disappeared. The worst was feared—that his bus had been hijacked and that the driver had been killed. But a few months later, both driver and bus were found in Florida. After driving his route in rush-hour traffic for years, the driver said he "just wanted a change." So instead of heading for the bus barn at the end of the day, he kept driving down the highway.

Of course, you don't have to take such a drastic step to make a fresh start, but there is something that each person can do to feel more alive and to make a positive mark on the time chart. It can be something that makes you feel you've used your gifts, however modest, or something that connects you with other people. Volunteering to help others is an obvious choice.

But it won't be therapeutic if it's out of a sense of *duty*. Simply adding one more obligation to your to-do list won't make you feel more fulfilled. What you should seek is a way to apply your particular life experiences, your talents, your philosophy, to the needs of others. It may sound counterintuitive, but by healthily giving yourself away, you will be replenished. It's the physics of life.

Consider the experience of Joan Kerr. She touches hundreds of lives each year just by giving four hours of her week on Fridays to a breast cancer helpline in Dallas. Those few minutes on the phone often mean the world to new cancer victims who are terrified of dying. It took Joan five decades of living to know what to say to them. Not long after going through a divorce, Joan was diagnosed with cervical cancer and had to have a hysterectomy. Then she was diagnosed with breast cancer and went through a mastectomy and chemotherapy.

And she's faced another hardship: Her daughter Stephanie was catapulted into the news headlines in 1995 when she was seriously disfigured by a hit-and-run motorboat accident on Lake Lewisville. She was sitting in a boat one evening with two friends near a marina when the driver of a high-speed cigarette boat plowed into and over their craft. The propeller sliced through the front of Stephanie's face, cutting through her nose, mouth, and cheek and shattering or knocking out most of her teeth. The culprit, who left the scene despite the cries from the boat, was never apprehended. During the next three years, Stephanie would endure more than twenty operations to restore as much of her face as possible. At one point, she needed thirty pills a day for pain in her face, arms, and back. Doctors used a piece of her skull to build a bridge for her nose and took a piece of her ear for a nose tip. Part of her palate was used to build up her gums for teeth implants. Throughout it all, Stephanie, who was only shown from the back or in shadow in multiple TV news interviews, showed admirable character. Though she admitted to reporters there were days she felt down, she said she was trying to keep a positive attitude, saying "I tell myself I'm going to make it through this." She said her mom had been her inspiration, spending virtually every waking hour with her. "My mother has wings and was sent down by God," she told one interviewer.

And indeed, while her father dealt with the news media, her mother watched over her during operations, eventually dressing her wounds day and night. "I learned to become Nurse Joan," she said. There was a flicker of pain across her face as those memories rushed forward. Then her inner reserves seemed to kick in and she added with a tension-breaking smile that "Nurse Joan" has now become her e-mail address. Asked how she endured the experience, she said her faith helped. "You learn to heal yourself," she said carefully. "You learn to be thankful for scars." Now that the operations have stopped, her daughter is trying to get back to as normal a life as possible. She even made herself visit a lake with friends, although not the one where she was injured. She explained to a reporter that her mother had taught her, "once you fall off a horse, you have to get back on."

No wonder Joan's friends use words like "upbeat" and "inspiring" to describe her. Her optimistic attitude not only has carried her through her own trials, but accounts for why she is a source of strength for many others. Joan was one of the first to volunteer back in 1992 when the Susan G. Komen Foundation was started to support women with breast cancer, even though she had barely recovered herself. For her, answering calls on the helpline is a way of paying back for her own recovery, like paying rent for the space you occupy. And she gets the satisfaction of easing troubled hearts.

"Thank goodness," she says, "I have always had a positive attitude. It is a gift." Still, it's not easy to find the words to help someone who has just been diagnosed with cancer, she admitted, so sometimes she just listens. One of the most difficult situations, she recalled, involved a young woman who had been raped. While the woman was being treated in the hospital for injuries from the rape, she was diagnosed with breast cancer.

"That was a *tough* call," Joan said. "My best asset is that I am a survivor. Sometimes it just helps them to know that someone else understands their pain. And sometimes I make helpful suggestions based on what I learned myself during treatment. I can explain what the doctors are talking about. I can explain to their family members why they may be acting the way they do.

"Sometimes they are worried they won't see their children grown. And they need to be able to say that safely to someone. Sometimes they are upset about losing their hair in chemotherapy. Then I can suggest that they cut their hair shorter, so they won't find long strands on their pillow or in the drain. When you are talking to people who know for sure they are dying, you just have to let them lead. Where I can, I try to uplift. I never proselytize, but if they express a faith and say something like they are praying thanks for me, then I will feel free to say I will pray for them, too. And sometimes, I'll encourage them to try to smile and laugh as much as possible. I'll tell them to go check out a silly video and laugh all they can, to get those endorphins going," she said. "But sometimes during treatment, it is tough to get through it physically . . . you can't keep food down or you may have sores in your mouth as a side effect . . . you can't go out because your immune system is so weak. It is difficult to feel positive when you feel so terrible. Then I'll tell them, it's fine to feel sorry for yourself, just not for six weeks."

Even when she is on vacation, she takes calls from cancer patients who call her for a needed boost. "I'll gladly spend a few minutes of my time if it makes somebody feel better. In the end, it also makes me feel better. Big deal. It's not an interruption. It makes my vacation better."

That's the spirit. Doing small things with great generosity of heart is what it is all about.

Jane Cresswell had known since she was a summer missionary in college that she wanted to do something to help people and she has found a way to use that desire in a different kind of way. She did not want to be a full-time missionary because she came from a family with little money. Her father suffered from bouts of unemployment. At times the family had to buy food with food stamps. "So I was *not* going into a career that wasn't lucrative," she says. "It was like Scarlett O'Hara: I'll never buy food with food stamps again!"

She majored in math and computer science and became an IBM software engineer working with NASA in Houston. However, she discovered that she was better at motivating other members of her team than she was at programming. She became a manager and was so effective that people from other areas asked to work in her department. As she neared her forties, she began taking classes by teleconference at Coaches U and started a private practice as a professional coach in the evenings. Both she and IBM realized coaching was what she should do full-time and IBM didn't want to lose her, so she became the first corporate coach at the giant computer corporation.

The results for IBM were terrific and it turned out to be the

> "Do not wait for leaders; do it alone, person to person."
>
> —MOTHER TERESA, HUMANITARIAN

perfect way to use her missionary training. She had found a way to make a living by helping others have a better life. Though she doesn't talk about spiritual things on the job, she radiates an upright character and convivial disposition that draws people to her. Over the years, many employees have come up to her and said, "Jane, there's something different about you. I know there is. What is it?" She invites them to go to lunch off-premises, where they can talk personally. "I've been called a chaplain, but I don't have to be vocal about my beliefs," she explained. "It comes through in the way you treat people. If they see people doing right things, then they think, 'I can, too.'"

In the meantime, Jane Cresswell's career has thrived. She now is vice president for organization development and was featured in a *Time* magazine article about the growing phenomenon of corporate coaching in the fall of 2000. Companies ranging from Dow Chemical to Marriott International are now using coaches. Basically coaching is a way to add the dimension of caring to the eight-to-five world. That's something you could do in any field. Ask yourself: Does your business allow you to model your ethics and values every day? How do you lift others up?

Sooner or later many women realize that each one of us can make a difference by the small things they do every day. It's like the parable of the Medieval cathedral—who built the cathedral? The architect? The stained-glass artist? The brawny carpenters? The master stone mason? Or the peasant woman who gave some of her precious straw to the ox who hauled the massive stone for the base? Every role has value and can be a force multiplier when combined with the contributions of others.

Being a force multiplier is the message of British anthropologist Jane Goodall. Of all the people I have interviewed in the last three decades, she is by far my favorite. She has a great decency and gentle intelligence that shines through. You feel a better person after having spent a few minutes with her. It's no exaggeration to say this unassuming woman, who is most comfortable in walking shorts or a simple shirtwaist dress, is a modern-day soul mate of St. Francis. She preaches on behalf of all creatures, great and small, lovable or not.

As I write, a large poster hangs on the wall over my desk, showing a chimp with its head thrown back in a big-lipped smile, and the gray-haired Jane, trying to pucker out her own little mouth in an answering smile. The chimp, which had been orphaned, was given a new home at a sanctuary in Kenya. Above the picture of the two of them, she has written, "Together we can make the world a better place for *all* living things."

Her story is the stuff that movies are made of. As a young girl in her twenties, she worked as a waitress in England and saved her money to go to Africa, where she got a job with renowned anthropologist Louis Leakey in Tanzania. She pioneered the practice of observing animals in their habitat by spending weeks alone in the wilds of Gombe forest. When leopards prowled by at night, she pulled her blanket over her head and stayed put. She overcame scientific skepticism (and malaria) to prove that chimpanzees in the wild could use tools and show affection. She became a real-life heroine to millions when National Geographic and PBS brought her story to millions. Today her chimpanzee study in Gombe is the longest-running research project of its kind. And children around the world now know her as "the chimp lady."

Yet there is a twist to her story that is not as well known. In October 1986, while she was attending a conference in Chicago, she had what she later described as "a road to Damascus experience." She was shaken to the core by the evidence showing how dramatically the chimpanzee population was declining around the world. The data showed human pressures on the natural environment were taking a dreadful toll on the wild animals. From that moment on, Jane Goodall's mission in life was changed. She had arrived at the Chicago session a research scientist; she left a crusader for global conservation. She was in her fifties, but rather than slowing down, she stepped up her speaking schedule. Rather than cashing in personally on her fame or settling for a comfortable academic role, she began a new phase. She became a champion of individual efforts to keep the earth livable.

Since that day, she has spent more time in airports than in the jungle. She travels most of the year to raise money for animal research and for a program she started called Roots and Shoots, which encourages children to respect the natural world. She turned sixty-six in 2000, but she has not slowed down. During one typical seven-week tour of North America, she went to 27 cities, made 71 speeches, gave 170 media interviews, and had just as many business meetings, lunches, dinners, and breakfasts.

In a soft, firm voice, rather like a patient teacher, she tells audiences that they can make a difference. "We all know the things we should or shouldn't do that are good or bad for the environment. With over six billion people in the world, we have the feeling it won't matter if I turn the tap off, turn the car engine off, pick up a piece of litter. What can one person do? If there were only *one* concerned person in the world, it would not make a difference. But there are *millions* of concerned people. And that *does* make a difference. You can start by turning off the tap when you are cleaning your teeth. Turn off the engine rather than idling while you are waiting for someone. Try walking or biking or taking public transport rather than using your car all the time. We could turn this around," she promises, "if we could have thousands and millions of people all being environmentally responsible. It would change things."

Those born in the affluent side of the world can make an ethical difference with everyday purchases, she suggests. They can choose products from environmentally sound companies. They can refuse to buy items from companies that test their products on animals, which is not necessary any longer. They can reject products made in slave camps. They can buy eggs from free-range hens. They can shop at natural food stores for produce that is grown without dangerous pesticides or additives. It takes more effort to find organic products, but she's right when she says the more people do so, the more the price will come down. It is already coming down in Great Britain.

Her Roots and Shoots conservation program now is being taught to children in fifty countries. It also is being used in retirement homes in Boulder, Colorado, and in women's prisons in Danbury, Connecticut. ("It's amazing how it has changed morale there. It has given the inmates a sense of purpose. It helps them face their friends when they get out, because they know there is something, no matter how small, that they can do that makes their life worthwhile.")

In truth, her philosophy is not just about protecting the environment, it's about a positive way of life. She likes to tell children, "Even when you meet somebody, you can make them smile or you can make them unhappy in some way. When you see a dog, you can make it happy and wag its tail, or you can reject it and cause it to put its tail between its legs and run away from you. When you see a plant that is withering, you can water it or walk on by. That's the simplest level of commitment. But just think. If everyone made two people a day smile, it would change your whole feeling inside yourself. Even just one would be good, but two would be more effective, wouldn't it?"

If that seems simplistic, just test yourself by asking if you made at least two people happy today. Or did you walk by people, dogs, and plants without noticing them? In her own gentle way, Jane Goodall makes people realize that they shouldn't be so self-absorbed that they ignore life around them. Her mission is to motivate people from all walks of life to be change agents in their own communities.

Maybe your life has made more difference than you realize. Sometimes it is a small thing that sets off a ripple effect in someone else's life. You may not even be aware of it. Once I was approached by a young African American woman at a civic luncheon who asked, "Do you remember me?" I said, "Yes, of course, how have you been?" out of politeness while I struggled to place her face. Only when she told me she used to be a clerk in a rental car agency did the memory come back. We had a short conversation at the rental car office, where I was renting a car while mine was being repaired after an accident.

"I've wanted to call or write you to say thank you," she said at the luncheon.

I was puzzled. "Thank me for what?"

It seems I had complimented her on how well she did her job, because her attitude had made a stressful experience a little easier. She told me she actually would like to find a more challenging job, but wasn't sure she could make the grade somewhere else.

"What would you like to do?" I had asked her.

"Oh, something to help other people, maybe something with a charity—if they would hire somebody like me," she said.

"Of course they would hire somebody like you," I reassured her. "You're bright and efficient. You'd be terrific. You should do it."

I rushed off to worry about daily minutiae and did not think of the exchange again. But as she told me at the luncheon, she had been encouraged by the brief exchange to look for another job and found one at a nonprofit that worked with women. She was beaming. She said, "I love what I do now."

Quite frankly, I was floored. Such a small intersection in our lives. Yet it was the hinge that enabled her to turn a different way. I walked away from the conversation with a new appreciation that a few words of encouragement may be just what someone needs at a crucial point. I should do that more often, I thought.

Often when I'm out in the community instead of at my desk, I am struck by the many anonymous people who do the work that keeps civic life together—the low-profile staffers at social agencies, the Cub Scout mothers, the soccer coaches, the election volunteers, the ushers at church. We don't do a very good job in my business of covering the people who try to do things right, who do things modestly. Yet in the process of researching this book, I ran across scores of them:

- Tanya Parieaux, a cancer survivor, founded the Threads of Life volunteer project to teach knitting to cancer survivors in the Seattle area.

- Kathy Garrett, a property manager, models an enlightened approach by offering job assistance, Bible studies, child care, and computer classes at the three low-income apartment complexes she supervises in Dallas.

> "Asking the proper questions is the central action of transformation. Questions are the key that causes the secret doors of the psyche to swing open."
> —CLARISSA PINKOLA ESTES, WRITER AND PSYCHOLOGIST

- Randy Fenton founded a business in Tucson called Happy Heads to provide attractive headwraps for people who lose their hair in chemotherapy.

- Betsy Frazier, a seventy-nine-year-old widow, reads books onto tape for Reading and Radio Resource in Dallas, so the sightless can enjoy good literature. For fun, she still treks to places like New Zealand and Machu Picchu, then records travelogues about the sights and recipes for home-bound listeners.

Are there some small steps that you could start taking to add a new sense of purpose to your life?

Is there a way to make your gifts intersect with the lives of others? For example, if you are a marvelous cook, could you write a cookbook and donate the proceeds to a deserving cause?

Are you good at gardening? Could you help beautify a park? If you have an artistic bent, perhaps you could put it to use teaching arts and crafts to runaways at shelters. If you think you have no talent, you might still gather clothes for the battered women's shelter or serve as an election monitor. You may be an anonymous soldier, but then, there's a great deal to be said for that.

Thinking of an entire life makeover can be overwhelming and may keep you from doing anything. Whether your next steps are donating your time, or starting a career, you can begin by taking one "chunk" at a time. Answer the following questions:

1. What is the one area that you are most interested in developing? You may start by identifying several areas and narrow down to the most interesting.

> "It made me feel as if I'd made a contribution. We just can't be cold automatons all our lives. Anyway, I made a difference. I made a small, little difference."
> —CAROL BELLAMY, FORMER CONGRESSWOMAN

2. What small step could you take first? Identify a tiny chunk to try out to see if in doing so, you are still passionate enough about it.

3. Did you feel excited about what you did? Did it seem purposeful and rewarding? If you determined interest by trying that first chunk, identify two or three more small pieces and try those out.

4. Are you beginning to see that this could really be an important next endeavor for you? If so, begin with a short outline of how the whole project could occur. Use the process above, of breaking the project down into do-able tasks, and proceed.

If you have tried an option and are not finding the potential there, then try another area of interest and go through the same process—checking out one possibility after another until you find just the right thing for you. You should ask yourself every day, Is this what I want to be doing? If the answer is no, you can tweak your plan a little every day. Adding new purpose to your life usually is a process, not an event. It's like losing weight, you have to do it a pound at a time, a step at a time. Just keep moving forward.

Chapter Sixteen

Just Do It! They Did It!

"There is always an enormous temptation in all of life to diddle around making itsy-bitsy friends and meals and journeys for itsy-bitsy years on end. . . . I won't have it. The world is wilder than that in all directions, more dangerous and bitter, more extravagant and bright. We are making hay when we should be making whoopee; we are raising tomatoes when we should be raising Cain or Lazarus."

—ANNIE DILLARD, FROM *PILGRIM AT TINKER CREEK*

Well, here you are at the brink, wondering, "Could I? Should I . . . ?"

Yes.

Say it out loud: YES!

The sound of your own voice is empowering. And finding your own voice is what this is all about.

It's important to live today.

It's time to just do it.

Try a new dream.

Try again, if need be. And then, maybe try again.

The good news is that there will be less pressure on you to succeed with the You Redux than you might fear. Relax. Cut yourself a little slack. You don't have to make the front page to feel more fulfilled. Penicillin has already been discovered. You just need to discover a healthy purpose for this stage of life. You can leave your own mark in your own way. Even if you flub up a little or a lot, at least you will get out of the rut you were in and learn a lot on the way.

For some, just a change of scene, on one's own terms, is enough.

Paula Price had been a nurse for twenty-five years. She delivered thirty-eight babies. She held her breath during "code" emergencies when the patient's life hung by a heartbeat. She helped stanch the blood as drunk drivers were wheeled into the emergency room. Then one morning she woke up and thought, "I don't want to do it anymore." The grind was getting her down. Her own health was suffering as she nursed others. So she quit. And went to work—surprise—at a gourmet food market. She's never been happier. Her mother told her she was "two tacos short of a combination plate" to leave a secure job just when she was getting to the age when she needed to think about security. But when her mom saw how relaxed and rejuvenated she was, she conceded that going to culinary school may have been the best thing her daughter had done in years. She was burned out. And she did something about it.

Others look up at midlife and realize their life took a wrong turn somewhere. They didn't end up the person they intended to be.

Martha Jackson was in her forties and completing her doctorate at the University of North Texas when she decided to "take a deep breath and look at where I was." She had been trained as a music teacher and loved both music and teaching.

When she had studied for her master's degree, she was told her plan of study was not "broad enough," that she needed to emphasize administration. Eventually she moved out of the classroom and into school administration, where she worked in community relations.

But moving onward and upward often takes people further away from the thing they love. It usually takes them away from the creative side of the business into the management track. And even if they try to approach management "creatively," it's not the same. A budget meeting is still a budget meeting. If you like counting beans, you're in the right place. If you're a woman of independent beans, you might be looking out the window.

When a photographer friend took Martha to a seminar for makeup artists, she felt that old creative buzz again. It was a different way to get involved with people than she might have imagined, but it got her juices flowing again. She left her education career to work as a makeup artist. As time went on, she was emboldened to step in front of the camera herself as an actress. As she was nearing the big five-oh mark, she said she is prepared to change again, or go back to teaching with new life experiences. "You learn to follow your gut feelings," she said. "You learn to listen to that little voice about what you should be doing. But I'm not sure you can hear that voice until you have some maturity—a lot of living. I learned what *wasn't* me."

Sometimes life forces you to change direction.

Remember Zoe Baird? She was the brainy attorney who had to give up her nomination from President Clinton to be the nation's first female attorney general in 1993. She withdrew after a storm of criticism that she had not properly reported payments for a nanny caring for her young son. The media feeding frenzy was intense. She could have been permanently scarred by the glare of the negative publicity. But instead, she regrouped and ended up the president of the Markle Foundation, one of the largest foundations in the country. At forty-seven, Zoe Baird has a new mission and a light in her eyes.

She was tapped by the foundation in 1998 after six years as general counsel at Aetna and a year as a visiting scholar at Yale Law School. In a short time, she started making new headlines for devoting more foundation resources to Internet projects. She has championed programs to provide information to voters on the Internet and to bridge the gap between the "haves" and "have-nots" in cyberspace. When the top foreign leaders in the world met in Japan in the summer of 2000, Zoe Baird was there to talk with them about the "digital divide" between rich and developing nations.

One of her first high-profile projects was a collaboration with Oxygen, the new cable television network trying to blaze new paths in providing programs for women. She hopes the Oxygen-Markle Pulse will become *the* comprehensive source for information about women. It's a long way from the Justice Department. But Zoe says it was a natural extension of her interests. "I probably fit in that category of people who have tried to live lives in different worlds for a long time. I came from a family of public service," she explains. "My father was a labor union official, so I grew up my whole life with him coming home talking about the guys who came into the labor hall that day with various problems on the job, with the kids, whatever. So I grew up in an environment of public service." Even when she worked in government or the private sector, she said, she was always involved in other things that she cared about. While she

> "You cannot hope to build a better world without improving the individuals. To that end each of us must work for his own improvement, and at the same time share a general responsibility for all humanity, our particular duty being to aid those to whom we think we can be most useful."
> —MARIE CURIE, SCIENTIST

was general counsel at Aetna, for example, she founded a program, Lawyers for Children America, that arranges for lawyers in private practice to represent abused and neglected children.

At some point, she explained, "you say to yourself you are going to put all you've learned together in your public service, which is what I deeply care about. For me, the opportunity to do that came when I was asked if I were interested in heading Markle. I think there is potentially a point in everyone's life where you have learned to do so much, how do you want to apply it? That's when you realize you only have one life to live and ask how do you want to live it?"

She was greatly influenced years ago by social organizer Sol Linowitz, who said that every August when he went on vacation, he would sit down by the lake and take a piece of paper and write down all the things he was doing and all the things that were taking up his time. Then he would cross off the things he should stop and write down the things he should add. "I don't have an annual ritual of that nature," she admitted, but she does periodically take stock of the commitments she has made and has been unable to live up to because of time pressures. She recently did so and decided to set aside more time for her family. And indeed, when we talked, she was vacationing at Martha's Vineyard with her husband, who teaches at Yale Law School, and their two young sons. It was late afternoon and the boys were resting, so she had some time to talk.

She was gracious and good-humored, even when asked whether the attorney general controversy had scarred her. "No, it made more people interested in my ideas than if they hadn't heard my name before," she said. "I'm unlike some people who go through these confirmation processes that become unbearable. For me it was just a few weeks and I got it out of my system. I had a fabulous job to go back to and a wonderful family, so no, it really didn't scar me. I learned a lot."

She said she now would encourage other women to think about what it is that they have found over the years that they are really skilled at and where they can make their most important contribution. "By midlife, you really have figured out who you are," she said. "You have accumulated your basic skills, but there is always more to learn and ways to stretch yourself. It's really important after that many years to take stock. Take stock and see where you can make the greatest contribution."

Ask yourself the question, What am I capable of doing? And believe your answer.

Even after a bruising primary fight for a judicial bench, Dallas attorney Karen Johnson says she was glad she took the plunge. Like many people, she thought she might make a good elected official, but she wasn't sure other people would think so. And she wasn't sure she had thick enough skin. Her life was changed when she happened to ask some politically active lawyers at a cocktail party how judicial appointments were made. She was surprised when the immediate response was, "You'd be great. You ought to consider it." In coming weeks, however, the party stalwarts made a giant leap from "She would

> "I believe that what woman resents is
> not so much giving herself in pieces as
> giving herself purposelessly."
> —ANNE MORROW LINDBERGH, WRITER

consider an appointment" to "She'll give up her practice and run for judge." Karen's first thought was, "There is no way!" Yet as people continued to encourage her, she felt honored by their trust. She looked into her heart and talked to her husband and three children. She decided, "I really wanted to do it."

She explains, "I teach my children that if they put their minds to something, they can do anything they want. When you're considering public office, you've got to take a reality check of your talents and what kind of risks you're taking on. Then you have to practice what you preach to your kids. Somewhere along the way, we forget the lessons we teach our children, that you can do what you want if you work hard enough. We tell them, 'reach for your dreams, reach for the stars.' We all teach our children that, but look around and the grown-ups don't do it!" She went on, "Somewhere in there, maybe it's the forties or the fifties or whenever, you have to do a check and say, 'Am I doing what I want to do? Am I doing what I am capable of doing?'"

She filed to run for judge in the 95th Civil District Court. That meant she was running against an incumbent, another woman. It turned out to be one of the toughest races of the election season. And when the votes were counted, Karen won with 55 percent of the vote. At forty-two, she became the first Asian elected official in all of North Texas. She was fortified by her conviction that "normal, rational people" need to get involved in politics, not just partisan activists or extremists. "If you want it to become a better place for you and your children, you've got to get a whole bunch of people like me to get involved. It's good to show the system sometimes works after all. I wanted to show my children that a normal person can stand up and decide to do something to make a difference."

She learned how to deal with criticism and move on. She stretched. And even after such a rocky beginning, she now says she would encourage others to consider public service. "If in their heart they want to try, if they feel there is a reasonable risk and there would be people out there to support them, I would advise it," she said. "Even people who ran and lost tell me that they are still glad they did it. It *is* important for people to get involved—and not leave everything up to 'other people.'"

Sometimes you can find a sense of purpose in a talent you haven't used.

In Austin, Cheryl Cash Koen had raised three children as a single mom, while struggling to get ahead in the real estate business. Just when she thought she had it made, with success in a swank real estate project and a new marriage, her twenty-four-year-old son Tobin committed suicide. It was agonizing for her. "As a single mom, you can't help but worry, 'I didn't do enough, I let somebody down.'" Though she had never studied art, she was moved one afternoon to sketch a portrait of her son. It was a startling likeness. The experience led her to start taking art lessons. Her impressionist paintings in warm colors proved very popular and before long she was exhibiting in two local galleries. Today, at fifty-two, she considers the prized portraits she does for families her way of giving something back that will be meaningful to others. "I get such an affirmation of what I'm doing when someone tells me how much it means to have a painting that they can look at every day and remember someone." Unfortunately, just as her art career was taking off, she was diagnosed in the summer of 2000 with a slow-growth leukemia. Her faith and her art meant more than ever. "Your life can change in a second and I'm here to tell you it can," she said. "This is going to be another one of those hurdles. I feel fortunate I have the art to focus on."

Sometimes your avocation can become your vocation.

Ann Hantzen Hughes is used to doing the unexpected. In 1955, after she was married and had children, she decided to go to medical school. Only 10 percent of each entering class at Southwestern Medical School was allotted for women, she was told, because women tended to have children and quit practicing. She told school officials the rules didn't apply to her because she already had children and she was ready to drop back in.

She spent the next few decades as a trailblazer in psychiatry, crafting innovative programs to help adolescents with serious behavior problems. She started a rugged outdoor camping treatment, called Discoveryland, for troubled youth near Bryan. Yet after years and years of intense day-to-day work with severely troubled youngsters, she was burned out. She tried a few administrative stints, then spent two years backpacking in the Rocky Mountains to clear her thoughts.

Instead of coming back to medicine, she started a gallery in Fredericksberg, the heart of the lovely Texas hill country, when she was in her sixties. She had collected art herself since her early married years. Art brought beauty and stimulating people into her life. It nurtured the creative side in her. She had connections at the galleries in Santa Fe, where she had a home, and knew enough to set up shop herself. She ultimately relocated from the hill country to Dallas, where there was more art traffic. It became one of the busiest galleries in town and she beams with every sale. Selling art at this time of her life is fulfilling. She says, "there was a time when women could only do what you were allowed to do. Now, if it isn't what you want to do, then you shouldn't be doing it. If it's your passion, then that's what you should be doing." She's not ruling out yet another career in her seventies. As she says with a twinkle, "I have a lot more to do. I tell people, don't tell me we can't do something. Tell me how we can."

Sometimes you can improve your own quality of life by serving others.

Evelyn Gregory of Denver, North Carolina, became a flight attendant at the age of seventy-two. She had wanted to be a "stewardess" since she was a little girl, but her father discouraged her, partly because he thought flying was dangerous. In those early airline days after World War II, attendants had to be trained as nurses. So she married instead and had three children. She also had a long career in banking, rising to assistant vice president and branch manager. Her husband passed away in 1989 and by the time she retired in 1993, her children were married with families of their own. She had a little place at the beach where she enjoyed having the seven grandkids visit, but after they were gone, she missed being around people. She did some volunteer work, teaching Sunday school at nursing homes in the area. But just as she would get attached to the patients, they would die, she says, so she longed for something more energizing.

So she applied to become a flight attendant at U.S. Airways

> "I say if it's going to be done, let's do it.
> Let's not put it in the hands of fate.
> Let's not put it in the hands of someone
> who doesn't know me. I know me best.
> Then take a breath and go ahead."
> —ANITA BAKER, SINGER

at the age of seventy. She was turned down. (On one of the questionnaire forms, she was asked what her career goals were for the next ten to fifteen years. She wrote in, "To keep on living."). Undaunted by the rejection, she applied again at seventy-one and was rejected again. So she went to work as a gate agent and applied for a flight attendant's job with Mesa Air Group. She was accepted. Her roommate in flight school was eighteen. The other members of flight school started calling her "Nana," the nickname her grandchildren had for her. Now the president of the company hugs her and calls her "Nana." And when she walks through Dulles International Airport, ramp agents ask for her autograph.

She has learned how to open forty-pound doors (cross-handed) and how to handle rowdy passengers (with southern charm). At an age when most women are winding down, she is winding her way to La Guardia and Little Rock. And loving it. She even asked for extra flights, explaining, "You know, my days are numbered." She treats passengers as if they were guests in her own home and breaks out extra snacks and drinks when there is a delay. Crews treat her like a beloved mother.

When we talked, she was in Phoenix, teaching at the ground school for other attendants. She spoke with me on her cell phone outside her dormitory. She's still flying and teaching part-time, she said. "They called me out on a Sunday last week and I got to fly to Monterey, California. It was the first time I had seen the Pacific Ocean. We just had time for lunch and then we were out again, but it is still wonderful to see other parts of the country."

It's also gratifying to her that her example has encouraged other older women to try airline work. "There's one woman in my class right now who saw an article about me. She's in her fifties. There have been several women in the classes in their fifties and late forties. There was a woman who was seventy-one in my last class, who also had read about me." She said most of the older attendants had turned out to be more dependable than some of the younger employees, so it was proving a good move for the airlines. And quite frankly, she said, the older workers would probably live longer if they are more productive. The seventy-one-year-old woman in her last class, she pointed out, jumped off the wing just like a twenty-year-old. "No problem."

Thanks to changes in federal law, employees can work past retirement age. Evelyn turned seventy-three in September 2000 and she said that her plans were to keep flying as long as she could. "My family thinks it is just wonderful," she said. "They are really proud. I think about my husband so often. When I would get a promotion at the bank, he would say 'I'm so proud of you.' So now I just look up at the sky and think, 'I know you're really proud of me now.' God has placed me where I need to be. People need me and I need them. If you have always wanted to do something in life, you should go do it. We have a mission in life. If we can do something that is useful to others, I say go for it."

If you feel a yearning to stretch yourself, a call that compels you and won't go away, listen to it.

Follow your instincts. If it's something that will make the world a better place, so much the better. Marcia Beauchamp did just that. People often compare her to the diminutive brunette actress Holly Hunter, the star of the movies *Broadcast News* and *The Piano*. Marcia is barely five feet tall. No bigger than a nickel, as they say in her native Oklahoma. Bright as all get-out and with a twang that will make you smile. Her story is proof you should not let your first career define you forever.

For eighteen years, Marcia was a hairstylist in Tulsa. As they say, she "did hair." Then she decided to go to Harvard Divinity School. Today she's a national coordinator for the Freedom Forum, training communities across the United States how to include religion in their curricula. How she made that transition is a testament to sheer gumption and faith.

When she was in high school, Marcia studied cosmetology and loved doing hair. So she eventually owned her own salon and was very successful. But at twenty-eight, she found herself with two divorces and a new high-end salon, Capelli, to run herself. "Doing hair" wasn't as much fun anymore. She had been taking courses at community colleges for some time, gaining a broader world view. The superficiality of what she did began to get to her, "especially when I had a picky customer." As she says, "I started seeing myself at fifty, and I thought, I cannot stand here and do this for another twenty years. I'll be bitter or diminished, or stunted." It was a wake-up call. She needed to look around for a solution. What else turned her on that she could do? She had been attending a church where the minister taught a course on world religions. She was intrigued by the great religious traditions of the world, but couldn't see how that added up to a paying job.

Then one day when she was reading the *New York Times*, an article caught her eye: it said several states had passed legislation requiring their public schools to offer Cultural Religious Studies. The concept was that as the United States has become more diverse, people need to understand each other better to solve problems. And one way to do that is to teach about the world's religions in the schools. Not from the point of view of indoctrination, but from an informational point of view.

She thought, "Here's something I can do. It was a moment of revelation." Her friends and colleagues were skeptical. They said, "You're not going to do that in Oklahoma or Arkansas or anyplace in the Bible Belt." Or, "That's illegal." But she knew it was not illegal. The Supreme Court decision that banned state-mandated prayer in public schools advocated the "objective" teaching about religion in public schools.

She became a full-time student, which she paid for by selling her salon. It was an adjustment. She had been used to a schedule where someone new sat down in her chair every forty-five minutes and she entertained them while she styled their hair. Now she had to get used to being an observer listening to someone else. She persevered and earned a bachelor's degree in philosophy and religion. Impressed by her dedication, one of her theology professors encouraged her to apply for graduate school at Harvard, where they had a program on Religion in Secondary Education. She scored well above the requirement on the graduate exam and soon found herself in Cambridge, Massachusetts, a world away from the salons she knew.

It was a chillier climate in many ways. When people at Harvard found out her background, some were fascinated; others wrote her off. When we talked she said, "I thought I was off-track a couple of times, but I'm glad I hung in there, because now I think I'm doing exactly what I am supposed to be doing. You have to follow what your heart tells you to do and trust that it will work out."

And oh yes, she has been back to Tulsa to do a seminar for several of the public schools there. As fate would have it, the

> "How can you hesitate? Risk! Risk any-thing! Care no more for the opinion of others, for those voices. Do the hard-est thing on earth for you. Act for yourself. Face the truth."
> —KATHERINE MANSFIELD, WRITER

workshop was held in a hotel across the parking lot from her old salon. She could look out the window and see where she came from. And then move on.

Lucretia Mott, the fearless little Quaker from Nantucket, made her life speak in the eighteenth century. She worked tirelessly for the abolition of slavery, for equal rights, and for higher education for women. She encouraged less active Quakers to let their "light shine" and become more involved in serving others. She would say: "What is thee doing?" A century later, another feminist, Betty Friedan, would ask, "Who knows what women can be when they are finally free to become themselves?"

And here we are, at the dawn of still another century, freer than ever before. It is possible for women to find a life of purpose, even at an age when they used to be thought "past their prime." Prime time has been extended. You can reach for the moisturizer with one hand and a new challenge with the other. You can become a person of new value. You can uplift others in the process.

Will it be easy? Absolutely not. But it certainly is no harder than living a life without purpose, day in and day out. Since all life takes effort, you might as well put your energy into something that feels good and does good. As Helen Keller said, "One can never consent to creep when one feels an impulse to soar."

If you've followed the script through the chapters, you probably have put together a fairly good outline in your mind, if not on paper, of what it is you intend to do that will make a difference in your life. You may need a chance to use your gifts or a change of scene. You may want to "give something back to the world." It is important to remember that you don't have to be a minister to have a "ministry" that makes this a better world in some way, as Donna Sanson shows in her restaurant and Jane Cresswell shows through her corporate coaching. The women in this book show how there are many different ways to make your life count for more than the ordinary.

Now it's time to put your feet to the plan and purpose. The following questions will help you get into action.

What does your intuition say you should do to get into action?

Listen to your biofeedback. Pay attention to the signs in your life. Is your pulse racing faster when you're on task? Or are you continually looking at your watch? What's that other thing you do that draws you in so deeply you never know what time it is? Pay attention to the truth in your body.

What do you most want to change about your life or try? Make a short-term plan. Include such things as collecting data on the possibilities, training or education that may be required, etc. Create an action plan that includes the next steps to feeling significant. Create a mission statement of the kind of person you want to be. What do you hope to do in your life? What would you like your legacy to include? Make sure your plan follows the deepest longings of your heart.

Have you defined your "calling"?

If you are a multitasker, you will need to get out of your overstimulated environment to hear your heart. If you are a creature of habit, you will need to ask for the courage to be quiet so direction can be revealed to you in a nonlinear way. You may not recognize it as the response to your quiet at first. In your prayers and meditations, you may have identified some of the spiritual elements of your prime time plan. When your work seems fun and rewarding, you know you're on the right track. It means that you're using the gifts God has given you.

Are you clear on "who" you are being as well as "what" you are doing?

Action plans sometimes get us concentrating on the "doing" of our lives. God created us to be human "beings." Pay attention to both factors to be congruent. Make sure that you develop a balance of your life with your work in your action plan. Block out time for the cookies of life.

What are you willing to give up?

Make a list of things you would like to change, but can tolerate. Then make a list of "intolerables" you must change. Most women making this shift find they only have to give up the "intolerables." What's left is the tolerable and the best—and the best contributes to the heart's desire. What is left behind are the roadblocks to your success.

What processes will you have in place when (if) you get discouraged? What processes will help sustain your progress?

Develop a "two-minute" drill—a quick sequence of behavior (meditation, prayer, list-making, counseling with your board of advisors) that gets you back into action and feeling confident. It really only takes a couple of minutes if you know what to do. Set up systems that assist you in midcourse corrections along the way, like journaling or checking in with your circle of supporters for more advice and acknowledgment.

Just remember:

- Lauren Bacall, who taught Humphery Bogart how to whistle, went back to Broadway at the age of seventy-six. As she put it, "I'm not a has-been. I'm a will-be." The play was *Waiting in the Wings,* a comedy about old age written by Noel Coward when he was sixty.

- Emily Post, having survived a philandering husband and a divorce, did not write her famous book of etiquette until she was in her late fifties.

- Gloria Stuart almost stole the show in the movie *Titanic* at the age of eighty-seven. In real life, she had given up movie acting in the 1950s to learn to become a painter in Europe. When she was fifty she had a gallery exhibit in New York. When she was seventy-three, she became a master printer, producing limited editions of museum-quality books.

- Philanthropist Brooke Astor wrote her highly regarded first novel, *The Last Blossom on the Plum Tree*, when she was in her late eighties.

- Grandma Moses (Anna Mary Richardson) was seventy-six when she took up painting because arthritis forced her to give up embroidery.

- At sixty-two, actress Jane Fonda has found a new faith in Atlanta and is leading the Georgia Campaign for Adolescent Pregnancy Prevention.

- Jan Karon was a forty-nine-year-old advertising copywriter in North Carolina when she came up with the idea of writing wholesome mystery novels. She introduced the reading world to Father Tim Kavanaugh in *At Home in Mitford* in 1994 and has had five books on the best-seller list since then.

- After a crazed gunman killed her husband and wounded her son on a Long Island train, Carolyn McCarthy, a nurse, ran for Congress to fight for gun control. She was elected at the age of fifty-two, and helped organize the Million Man March in 2000.

- Betty Furness moved from acting in B movies to selling refrigerators on TV, which led to her appointment as a special assistant on consumer affairs in the Johnson administration. That in turn opened a whole new career as a consumer protection expert on *The Today Show* while she was in her sixties.

- When she was sixty-six, U.S. Senator Margaret Chase Smith made a bid for the GOP presidential nomination, which went instead to Sen. Barry Goldwater. She served in the Senate six more years.

- Fashion designer Anne Klein founded her women's clothing company "somewhere between the age of forty-seven and sixty-three."

- Golda Meir was sworn in as Israel's premier at seventy.

- Philadelphia activist Maggie Kuhn founded the Gray Panthers at age sixty-five to fight for the rights of retired Americans.

- Chita Rivera returned to Broadway at the age of sixty to sing and dance in *Kiss of the Spider Woman.*

- Pianist Marian McPartland recorded *Silent Pool,* a critically treasured jazz album, at the age of seventy-eight. It included twelve of her own compositions.

- At sixty, Germaine Greer was still challenging conventional thinking about women and sex in her book *The Whole Woman.*

- Tony Award–winning actress Jane Alexander was named chair of the National Endowment for the Arts at fifty-three.

- Pamela Harriman was in her seventies when she was named U.S. ambassador to France.

- At eighty, actress Maureen O'Hara returned to work to make a TV movie about a retired teacher called *The Last Dance.*

- At eighty-seven, Margaret Carson, a press agent who is considered a force of nature in the New York music world, is still representing conductor Michael Tilson Thomas.

So there is plenty of precedent for producing fruit from seasoned wood. According to the Bureau of the Census, today's women can expect to live at least twenty years longer than their parents and grandparents. In 1900 the life expectancy was forty-seven. By 1998 it was seventy-seven. You can watch and wait, or you can be an active participant in that life. It's your choice. The meter is running.

I hope that as you deal with the halftime of your life, you will give yourself permission to be brave. Be yourself. Do important things. Do something to make this a better world. Live the rest of your life as if you were just beginning. Dance as if no one were watching.

Remember what British writer George Eliot (Mary Ann Evans) advised more than a century ago:

"It's never too late to be what you might have been."

Epilogue

"The need for change bulldozed a road down the center of my mind."

—MAYA ANGELOU, POET

I must admit that when I started this project, I didn't have a map to show me where I was going. But as Gloria Steinem once said, you have to convince yourself that not knowing what is going to happen is good, because if you don't know, it could be terrific.

And it has been.

For the last three years, I have talked to countless dozens of women about how they changed their lives in the prime of life and what helped. I think I am a different woman today because of that process, a stronger person. This journey changed my DNA, my wiring, because learning from these women taught me to deal with life differently than I did before.

Let me share with you a few things I learned:

1. *If you want to change,* change.

I know that sounds simple, but it's the crux of the matter. I had thought about writing a book for a long time. Once I started this project, it was embarrassing to me to tell friends that I couldn't go to the movies because I was working on a book. It seemed pretentious to me. But once I said it out loud, it put pressure on me to actually do it. You may feel the same about some suppressed desire you have. Blurt it out. It's not the distance that's so difficult, it's that first step.

2. You can't pursue two major things at the same time.

There's an old saying that if you chase two rabbits, one will get away. I discovered that I couldn't just layer my new goals on top of my old ones. I had to give up many of the things I used to do in the first part of my life. I cut back on nighttime civic meetings and virtually stopped watching TV so I would have time to write at night. You can't keep up the same social life if you want to seriously stretch yourself to learn something new. There isn't enough time, my friends. Something will have to give. But these are replaced with a newfound sense of direction.

3. The process may take longer than you think and may be more difficult than you would like.

I thought it would take half a year. It took more than three. I went through two computers and three printers. I was turned down by more agents than I care to count. Some women declined to be interviewed. I flew all the way to Los Angeles to interview an actress who stood me up. The first publishers I approached politely said I would be happier somewhere else. (They were right.) I erased several chapters accidentally at one in the morning. I have typed more than I ever typed in all of the other fifty years of my life. But as Tom Hanks said to the ragged team of female baseball players in the movie *A League of Their Own,* "It's supposed to be hard. The 'hard' is what makes you do it. If it wasn't hard, anyone could do it. The 'hard' is what makes you great."

4. You have to let other people help you.

I was mortified to reveal my fledgling efforts to others and ask for an opinion or assistance. But I gritted my teeth and did. Friends used their connections to help me get interviews. My tennis partner critiqued my early chapters. My secretary did proofreading. Bob Buford steadily provided suggestions, once gently suggesting that maybe even editors needed editing. One friend gave legal advice and others reviewed manuscripts. And several times, late at night, I had to wake my sons up to give me computer assistance. I felt as if I were imposing on them, but they were all incredibly darn nice about it. I'm betting that you will find at many points along the way, whatever your transition, you will need to ask other people to tell you the truth or lend you a hand.

5. You may have to change your financial habits.

Inspired by the example of Maggie Lichtenberg and Cynthia Gonzalez, I took several steps to prepare for new opportunities. I began paying down my credit card debt, to reduce obligations. I studied ways to get a better return on my retirement savings. I invested in a small vacation home where I could get away to write. Then I drew up several contingency budgets that would match different options—Plans A, B, C, D, E.

6. *Reviewing your life truthfully can be brutal. And liberating.*

It's like trying on a bathing suit with knee-high hose on. It's not pretty to look in the mirror sometimes. But in charting your life, you will probably discover how many things connect and lead to another. One episode of *Star Trek* has stuck in my mind for years: Captain Piccard got the chance to go back in his past and relive his life. He decided to avoid getting into a bar fight in which he was stabbed in the chest as a young man. Another man had died in the fracas and Piccard nearly did. When he returned to the present, he discovered he was no longer the captain of the spaceship *Enterprise,* but a lowly crewmember. The remorse from the fight, and his agonizing recovery in the hospital, had made him the man he ultimately became. Character, you discover as you look back, is a series of decisions, not all wise.

7. *They were right about solitude and enjoying nature.*

I have a new appreciation for peace and quiet. I never walk in the house and turn on the TV anymore. I love it when it is so quiet I can hear the clock chime. I turn off the cell phone and the car radio when I want to relax more on the way to work. Thoughts happen. I started going for walks five or six times a week and try to listen to the sounds of nature. I saw a golden crowned night heron the other day that was standing regally in a creek. It made me feel part of the universe and a little wilder and freer myself.

8. *A positive attitude works.*

Beverly Sills's indomitable spirit was inspiring. It reminded me of Rose Kennedy's advice, "Birds sing after a storm, why shouldn't we?"

9. Once you have a goal to shoot for, mundane problems seem less important.

As I began to focus on this project, old everyday problems that used to preoccupy me moved to the periphery. I didn't have time to think about them. They didn't go away, but I just didn't worry as much about them anymore.

10. Prayer works.

I use Alma Powell's "finger prayer" often and it is a good reminder to praise God first before I start giving him my shopping list. Taking another cue from her, I started saying a prayer to God to thank him for my blessings first thing in the morning, which changed my outlook about getting out of bed and going to work. Then, too, the prayers with my businesswomen's Bible study group have been truly elevating. I feel less awkward about praying in front of others and am more dutiful about praying *for* others. I'm trying to pass this on to my sons, by saying a blessing more often at meals and praying with them as they prepare for challenges, often as they head out the door. Now I understand what all those women meant when they said it was like a continuous conversation.

11. Faith means more now.

One of the most rewarding experiences of all was having perfect strangers speak so candidly about their deepest spiritual beliefs and their philosophy about life. I had more thoughtful conversations with these women than I have had with many longtime friends. I couldn't help but feel a twinge of mortalilty when Cheryl Koen said her leukemia had made her realize "I want to see my grandchildren grown." Many of these women had seen their lives crumple like a paper cup and yet, through faith, had fashioned a new life. As a result, I began to work harder at my own faith, studying commentaries, reading books about women of the Old and New Testament, attending special programs, and thinking seriously about what I believed. I realized I had been going through the motions, skimping on the kind of study you need to do to grow. I had been going to church on autopilot, hoping the minister would be in good form and say something that would apply to problems I was facing. Now I try to go with the attitude that I am there to worship God and be grateful for my blessings and problems. To paraphrase Mother Teresa, I don't pray for success anymore. I pray for faithfulness.

12. Friends mean more.

I read somewhere once that novelist Charles Kingsley once asked Elizabeth Barrett Browning, "What is the secret of your life? Tell me, that I may make mine beautiful also." Thinking a minute, the poet replied, "I had a friend."

13. Getting older has its benefits if you have a sense of humor.

Gray hair does have more body. And you have more perspective. Remember she who laughs, lasts.

14. Baby boomers still have something to teach the world.

There are some who think aging boomers have merely become jaded hippies with a wine cellar and a face-lift. True, there are some who simply segued from rock music and marijuana to merlot and brie. Good-bye VW bus, hello BMW. Instead of going to Woodstock, the yuppies in the nineties went to Tuscany. They dream of cashing in their 401(k)s and moving to Montana. But there's another side to that sustained prosperity. What I found was woman after woman who wanted to pare down the multiplicity of her life so she could contribute more to others. I believe the same idealism that motivated people to join the Peace Corps, support equal rights, and oppose war will compel them to use their remaining years more altruistically. Most of them have gotten the children they deserve and have discovered that corporate victories and defeats are both short-lived. Boomers have been notorious for rushing to embrace the latest recipe for happiness— casual drugs, casual sex, EST, the high of marathon running and the burn of aerobics—only to discover the answer to their restlessness was right there all the time. Many have rediscovered faith, although they may not be traditional churchgoers. I won't be surprised if there is another awakening of the postwar generation that will make an impact. We have gone through an era of commercialism where everything seemed an advertisement. We have gone through an era of cynicism and irony where nobody trusted anybody; like Seinfeld, we were too cool to really care. We are going through an era of rapid technological change that does not leave time to touch other lives. But it is that lack of touching and believing that people seem to miss. That's what the women in this book are trying to say with their lives. That touching each other and those in need is the antidote to the skepticism of the last few decades. It is the best hope for the next few.

> "That's what learning is. You suddenly understand something you've understood all your life, but in a new way."
> —DORIS LESSING, AUTHOR

15. *The value of things and time changes.*

Centuries ago, Socrates asked, "What is the good life?" I must admit my answer to that today is much different than it would have been when I was in my twenties.

16. *If I can do it, so can you.*

As that sage survivor Cher once said, "If you really want something, you can figure out how to make it happen." Amen to that. I hope as you near the prime of your life, you will give yourself permission to be brave. Be yourself. Use your gifts. Do whimsical things. Do something to make this a better world. Live the rest of your life with meaning. Breathe deeply. You can do it. I have this really great feeling you are going to start now.

Good Company

(Ages as of the year 2000, give or take a little)

Kristin Scott Thomas, actress—40
Daryl Hannah, actress—40
Julianne Moore, actress—40
Greta Scacchi, actress—40
Tracy Ullman, comedian—41
Linda Blair, actress—41
Sarah Ferguson, Duchess of York—41
Ellen Degeneres, comedian—42
Deborah Norville, TV journalist—42
Annette Bening, actress—42
Tanya Tucker, singer—42
Jamie Lee Curtis, actress—42
Brett Butler, comedian—42
Madonna, actress-singer—42
Michelle Pfeiffer, actress—43
Caroline Kennedy Schlossberg, author—43
Geena Davis, actress—43
Melanie Griffith, actress—43
Leeza Gibbons, TV personality—43
Gloria Estefan, singer—43
Katie Couric, TV host—43
Frances McDormand, actress—43
Princess Caroline of Monaco—43
Paula Zahn, news anchor—44

Martina Navratilova, tennis player—44
Debbie Boone, singer—44
Linda Hamilton, actress—44
Mimi Rogers, actress—44
Jerry Hall, model—44
Carrie Fisher, actress-author—44
Debra Winger, actress—45
Maria Shriver, journalist—45
Sandra Bernhard, comedian—45
Kate Mulgrew, actress—45
Olga Korbut, gymnast—45
Kirstie Alley, actress—45
June Pointer, singer—46
Oprah Winfrey, talk show host—46
Patty Hearst, newspaper heiress—46
Rene Russo, actress—46
Rickie Lee Jones, singer—46
Beverly D'Angelo, actress—46
Chris Evert, tennis player—46
Kim Basinger, actress—47
Mary Steenburgen, actress—47
Kathie Lee Gifford, TV personality—47
Marcia Clark, attorney—47
Alfre Woodard, actress—47

Mary Matalin, political consultant—47

Anna Quindlen, novelist-columnist—47

Cathy Rigby, gymnast—48

Christine Baranski, actress—48

Pat Benatar, singer—48

Christie Hefner, publisher—48

Susan Dey, actress—48

Lorna Luft, singer—48

Roseanne Barr, comedienne—48

Juice Newton, singer—48

Patricia Richardson, actress—49

Heloise, columnist—49

Jane Seymour, actress—49

Annie Potts, actress—49

Melissa Manchester, singer—49

Ann Jillian, actress—49

Lisa Halaby Noor, former queen of Jordan—49

Luci Arnaz, actress—49

Sally Ride, astronaut—49

Lynda Carter, actress—49

Charo, actress-singer—49

Angelica Huston, actress—49

Crystal Gayle, singer—49

Morgan Fairchild, actress—50

Cybill Shepherd, actress—50

Jane Pauley, journalist—50

Cathy Guisewite, cartoonist—50

Debbie Allen, choreographer—50

Natalie Cole, singer—50

Patty Murray, U.S. senator—50

Victoria Principal, actress—50

Princess Anne, British royal family—50

Susan Anton, singer—50

Tess Harper, actress—50

Joan Lunden, TV personality—50

Shelley Duvall, actress—51

Sissy Spacek, actress—51

Bonnie Raitt, singer—51

Sigourney Weaver, actress—51

Annie Leibovitz, photographer—51

Twiggy, model-actress—51

Meryl Streep, actress—51

Lindsay Wagner, actress—51

Shelley Long, comedian—51

Brooke Adams, actress—51

Marilyn Quayle, attorney-author—51

Phyllis George, former Miss America—51

Anne Reinking, dancer—51

Maureen McGovern, singer—51

Kathleen Battle, opera singer—52

Kathy Bates, actress—52

Linda Bloodworth-Thomason, TV producer—52

Barbara Hershey, actress—52

Olivia Newton-John, singer—52

Kate Jackson, actress—52

Margot Kidder, actress—52

Julie Eisenhower, Nixon daughter—52

Tipper Gore, photographer—52

Sally Struthers, actress—52

Georgia Engel, actress—52

Barbara Mandrell, singer—52

Farrah Fawcett, actress—53

Hillary Rodham Clinton, U.S. senator—53

Danielle Steele, writer—53

Luci Baines Johnson, LBJ daughter—53

Lois Chiles, actress—53

Cheryl Tiegs, model—53

Mary Kay Place, actress-singer—53

Jane Curtin, comedian—53

Betty Buckley, singer—53

Camille Paglia, writer—53

Sondra Locke, actress—53

Jaclyn Smith, actress—53

Susan Sarandon, actress—54

Tyne Daly, actress—54

Susan St. James, actress—54

Linda Ronstadt, singer—54

Tricia Nixon, Nixon daughter—54

Suzanne Somers, actress—54

Lesley Gore, singer—54

Hayley Mills, actress—54

Sally Field, actress—54

Diane Keaton, actress-director—54

Dolly Parton, singer—54

Sandy Duncan, actress—54

Liza Minelli, singer—54

Patty Duke, actress—54

Connie Chung, journalist—54

Laura Bush, First Lady—54

Christine Todd Whitman,
governor—54

Susan Lucci, TV actress—54

Naomi Judd, singer—54

Loni Anderson, actress—54

Cynthia Gregory, ballerina—54

Mia Farrow, actress—55

Lauren Hutton, model—55

Goldie Hawn, actress—55

Diane Sawyer, TV anchor—55

Carly Simon, singer—55

Adrienne Barbeau, actress—55

Priscilla Presley, actress—55

Bette Midler, singer—55

Jessye Norman, opera singer—55

Maud Adams, actress—55

Bianca Jagger, human rights
activist—55

Patricia Ireland, feminist—55

Bonnie Franklin, actress—56

Dame Kiri Te Kanawa, opera
singer—56

Jacqueline Bisset, actress—56

Angela Davis, professor—56

Gladys Knight, singer—56

Diana Ross, singer—56

Alice Walker, author—56

Stockard Channing, actress—56

Jill Clayburgh, actress—56

Lauren Hutton, model—56

Linda Ellerbee, journalist—56

Patti LaBelle, singer—56

Kay Bailey Hutchison, U.S.
senator—57

Lynn Redgrave, actress—57

Billie Jean King, tennis player—57

Sharon Gless, actress—57

Cokie Roberts, journalist—57

Joni Mitchell, singer—57

Toni Tennille, singer—57

Catherine Deneuve, actress—57

Diane Ladd, actress—57

Tuesday Weld, actress—57

Doris Kearns Goodwin,
historian—57

Judy Shandlin, judge—57

Barbara Streisand, singer-actress—
58

Carole King, singer—58

Stephanie Powers, actress—58

Annette Funicello, actress—58

Shere Hite, author—58

Erica Jong, author—58

Martha Stewart, lifestyle expert—59

Nora Ephron, author-director—59

Anne Rice, novelist—59

Faye Dunaway, actress—59

Jackie Collins, author—59

Lesley Stahl, TV reporter—59

Raquel Welch, actress—59

Joan Baez, folk singer—59

Maureen Reagan, Reagan
daughter—59

Ellen Goodman, columnist—59

Donna Shalala, Cabinet
secretary—59

Helen Reddy, singer—59

Raquel Welch, actress—60
Valerie Harper, actress—60
Pat Schroeder, former
　congresswoman—60
Nancy Sinatra, singer—60
Dionne Warwick, singer—60
Linda Gray, actress—60
Natalia Makarova, ballerina—60
Sue Grafton, author—60
Barbara Boxer, U.S. senator—60
Marion Wright Edelman, children's
　advocate—61
Tina Turner, singer—61
Grace Slick, singer—61
Jane Alexander, actress—61
Claudia Cardinale, actress—61
Liv Ullmann, actress—61
Elizabeth Ashley, actress—61
Germaine Greer, author—61
Jane Bryant Quinn, economist—
　61
Paula Prentice, actress—61
Roberta Flack, singer—61
Joan Rivers, comedian—61
Lily Tomlin, comedian—61
Etta James, singer—62
Ali MacGraw, actress—62
Janet Reno, U.S. attorney
　general—62
Diana Rigg, actress—62
Judy Blume, author—62
Loretta Swit, actress—63
Dyan Cannon, actress—63
Grace Bumbry, opera singer—63
Mary Tyler Moore, actress—63
Jane Fonda, actress—63
Marlo Thomas, actress—63
Suzanne Pleshette, actress—63
Vanessa Redgrave, actress—63
Madeleine Albright, U.S. secretary
　of state—63
Shirley Bassey, singer—63

Eleanor Holmes Norton, civil
　rights leader—63
Elizabeth Dole, former Red Cross
　leader—64
Ruth Buzzi, comedian—64
Betty Rollin, journalist-author—64
Barbara Mikulski, U.S. senator—
　64
Renata Scotto, opera singer—65
Julie Andrews, singer-actress—65
Lee Meriwether, beauty
　queen–actress—65
Diahann Carroll, actress—65
Geraldine Ferraro, former U.S.
　congresswoman—65
Dame Maggie Smith, actress—66
Dame Judi Dench, actress—66
Gloria Steinem, feminist—66
Kate Millett, feminist—66
Sophia Loren, actress—66
Barbara Eden, actress—66
Shirley Jones, actress—66
Joan Didion, writer—66
Tina Louise, actress—66
Brigitte Bardot, actress—66
Shirley MacLaine, actress—66
Ruth Bader Ginsburg, Supreme
　Court justice—67
Diane Feinstein, U.S. senator—67
Joan Collins, actress—67
Ann Richards, former governor—67
Kim Novak, actress—67
Yoko Ono, artist-poet—67
Susan Sontag, author—67
Chita Rivera, actress—67
Ellen Burstyn, actress—68
Miriam Makeba, singer—68
Debbie Reynolds, actress—68
Elizabeth Taylor, actress—68
Piper Laurie, actress—68
Angie Dickinson, actress—69
Anne Bancroft, actress—69

Rita Moreno, actress—69
Toni Morrison, author—69
Leslie Caron, actress—69
Barbara Walters, journalist—69

Sandra Day O'Connor, Supreme
  Court justice—70
Princess Margaret, British royal
  family—70
Polly Bergen, actress—70
Leona Helmsley, hotel owner—70
Beverly Sills, opera star—71
Liz Claiborne, designer—71
Joan Ganz Cooney, *Sesame Street*
  creator—71
Edie Adams, actress-singer—71
Jean Simmons, actress—71
Dr. Ruth Westheimer, sexual advice
  personality—72
Shirley Temple Black, actress-
  diplomat—72
Maya Angelou, poet—72
Gina Lollobrigida, actress—72
Rosalynn Carter, former First
  Lady—72
Rosemary Clooney, singer—72
Jeanne Moreau, actress—72
Judith Krantz, author—72
Janet Leigh, actress—73
Patti Page, singer—73
Leontyne Price, opera singer—73
Eartha Kitt, singer—73
Coretta Scott King, civil rights
  leader—73
Dr. Joyce Brothers, psychiatrist—
  74
Julie London, singer—74
Cloris Leachman, actress—74
Jeanne Kirkpatrick, former U.N.
  ambassador—74
Charlotte Rae, comedian—74
Patricia Neal, actress—74

Queen Elizabeth II, British royal
  family—74
Barbara Bush, former First Lady—
  75
Maureen Stapleton, actress—75
Angela Lansbury, actress—75
Margaret Thatcher, former British
  prime minister—75
Shirley Chisholm, former U.S.
  congresswoman—76
Lauren Bacall, actress—76
Phyllis Schlafly, conservative
  activist—76
Margaret Whiting, singer—76
Gloria Vanderbilt, fashion
  designer—76
Doris Day, actress—76
Rhonda Fleming, actress—77
Kim Hunter, actress—77
Liz Smith, gossip columnist—77
Helen Gurley Brown, magazine
  editor—78
Eleanor Parker, actress—78
Nancy Reagan, former First
  Lady—79
Janet Blair, actress—79
Betty Friedan, feminist—79
Jane Russell, actress—79

Virginia Mayo, actress—80
Shelley Winters, actress—80
Maureen O'Hara, actress—80
Abbie Van Buren and Ann
  Landers, advice columnists—82
Betty Ford, former First Lady—82
Celeste Holm, actress—81
Pauline Kael, movie critic—81
Katharine Graham, publisher—83
Joan Fontaine, actress—83
Phyllis Diller, comedian—83
Olivia de Havilland, actress—84
Jane Wyman, actress—86

Rosa Parks, civil rights pioneer—
   87
Lady Bird Johnson, former First
   Lady—88
Julia Child, chef—88
Dale Evans, cowgirl singer—88
Luise Rainer, actress—90

Molly Yard, feminist—90
Anne Southern, actress—91
Estee Lauder, businesswoman—92
Katharine Hepburn, actress—93
Fay Wray, actress—93
Anne Morrow Lindberg, writer—
   94

Recommended Reading

Barnes, M. Craig. *Yearning*. InterVarsity Press, 1991.

Blackaby, Henry, and Claude V. King. *Experiencing God*. Broadman and Holman, 1994.

Bolles, Richard. *What Color Is Your Parachute?* Ten Speed Press, 1999.

Bridges, William. *Transitions and Managing Transitions*. Perseus, 1991.

Cameron, Julia. *The Vein of Gold*. Tarcher, 1997.

———. *The Artist's Way*. Tarcher, 1992.

Chambers, Oswald. *My Utmost for His Highest*. Dodd Mead and Co., 1992.

Child, Julia. *Mastering the Art of French Cooking*. Knopf, 1983.

———. *In Julia's Kitchen*. Random House, 1999.

———. *Julia and Jacques Cooking At Home*. Knopf, 1999.

———. *Julia's Kitchen Wisdom*. Knopf, 2000.

———. *The Way To Cook*. Knopf, 1993.

Chittister, Ruth. *The Rule of Benedict*. Crossroad, 1992.

Ferguson, Marilyn. *The Aquarian Conspiracy*. Tarcher, 1980.

Foster, Richard. *Celebration of Discipline*. HarperCollins, 1978.

Gillmor, Verla. *Reality Check: A Survival Guide for Christians in the Marketplace*. Christian Publications, 2001.

Hagberg, Janet. *Real Power*. Sheffield, 1993.

Hagberg, Janet and Richard Leider. *The Inventurers*. Perseus, 1988.

Helmstetter, Shad. *What To Say When You Talk To Yourself*. Grindle, 1986.

Jenson, Margaret. *A Nail in a Sure Place*. Harvest House, 1997.

Jones, Laurie Beth. *The Path*. Hyperion, 1996.

Leider, Richard and David Shapiro. *Repacking Your Bags: How To Live With A New Sense of Purpose*. Fine Communications, 2000.

MacDonald, Gordon. *Ordering Your Private World*. Thomas Nelson, 1997.

Morgan, Marlo. *Mutant Message Down Under*. HarperCollins, 1995.

Myers, Ruth. *31 Days of Praise*. Multinomah, 1998.

Nouwen, Henri. *Seeds of Hope*. Image, 1989.

———. *The Inner Voice of Love*. Doubleday, 1996.

———. *Intimacy*. HarperSanFancisco, 1969.

———. *Life of the Beloved*. Crossroad, 1997.

———. *Reaching Out*. Doubleday, 1986.

———. *The Return of the Prodigal Son*. Doubleday, 1994.

———. *The Way of the Heart*. Ballantine, 1982.

———. *The Wounded Healer*. Image, 1972.

Orman, Suze. *The Nine Steps To Financial Freedom*. Crown, 1997.

———. *The Courage to Be Rich*. Riverhead, 1999.

Ortberg, John. *The Life You've Always Wanted*. Zondervan, 1997.

Pollan, Stephen M. *Die Broke*. HarperBusiness, 1997.

Russell, A. J. *God Calling*. Barbour, 1989.

Stanley, Thomas J. and William D. Danko. *The Millionaire Next Door*. Simon and Schuster, 1998.

Tieger, Paul and Barbara. *Do What You Are*. Little, Brown, 1995.

Wilkinson, Bruce. *Personal Holiness*. Harvest House, 1999.

Bibliography

Books

Ash, Mary Kay. *You Can Have It All*. Prima, 1995.

———. *Mary Kay*. Harper Perennial, 1994.

———. *Paychecks of the Heart*. Mary Kay, 2000.

Batchelor, Mary. *The Doubleday Prayer Collection*. Doubleday, 1996.

Breathnach, Sarah Ban. *Simple Abundance*. Warner Books, 1995.

———. *Something Else*. Warner Books, 1998.

Buford, Bob. *Game Plan*. Zondervan, 1997.

———. *Halftime*. Zondervan, 1994.

Dillard, Annie. *Tinker At Pilgrim Creek*. HarperCollins, 1998.

Dole, Elizabeth and Bob, with Richard Norton Smith. *The Doles—Unlimited Partners*. Simon and Schuster, 1988.

Ellerbee, Linda. *And So It Goes*. G.P. Putnam's Sons, 1986.

———. *Moving On*. G.P. Putnam's Sons, 1991.

Fitch, Noel Riley. *Appetite For Life, The Biography of Julia Child*. Doubleday, 1997.

Giese, Jo. *A Woman's Path*. Golden Books, 1998.

Gill, Brendan. *Late Bloomers*. Artisan, 1996.

Goodall, Jane. *In The Shadow of Man*. Houghton Mifflin, 1971.

———. *Through A Window*. Houghton Mifflin, 1990.

Goodall, Jane with Phillip Berman. *Reason for Hope, A Spiritual Journey*. Warner Books, 1999.

Grizzle, Anne. *Going Home Grown Up*. Shaw, 1998.

Heilbrun, Carolyn G. *Writing A Woman's Life*. Ballantine, 1998.

Hutton, Shirley with Constance deSwaan. *Pay Yourself What You're Worth*. Bantam 1988.

Lindberg, Anne Morrow. *Gift from the Sea*. Pantheon, 1975.

McDowell, Lucinda Secrest. *Women's Spiritual Passages, Celebrating Faith After 40*. Harold Shaw, 1996.

Molinari, Susan, with Elinor Burkett. *Representative Mom*. Doubleday, 1998.

Norris, Kathleen. *The Cloister Walk*. Riverhead, 1996.

Quindlen, Anna. *A Short Guide to a Happy Life*. Random House, 2000.

———. *Living Out Loud*. Random House, 1988.

———. *Object Lessons*. Random House, 1991.

———. *One True Thing*. Dell, 1995.

———. *Black and Blue*. Random House, 1998.

———. *Thinking Out Loud*. Fawcett, 1994.

Quindlen, Anna, with Nick Kelsh. *Naked Babies*. Penguin, 1996.

Sills, Beverly. *Bubbles*. Bobbs Merrill, 1976.

Sills, Beverly and Lawrence Linderman. *Beverly, An Autobiography*. Bantam, 1987.

Sinclair, Ward. *Truckpatch: A Farmer's Odyssey*. American Botanists Booksellers, 2000.

Smith, Robert Lawrence. *A Quaker Book of Wisdom*. Eagle Brook, 1998.

Wells, Rebecca. *Divine Secrets of the Ya-Ya Sisterhood*. Harper Perennial, 1996.

Yager, Jan. *Friendshifts: The Power of Friendships and How It Shapes Our Lives*. Hannacroix Creek Books, 1999.

Index

About the Authors

Rena Pederson currently is vice president/editorial page editor of the *Dallas Morning News,* the largest newspaper in Texas and the Southwest. She has been a finalist for the Pulitzer Prize in editorial writing and currently is a member of the Pulitzer Prize board. Ms. Pederson has been recognized by *Texas Monthly* as one of the "Most Powerful Women in Texas."

She is a former president of the National Conference of Editorial Writers and currently is coeditor of *The American Editor* magazine. She is a member of the Council on Foreign Relations in New York and the American Society of Newspaper Editors. She has a bachelor's degree in journalism with honors from the University of Texas at Austin and a master's degree in journalism from Columbia University in New York.

Her civic awards include being named a "Pioneer Woman of Dallas" and "Mother of the Year." Her writing has won awards from the Headliners Club, Dallas Press Club, and Associated Press Managing Editors.

Rena Pederson writes a weekly newspaper column, which is carried by the Knight-Ridder newswire and is often featured in daily newspapers around the country. She has had articles published in *American Way* magazine, *D* magazine, the *Christian Science Monitor,* and *Congressional Quarterly.*

Dr. Lee Smith is an executive coach who works with business leaders around the world to be the best they can be and direct their companies in a values-based way. As President of Coach Works International (*www.coachworks.com*) she has been instrumental in developing the concept of Legacy Leadership. Those leaders learn to become aware of what their lives and/or their leadership says to others and to the world. She also serves as a coach to women who are moving into "Act Two," the prime time of their lives.

She is one of the first internationally credentialed Master Coaches. Her clients are leaders from companies such as Tricon, Northern Telcom, Ford Motor Company, Levi Strauss, American Airlines and Baxter Healthcare. Dr. Smith has served as an adjunct professor and guest lecturer at the University of Texas at Dallas Executive MBA Program, the University of North Texas and Abilene Christian University. She has been a show-cased speaker at the IACMP Post Conference on Executive Coaching in Washington, D.C., and the Professional Mentor and Coaches Association on the Language of Leadership.

Dr. Smith has been featured in *Newsweek,* a PBS special in 1995 titled, *Ready, Set, Succeed* and a 1998 PBS special about executive coaching titled *Inspiring Businesses and Individuals to Win.*

Rena Pederson   *Dr. Lee Smith*